Colour Terms in Greek Poetry

Colour Terms
in
Greek Poetry

Eleanor Irwin

Hakkert
Toronto
1974

Cover design by R. Mitchell Design
Book design by Anya Humphrey

This book has been published with the help of a grant from the Humanities
Research Council of Canada, using funds provided by the Canada Council.

International Standard Book Number 0-88866-519-9
Library of Congress Catalogue Card Number 72-78018

Printed and bound in Canada
by The Hunter Rose Company

A. M. Hakkert Ltd., 554 Spadina Crescent, Toronto, Canada M5S 2J9

TO MY HUSBAND

οὐ μὲν γὰρ τοῦ γε κρεῖσσον καὶ ἄρειων,
ἢ ὅθ᾽ ὁμοφρονέοντε νοήμασιν οἶκον ἔχητον
ἀνὴρ ἠδὲ γυνή

Contents

Acknowledgements

Grateful acknowledgement is here made to Professor L. E. Woodbury who directed the thesis out of which this study developed, for the time he spent in discussion with me and his helpful comments on earlier drafts; to the members of my Ph.D. Committee, Professors D. J. Conacher, D. P. de Montmollin, and J. J. Sheridan, who read this work when it was presented as a thesis, in whole or in part; to Professor F. E. Winter for his advice on archaeological matters; to my colleagues at Scarborough College, especially Professor P. H. Salus and Professor N. E. Collinge (who has since been appointed Director of the Centre for Linguistic Studies at the University of Toronto) for their assistance in etymological discussions; to Professor W. B. Stanford of Trinity College, Dublin, who acted as an outside appraiser for the thesis and gave me encouragement to continue; and to all who at various times contributed to my understanding of the problem.

I wish also to thank the librarians and secretarial staff at Scarborough College; my publishers who have been most helpful in the editing of the manuscript; and my husband and family for their co-operation and encouragement. For those faults which remain I am, of course, entirely responsible.

Scarborough College,
University of Toronto,
June, 1973.

Abbreviations and Sources for Quotations

LSJ Liddell-Scott-Jones *A Greek-English Lexicon*, Oxford 9th ed., 1940

ONED: *Oxford (New) English Dictionary*, ed. J. A. H. Murray, H. Bradley, W. A. Craigie, C. T. Onions, Oxford, 1933

Emile Boisacq: *Dictionnaire étymologique de la langue grecque*, Heidelberg 4th ed., 1950

Hjalmor Frisk: *Griechisches etymologisches Wörterbuch*, Heidelberg, 1954, in progress

Pierre Chantraine: *Dictionnaire étymologique de la langue grecque: Histoire des mots,* Tome 1 A-Δ, Tome 2 E – K, Paris, 1968, 1970

Quotations in this work are made from the following editions:

Homer   ed. D. B. Munro and T. W. Allen, Oxford, 1920

Hesiod ed. R. Merkelbach and M. L. West, Oxford, 1970

Sappho and Alcaeus from *Poetarum Lesbiorum Fragmenta* ed. E. Lobel and D. L. Page, Oxford, 1955 (*PLF*)

Bacchylides ed. B. Snell, Leipzig, 1961

Pindar ed. B. Snell, Leipzig, 1954

The other melic poets from *Poetae Melici Graeci* ed. D. L. Page, Oxford, 1962 (*PMG*)

The elegiac and iambic poets from *Anthologia Lyrica Graeca* ed. E. Diehl, fasc. I, Leipzig, 1951, fasc. III, 1952 (D.)

Theognis ed. D. Young, Leipzig, 1961

Aeschylus ed. G. Murray, Oxford, 1937
Sophocles ed. A. C. Pearson, Oxford, 1928
Euripides ed. G. Murray, Oxford, 1913
Aristophanes ed. F. W. Hall and W. M. Geldart, Oxford, 1912
Fragments of the tragic poets in *Tragicorum Graecorum Fragmenta* ed. A. Nauck, Leipzig, 1889 (N.)
Fragments of the comic poets in *Comicorum Atticorum Fragmenta* ed. T. Kock, Leipzig, 1880-1888 (K.)
Fragments of the Presocratics in *Die Fragmente der Vorsokratiker* ed. H. Diels, W. Kranz, Zurich/Berlin, 1964

Colour Terms in Greek Poetry

One
The Problem and Its History

Our consideration of Greek colour terms begins with Homer, the most widely read of Greek poets and one who is apt to use colour terms in strange ways. The reader may find himself disappointed, for instance, by Homer's lack of scenic descriptions and appreciation of nature's beauties. Passing references to "saffron-robed" or "rosy-fingered" dawn, epithets portraying the colours of the early morning sky, will probably seem abrupt in comparison with the extensive descriptions of later European poets.[1] He will not find word-pictures of fields of green grass, the expanse of blue sky overhead, and the azure depths of the sea. In their place he will find "black" earth (μέλας, *Il.* 2.699), sky which is "bronze" (κολύχαλκος, *Od.* 3.2), or "iron" (σιδήρεος, *Od.* 15.328) by day and "starry" (ἀστερόεις, *Od.* 9.527) by night, and sea which is "black" (μέλας, *Il.* 24.79, κελαινός, *Il.* 9.6), "white" (λευκός, *Od.* 10.94, *h. Hom.* 33.15), "grey" (πολιός, *Il.* 1.350, γλαυκός, *Il.* 16.34), "purple" (πορφύρεος, *Il.* 16.391, ἰοειδής, *Od.* 5.56), or

---

1. Cf. Milton *On the Morning of Christ's Nativity*, Stanza 26:

> So, when the sun in bed,
> Curtained with cloudy red,
> Pillows his chin upon an orient wave . . .
> . . . the yellow-skirted fays
> Fly after the night-steeds, leaving their moon-loved maze.

Cf. also Shelley *The Cloud*, Stanza 3:

> The sanguine Sunrise, with his meteor eyes,
> And his burning plumes outspread, . . .
> In the light of its golden wings . . .
> And the crimson pall of eve may fall.

"wine-dark" (οἶνοψ, Od. 5.132). He will be particularly puzzled no doubt that the only hue attributed to the sea is purple or wine.[2] The Homeric world will seem rather colourless because of Homer's preference for "black" and "white" over terms which indicate a hue.[3] On the other hand, certain phrases may strike the reader as particularly suitable: the god of the sea is "blue-haired" Poseidon (κυανοχαίτης, Il. 13.563); the (fabulous) sheep of the Cyclops have "violet-dark" fleece (ἰοδνεφής, Od. 9.426). Again, he may be bewildered by a word like ἀργός which is generally translated "white" when it describes geese, "flashing" when the tusks of the white-toothed boar, and "swift" when dogs. In spite of scholarly explanations it is hard to believe that one epithet can have so many meanings and even harder to feel any sympathy with a poet who uses it in this way. So also with the rare λειριόεις which describes the voice of the grasshopper (auditory) and the appearance of flesh (visual); such connections do not seem reasonable.

Matters do not improve much in the later poets. It is true that there are references to the greenness of vegetation and the blueness of the sea, and that certain passages show an effective use of colour terms, but one still finds strange phrases.[4] What is one to make of the "black-leaved" laurel (μελάμφυλλος, Anacr. fr. 443 PMG), nightingales "with green necks" (χλωραύχην, Simon. fr.

2. I have used traditional translations of the various colour terms in presenting the problem, but it will be clear from my discussion that I do not always agree with these translations. For discussions of individual colour terms, see Index. For a discussion of Homer's disregard for the blueness of the sky, see J. Werner "Blauer Himmel bei Homer?" in *Forsch. u. Fortschr.* 33 (1959) 311-316. Werner assembled the conclusions of many who referred to the problem, in particular he examined and rejected the suggestion that the common Homeric epithets of sky σιδήρεος and χάλκεος might be references to blueness.

3. The inclusion of "black" and "white" as colour terms in Greek is justified by the treatment of the colour theorists (see pp. 22-27). F. E. Wallace remarks that "83 per cent of the color-words in the *Iliad* are those words expressing value rather than hue, and 60 per cent in the *Odyssey* . . . So the use of black-and-white words is actually far greater than that of red-to-violet words in the poem"; *Colour in Homer and in Ancient Art,* Smith College Classical Studies 9 (Northampton 1927), p. 29.

4. Simonides is first to use κυάνεος of the sea (chapter three, p. 103) but it is not at all certain whether he intended it to mean "blue." Effective use of colour is found notably in Pind. *Olymp.* 6. 39-45, 55, Soph. *O. C.* 668-719, Eur. *Helen,* 179-182. See C. M. Bowra *Greek Lyric Poetry* (Oxford 1961) p. 392 for Simonides' pictorial use of colour; and A. E. Harvey in *CQ* N.S. 7 (1957), 216-217 for the juxtaposition of colours in Anacreon.

586.2 *PMG*), a "saffron-dyed" drop, usually interpreted as blood (κροκοβαφής, Aesch. *Ag.* 1121), "blue" earth (κυάνεος, Pind. fr. 33b4), and, perhaps most incredible of all, "green" blood (χλωρός, Eur. *Hec.* 127).[5] In the face of these and other colour descriptions there are several possible reactions. One may, of course, ignore the problem and regard such descriptions as I have repeated here with tolerant affection. There are, for example, staunch defenders of Homer's "wine-dark sea" who claim that the Mediterranean really is "wine-coloured," especially at sunset. Some of them may argue that since such descriptions occur in poetry, they ought to be accepted as "poetic," i.e. not literally true. (On the distinction between prose and poetry, see p. 17). But, the majority of those who considered the problem seriously generally came to one of two conclusions. Some reasoned that the colour vision of the Greeks was at fault, that they were, in fact, colour blind. Others disagreed, concluding that it was Greek colour terminology that was frankly defective, although presumably their faculty was not.

The problem of Greek colour perception and colour terminology seems first to have been raised by Goethe in his *Zur Farbenlehre*, published in 1810.[6] Over one hundred years before, in 1704, Sir Isaac Newton published his conclusions about the nature of light in the *Opticks*. In this work, the experiments for which were begun in 1666, Newton established two important facts about colour and colour perception. First, he demonstrated that the colours of the spectrum could be recombined by a second lens or prism to form white light again. (Previous experiments had shown that white light could be broken by a prism into the colours of the spectrum.) Secondly, he explained that the reason bodies appeared coloured under white light is that they reflect some of its spectral components more strongly than others. These two observations were extremely important in the scientific understanding of colour. But Goethe did not accept Newton's findings and attempted to disprove them in *Zur Farbenlehre*.

In 1794, John Dalton, an English chemist best known for the

5. For a discussion of these passages, see Index Locorum.
6. Goethe *Zur Farbenlehre* in *Sämtliche Werke* (Munich 1913) vol. 22 pp. 7-42, esp. pp. 39-42.

development of modern atomic theory, presented a paper to the
Manchester Literary and Philosophical Society entitled "Extra-
ordinary Facts Relating to the Vision of Colours." In this, the
earliest account of the optical peculiarity known as Daltonism or
colour blindness, Dalton summed up its characteristics as he
observed them in himself and others.[7] It is significant, I think, that
Goethe's examination of the colour perception of the Greeks and
his conclusion that their colour perception was faulty followed
this paper by a very short interval. Many odd colour descriptions
in Greek considered in the light of Dalton's account seemed to be
explicable as the result of defective colour vision in the Greeks.
Gladstone, in the middle of the nineteenth century, concluded
"that the organ of colour and its impressions were but partially
developed among the Greeks of the heroic age."[8] Gladstone does
not describe this lack as colour blindness, but he does mention
studies which show that some creatures perceive only light and
dark, not colour, suggesting by implication that the Greeks might
have been in the same state. There may be significance in the fact
that Charles Darwin's work *On the Origin of Species* appeared in
1859, later than Gladstone's first writings on the subject of Homer
and colour, but before the flood of works in the 1870's. Others
before Darwin had proposed a theory of evolution; so the idea
itself was not new, though the working out through natural
selection was his, and with the publication of his *Origins* public
interest in the topic was roused.[9] The assumption that develop-
ment (or evolution) is both possible and probable underlies much
of the writing on the matter of colour perception in the ancient
world. Arguments about Greek colour blindness or defective
colour vision continued. In 1867, Alfred Geiger addressed an
assembly of natural scientists in Frankfurt on the subject of the

7. An account of Newton, Dalton, and their contributions can be found in
Encyclopaedia Britannica ed. W. B. Preece (Chicago 1966) vols. 6 and 7, s.vv. Colour,
Colour Blindness, and Dalton.

8. W. E. Gladstone *Studies on Homer and the Homeric Age* vol. 3 (Oxford 1858)
pp. 457-499, "Homer's Perception and Use of Colour." Gladstone also wrote an article
on the subject in *Nineteenth Century* 2 (1877) 366-388 entitled "The Colour Sense."

9. On Darwin and his predecessors, see *On the Origin of Species, a Facsimile of
the First Edition*, with an introduction by Ernst Mayr (Cambridge, Mass. 1964) pp. ix,
xx-xxiii.

colour sense in antiquity and its development.[10] He pointed out that in many early literary works words for blue and green were lacking and that words which later came to mean "blue" often originally meant "black." He concluded from his examination of the literary evidence that in Greek the earliest colours perceived were black, red and gold (or yellow). He was familiar with the work of Gladstone and Goethe in this field and the fact that men differed in ability to perceive colour.

In 1877, Hugo Magnus, who was interested in vision both as a medical doctor and as a student of the classics, published a discussion developing Geiger's argument further: *Die geschichtliche Entwickelung des Farbensinnes* (Leipzig 1877). He concluded that at an early period men could perceive light but no colour; then red was perceived, although there was confusion between bright and "light-rich" colours, as between white and red; next reds and yellows were recognized, then greens; finally blues and violets which are weakest in light. He related this development of colour perception to the ability of the retina to perceive each of the colours.[11] In 1878, O. Weise supported the work of Geiger and Magnus and examined some Indo-European roots from which some colour terms are derived in an article "Die Farbenbezeichnungen der Indogermanen."[12] A discussion which disagreed with the theory that the eye gradually developed the ability to perceive colours was advanced in 1879 by Anton Marty in *Die Frage nach der geschichtlichen Entwickelung des Farbensinnes* (Vienna 1879). He argued that such a development as posited by Geiger and

10. *Zur Entwickelungsgeschichte der Menschheit* (Stuttgart, first edition 1871, second 1878). The relevant section is from p. 45 to p. 60, second edition. For his discussion of "blue," see pp. 49, 52; for the earliest colours perceived, see pp. 54, 57. He refers (on pp. 50-52) to the case mentioned by Goethe (*Werke* vol. 40 p. 49, in a letter to Dr. Brandis) of two young men with otherwise good vision who saw no blue; for them the sky was rose-coloured, and greens varied from yellow to brown.

11. Magnus' interest in relating medical knowledge to classics can be illustrated by another of his works, *Die Anatomie des Auges bei Griechen und Römern* (Leipzig 1878). It is an index of the interest in the subject of colour perception that his work on the colour sense was translated into French the following year by J. Soury as *Histoire du sens des couleurs* (Paris 1878). The references of particular interest: *Die geschichtliche Entwickelung des Farbensinnes* pp. 41-42, 55-56.

12. In *Beiträge zur Kunde der Indogermanischen Sprachen* ed. A. Bezzenberger (Göttingen 1878) vol. 2 pp. 273-290. See also Weise's later article along similar lines "'Die Farbenbezeichnungen bei den Griechen und Römern" in *Philologus* 46 (1888), 593-605.

Magnus was unlikely on deductive grounds. "Where in our experience with savage tribes," he asked, "could we find any evidence that they saw colour differently from more civilized peoples?"[13] On historical grounds, too, he argued against such a development, inferring from the remains of paintings and decorations that ancient peoples enjoyed a wide range of colours. In literature, he suggested that some of what are considered peculiar colour usages may be explained by poetic licence, remarking that the poets are sometimes more interested in brightness or tone than colour hue. He pointed out that the need for technical colour designations is not felt in the early Greek period and that this influenced the development of terminology.[14] Marty's reading on the subject of colour perception was wide and he showed himself familiar with the views of his predecessors and contemporaries.[15] His weakness lay in not considering the actual colour terms in their literary context, but armed with a few references and statistics, basing his conclusions on deduction and probabilities. Nonetheless, the points he raised are valuable: that evidence from archaeology suggests that the Greeks could see a full range of colours; that the Greeks in the early period did not feel a need for technical colour vocabulary; that writers may not be intending to describe "colour" in every instance. He reminded those involved in the discussion that factors other than physiological might be at the base of the problem.

---

13. Marty *Die Frage* pp. 7-22.

14. *Ibid.* pp. 53-57 for painting; pp. 62-73 for speech development; pp. 78-94 for poetic treatment; pp. 95-105 for the development of a technical vocabulary.

15. Marty mentions on pp. 3-5 the following references: Gladstone *Der Farbensinn, Mit besonderer Berücksichtigung der Farbenkenntnis des Homer* (Breslau 1878); Geiger lecture, Sept. 24, 1867 and *Ursprung und Entwickelung der menschlichen Sprache und Vernunft*, part 1 (Stuttgart 1868) and part 2 (Stuttgart 1872); Schuster (article) in *Zeitschrift für das Gymnasialwesen von Mützell* 1861, 1.b, 712ff; W. Jordon "Novelle zu Homeros" in *Jahrbücher für klassische Philologie von A. Fleckeisen*, 1876 pp. 161ff; H. Steinthal *Ursprung der Sprache in Zusammenhang mit den letzten Fragen alles Wissens* (1877); H. Magnus *Die geschichtliche Entwickelung des Farbensinnes* (Leipzig 1877); B. Günther, a lecture to the 50th assembly of German scientists and doctors; E. Kraupe and G. Jäger, *Kosmos: Zeitschrift für einheitliche Weltanschauung auf Grund der Entwickelungslehre* (I Jahre, 3. Heft p. 264ff, 5. Heft p. 428ff, and 6. Heft p. 486ff). In addition on p. 151 Marty gives as references: I. Stilling *Ueber Farbensinn und Farbenblindheit* (Cassel 1878); Fr. Hildebrand *Die Farben der Blüthen in ihrer jetzigen Variation und früheren Entwickelung* (Leipzig 1879). He makes it clear on pp. 152-153 that he knew Goethe's work on the subject.

In the same year in which Marty's reply was published, Grant Allen made a more general answer, *The Colour-Sense: its Origin and Development* (Boston 1879). Allen, a comparative psychologist, argued that the rate of evolution in the theory of Geiger and Magnus was much too rapid to be compatible with other facts. He produced a questionnaire addressed to missionaries, government officials and other persons working "amongst the most uncivilized races" asking, among other questions, "Can the members of a given language group distinguish between colour x (blue) and colour y, (green, violet)?" and then "Have they separate names for x and y?" He found no instances of inability to distinguish colours, in spite of a recurrent lack of colour terms.[16]

In 1904, W. Schultz produced a study which examined far more thoroughly than his predecessors the actual colour terminology of the Greeks: *Das Farbenempfindungssystem der Hellenen* (Leipzig). In the first section of this work he discussed colour terms individually, with particular reference to the work of the colour theorists and lexicographers, in an attempt to define the precise hue indicated by each term. In his second section, he assembled ancient evidence on the appearance of the rainbow, the colour theories of Democritus and Plato, and a discussion of Phidias' statue of Zeus at Olympia. In discussing the various texts, he found evidence of anomalies in Greek colour vision. Let this example suffice: it is said that blue is produced by mixing black and green, τὴν δ᾽ ἰσάτιν ἐκ μέλανος σφόδρα καὶ χλωροῦ and that green results from the mixture of purple and blue, τὸ δὲ πράσινον ἐκ πορφυροῦ καὶ τῆς ἰσάτιδος (Theophr. *De Sens.* 77). In his final section Schultz discussed normal and abnormal colour vision, ending with a diagnosis of the anomaly of Greek colour vision. Based on such peculiarities as mentioned above, he concluded that the Greeks were all blue-yellow blind.[17]

What then is colour? How do we see it? What is colour blindness? Newton declared that white light could be broken up

---

16. Allen *The Colour Sense* p. 205. For a further account of the history of this discussion, see M. H. Segall, D. T. Campbell, M. J. Herskovits *The Influence of Culture on Visual Perception* (New York 1966) pp. 38-41.

17. *Das Farbenempfindungssystem der Hellenen* p. 187. An answer to this theory with regard to the Roman poets was given by K. E. Goetz "Waren die Römer blaublind?" in *Archiv f. lat. Lex. u. Gram.* 14 (1905) 75-88; 15 (1908) 527-547.

into seven colours: red, orange, yellow, green, blue, indigo, and violet,[18] which always appeared in the same order, in bands whose width varied from colour to colour. This spectrum appears in nature as the rainbow, but of course the scientific explanation was not known to its earliest observers.[19] Modern colour theory uses the spectrum as one of the measurements by which a colour is described. Munsell, whose colour system has been widely accepted, specifies three measurements for colour: *hue*, which indicates position on the spectrum; *value*, which measures the lightness or darkness of a hue; and *chroma*, which describes the intensity of a hue.[20] (See diagram.) Pictorially he represents hue as a circle around which each colour merges into its neighbour in a mathematically determined progression, so that yellow for example is next to yellowish-green (two parts yellow to one part green), next to which is yellow-green (one part to one) then greenish-yellow (two parts green to one yellow) and finally green. (Such a process could be further subdivided.) Value is depicted as a

18. Newton's seven colours are more usually reduced to six, with indigo omitted. Part of Newton's reason for naming seven was an attempt to establish an analogy between the colours of the spectrum and the seven notes of the diatonic scale (cf. our comments below).

19. The rainbow is seen when the rays of the sun (white light), coming from behind us, are broken up into the component colours by the drops of rain which act as prisms. In addition to Homer's description of the rainbow as πορφύρεος (*Il.* 17.547, see p. 28), we have three Greek attempts to give the colours found in it. The earliest, that of Xenophanes, says it is a cloud πορφύρεος, χλωρός, and φοινίκεος; Aristotle gives the colours as ἀλουργής πράσινος, ξανθός, and ἐρυθρός; Poseidonius as ἀλουργής, κυάνεος, πράσινος, and ἐρυθρός. The red and violet ends are represented in all three accounts; the weaker colours, yellow, green, and blue, are not so well represented. For a discussion of ancient attempts to analyse the colours of the rainbow, see André *Etude sur les termes de couleur dans la langue latine* p. 13, Schultz *Das Farbenempfindungssystem der Hellenen* pp. 99-114.

A mosaic which apparently attempts to depict a rainbow has been found at Pergamon and dated by the excavators to 197-159 B.C. G. S. Merker (*AJA* 71 [1967] 81-82) thinks that the artist was influenced by Aristotelian colour theory. The mosaic consists of thirty rows of tesserae which shade in bands gradually from red through yellow and yellow-green to green-blue. The orange band and the blue-violet are lacking. Merker argues that this accords with Aristotle *Meteorologica* 3.4.375a4-11, where the effect of the neighbouring colours (red and green) in the rainbow is said to produce yellow. I am not at all convinced that one need resort to Aristotle to explain the colour choice of the artist; it might fit other descriptions as well. The strangest part of the mosaic is the reversal of the colour order in nature; the artist has placed the red band on the inner edge. Merker takes this reversal as evidence that the artist in not imitating nature, and as support for her view that he is putting colour theory into practice.

20. For the Munsell system of colour measurement, see *Encyclopaedia Britannica* ed. W. B. Preece (1966) vol. 6 s.v. Colour.

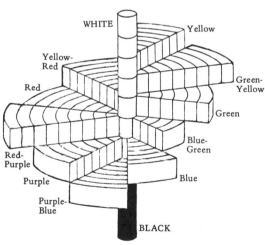

The original Munsell Color Tree and a modern representation of the same theory.

vertical pole ranging from black (0) to white (10). Hue combined with value measures shade variations, in red for example from pink (light in value) to maroon (dark). Chroma is represented as stretching horizontally from the value pole. Different colours reach their maximum intensity at different values. Red, for example, reaches its maximum at value 4, yellow at value 9. Some colours attain a stronger chroma than others. Red and yellow are pictured as stretching twice as far from the value pole as blue and green. Munsell observes that the higher in value the point at which a hue reaches its maximum chroma, the more powerful it is reckoned to be. This statement is represented by the equation "power equals value times chroma." In his system of colour measurement, the colours which are most powerful are the reds and yellows, those least powerful the greens and blues. Based on these observations one might expect that reds and yellows make more impact than greens and blues, light colours more than dark ones.[21]

By this system of measurement it is possible to be extremely accurate in describing a colour. In ordinary experience we do not

21. There are systems of colour measurement other than Munsell's, but his is widely accepted in North America. For the Ostwald system, see *Wilhelm Ostwald: A Basic Treatise on the Color System of Wilhelm Ostwald The Color Primer* ed. with foreword and evaluation by Faber Birren (New York 1969). This contains the translation of Ostwald's *Color Primer* originally published in 1916 under the title *Farbenfibel*. Ostwald differs from Munsell (who uses the six colours of the spectrum as his basis) in having eight principal hues. These are the four "fundamental" colours — yellow, red, blue, and sea-green — and four others, one midway between each pair of fundamental colours — orange, purple, turquoise, and leaf-green. His arrangement puts more emphasis than Munsell's on varieties of green. The system is based on a pyramid shape, as Munsell's on the circle of the spectrum. Each colour can be represented by a triangle with white at one apex, black at another and the pure, saturated colour at the third.

On the matter of the relatively low impact of green, I offer as contemporary evidence the song sung by Kermit the frog, a puppet character on "Sesame Street" (production of the Children's Television Workshop). Kermit ponders his greenness in the following lyrics:

> It's not that easy being green;
> Having to spend each day the colour of the leaves,
> When I think it could be nicer being red, or yellow, or gold —
> or something much more colorful like that.

> It's not easy being green.
> It seems you blend in with so many other ordinary things,
> And people tend to pass you over 'cause you're not standing out
> like flashy sparkles in the water — or stars in the sky.

attempt to be so exact, but we are none the less influenced by such studies. People with normal colour vision are described as trichromatic because "the subjective sensation elicited by any single spectral colour can be reproduced or matched ... by a mixture of three so-called primary colours, red, green, and blue."[22] The proportions in which these colours are mixed to produce a given colour do not vary in people of normal vision (about 92 per cent of males, 99.5 per cent of females).[23] The rest of the population lacks the ability (in whole or in part) to see red and green or (less commonly) blue and yellow. The rare cases of total colour blindness, in which the subject sees only blacks and whites, is, unlike red-green or blue-yellow blindness, usually associated with other visual defects. A severely red-green blind person cannot distinguish red from green; he finds it difficult to see red berries on a green bush and to tell which are ripe when he does find them.[24] Colours have a stronger than normal blue or yellow content. A race of red-green blind men might be expected to have terms for blue and yellow and perhaps one term for red and green. Similarly, a race of blue-yellow blind people might have terms for red and green, the colours they can see, and one term to cover

22. For a medical analysis of colour vision, see B. H. Crawford "A Sketch of the Present Position of the Young-Helmholtz Theory of Colour Vision" in *Ciba Foundation Symposium on Colour Vision* (London 1964) pp. 152-172. I wish also to express my debt to the late A. G. S. Heathcote M.D. who did many studies among school children in the Metro Toronto area to diagnose colour blindness and to attempt to determine which colours were most confusing to children with colour defective vision. He generously made his research available to me.

23. Colour blindness is found in more males than females because it is a sex-linked recessive factor, i.e. it is found in the X-gene, of which women have two and men one. Because it is recessive, a woman must have the factor in both X-genes to cause her to be colour blind, i.e. she must inherit it from both parents. A man, who has only one X-gene, will be colour blind if the factor is present in this one gene which he can inherit only from his mother. A woman may be a carrier without being affected and may pass this factor to her sons, who will then be colour blind, and to her daughters, who will be carriers. I find myself part of this pattern. My brother is red-green blind (a protanope); he must have inherited the colour blind factor from our mother whose colour vision was normal. I knew I might be a carrier, but this would be apparent in me only if I had a son who was colour blind. My oldest son, now eight, has evidently defective colour vision; therefore I am a carrier. (He and I have had differences of opinion about colour since he first learned a colour vocabulary.)

24. There are two types of red-green blindness, protanopia and deuteranopia (or deutanopia), the difference being that in protanopia the red end of the spectrum is shortened, but in deutanopia it is not. Thus protanopes "see" colour differently from deutanopes, but in both there is red-green confusion.

blue and yellow which appear the same. The complaint against the Greeks, however, is that they lacked terms for blue and green and yet had a variety of terms for red and yellow.

We conclude, then, *pace* Schultz, that the Greeks were not colour blind in a medical sense. (Moreover, because of the genetic pattern in the transmission of Daltonism it is highly unlikely that a whole race has ever suffered from colour blindness; see n. 23.) We shall see later that training and learning play an important part in our concept of colour. Recent studies of colour in Greek literature conclude, for the most part, that Greek vision was normal, but their terminology was at fault. In an article in 1921, Platnauer assembled some of the more startling colour descriptions in Greek prose and poetry from Homer to Xenophon.[25] He was attempting not to answer the problem, but to present it; he did, however, make certain observations. The difference between colours is quantitative rather than qualitative; black and white are considered colours, and (other) colours shades between these extremes; there is no real distinction between chromatic and achromatic; lustre or superficial effect is important, not colour or tint. Platnauer has drawn to our attention an important point, that "colour" did not mean to the Greeks what it means to us.

In 1927 Miss F. E. Wallace published her dissertation, *Colour in Homer and in Ancient Art*, in which she examined the colour terms used by Homer, tried to specify as closely as possible their hue and compared these hues to remains in ancient art.[26] 1933 saw the publication of Miss A. E. Kober's dissertation, *The Use of Color Terms in the Greek Poets, Including all the poets from Homer to 146 B.C. except the Epigrammatists*. She collected the colour usages of these poets, specifically excluding what she termed the "non-colour" occurrences, and attempted to define the

25. M. Platnauer "Greek Colour Perception" in *CQ* 15 (1921) 153-162.
26. There are certain difficulties involved in comparing the evidence of literature and archaeology in the matter of colour terms. First, one cannot be sure what name the artist gave to the colour he used; secondly, one does not know whether the colour in its present state is the same as when it was produced first, or whether it has suffered change; thirdly, and this is less well understood than the other points, one cannot know whether the artist saw what we see. Until an abstract concept of colour is developed, a people may not look at things in terms of colour. For a discussion of literary and archaeological evidence concerning colour in Greek painting, see H. Osborne "Colour Concepts of the ancient Greeks" in *British Journal of Aesthetics* 8, no. 3(1968) 269-283, esp. 274-278.

exact hue indicated by each word. Apparently both authors thought that by defining colour terms it was possible to prove the Greeks perceived colour normally and that the "problem" of colour perception did not really exist. Kober's study which covers a very long period of time, does not make observations on the development of words and changes in meaning from the beginning to the end of this period. Both works are valuable for reference, however.

R. A. Cole in his unpublished Dublin dissertation, "Adjectives of Light and Colour in Greek Lyric Poetry from Alkman to Bacchylides" (1952), presented the instances of colour in Homer, Hesiod, and the Homeric cycle (volume 1), the pre-Pindaric lyricists (volume 2), Pindar (volume 3), and Aeschylus and Bacchylides (volume 4). He too tended to define each word in terms of its hue and to ignore the problem of the Greek understanding of colour and the "non-colour" aspects of words.[27] The problem was explored again in 1958 in an article by R. D'Avino "La visione del colore nella terminologia greca," in which the terms ἀργός, πορφύρεος, πόλιος, ξανθός and χλωρός were explored with particular attention to etymology.[28]

1962 saw the publication of the most recent discussion of Greek colour terms known to the author G. Reiter's *Die Griechischen Bezeichnungen der Farben Weiss, Grau und Braun* (Innsbruck). As the title indicates, this examination covers only the colours white, grey and brown and the terms used by the Greeks for them. Unlike the dissertations of Kober, Wallace, and Cole, this examination takes into consideration uses of prose as well as poetry. The author discussed many terms whose earliest occurrence is post-classical and hence beyond the range of this study; e.g. under "white" he treated μαλός, ἀλφός, γαλάκτινος, ἐλεφαντῖνος, ἀφυώδης, γοψοειδής. He devoted more time than

27. I have had access to this unpublished dissertation through the kindness of Professor W. B. Stanford who allowed me to retain his copy for consultation over a period of several years. Professor Stanford's books and articles on aspects of Greek poetic diction have been of great assistance in the examination of Greek colour terms; in particular *Greek Metaphor* (Oxford 1936), *Ambiguity in Greek Literature* (Oxford 1939) *Aeschylus in his Style* (Dublin 1942) and *The Sound of Greek* (Berkeley and Los Angeles 1967).

28. In *Ricerche Linguistica* 4 (1958) 99-134 (Univ. of Rome, Inst. di Glottologia).

previous writers to a critical consideration of the problem, without, however, directing much attention to the development of the concept of colour.

I refer as a matter of interest to a study of Latin colour terms: J. André *Etude sur les termes de couleur dans la langue latine* (Paris 1949). André refers briefly in his introduction to the problem of Greek colour terminology and perception and to the work of his predecessors in this and the Latin field. He has divided the main body of his work into three sections. A semantic study presents the colour terms, arranged in "families" according to hue. This arrangement is possible in the Latin field, because the Latin authors are post-Aristotelian. In the early Greek period such an arrangement can lead to frustration because of the so-called "non-colour" uses. (See below for the development of the concept of colour.) Following the semantic study come lexicological and stylistic studies. The latter contains a discussion of colour symbolism, poetic and prose style, imitation of earlier passages by later authors, and the personality of authors as it is revealed by their use of colour. This final section makes a valuable contribution to the study of Latin colour terms. Following publication of André's work, French scholars seemed to show a renewed interest in colour in the ancient world. In 1954 André took part, with many others, in a seminar which examined questions related to colour in respect of the physics, physiology, and psychology of colour perception, the manufacture and use of pigments, the use of colour in the plastic arts, and the names of colours in several languages. These studies were edited by I. Meyerson and published as *Problèmes de la couleur*, Exposés et discussions du Colloque du Centre de Recherches de Psychologie comparative tenu à Paris les 18, 19, 20 Mai 1954.

Scholars have examined more specific topics within the larger field of Greek colour usage: individual words, passages where a colour term presents a problem, and in particular the Greek interest in light and darkness rather than hue. Only a few of the many studies can be mentioned here. Two of these are concerned with cult among the Greeks and Romans: K. Meyer *Die Bedeutung der weissen Farbe im Kultus der Griechen und Römer* (Freiburg 1927) and G. Radke *Die Bedeutung der weissen und schwarzen*

Farbe in Kult und Brauch der Griechen und Römer (Jena 1936). A study of colour and contrast in Greek epic was made recently in a Hamburg dissertation (1958): Horst Fahrenholz *Farbe, Licht und Dunkelheit im älteren griechischen Epos*. The contrast of light and dark is studied along with other examples of polarity in a book by G. E. R. Lloyd: *Polarity and Analogy: Two Types of Argumentation in Early Greek Thought* (Cambridge 1966).[29]

I Poetic Imagery

Two other matters connected with Greek colour usage deserve comment: the questions of poetic imagery and the abstract concept of colour. Today we are very conscious of the difference between prose and poetry and the language proper to each, but this distinction is not made in the early Greek world. Poetry, of course, predates prose as a literary form, and among the earliest poets are some whom we might call "versifiers" because the content of their poetry could be expressed as well in prose. Rhetoric, the art which taught the effective use of figures of speech, came to Athens with Gorgias the Sophist in 427. The earlier poets, unconscious of this "art," wrote as they saw. It would be a mistake to think that these poets were deliberately striving for effect by using "poetic" devices as seen by the rhetoricians. Rather we should say that poetry was analysed for its methods by the rhetoricians of the sophistic age and that these methods were imitated, especially by the orators, to embellish their writings. Since our discussion ends with the fifth century, it is clear that rhetoric and the sophistic movement will have had very little influence on any of the poets, except Euripides, investigated here. Although perhaps aware of poetic figures, Euripides also used archaic language and often elaborated a Homeric description. He could appreciate the words he used from the sincere, uncontrived viewpoint of the earlier poets, employing them like his precursors to render a faithful representation of his world: in the present work the poets have been taken seriously.

A story told by Ion of Chios will help us to see the gulf

---

29. In particular pp. 376-377 for a discussion of Aristotle's view of the way colours are produced from black and white; also pp. 16, 42-43, 46-47, 49.

between the poets and the sophists. At a dinner party, Sophocles (the tragedian) quoted with approval Phrynichus' line (fr. 13 N.) λάμπει δ' ἐπὶ πορφυρέαις παρῆισι φῶς ἔρωτος "the light of love shines on purple [?] cheeks." When a schoolmaster objected that πορφύρεος was no better a description of a beautiful boy's cheeks than the effect would be pleasing if a painter painted his cheeks πορφύρεος, Sophocles laughed and said, "well, you won't like Simonides' lines either, although they please most people," and he quoted Simonides (fr. 585 PMG): πορφυρέου ἀπὸ στόματος / ἱεῖσα φωνὰν παρθένος "a girl sending forth a sound from her purple [?] mouth." Lorimer calls this use of πορφύρεος "the poetical heightening of a real colour to a literal hideousness."[30] It is plain that the schoolmaster saw and disliked the literal hideousness. Why did not Sophocles, who was far more sensitive to beauty, also dislike it? It is possible that Lorimer's explanation, based on the sophistic view, is not right. She and the schoolmaster both give a strictly chromatic meaning to πορφύρεος; to them the earlier use of the word in which the significance of hue is not dominant does not make sense. In early poetry πορφύρεος is not definitely chromatic, but describes the appearance which purple-dyed material and certain other objects have in common. This may be sheen or iridescence, the apparent mixture of light and dark on a changing surface. When πορφύρεος describes cheeks, "blushing" seems a felicitous translation, because it conveys for us the change of colour which traditionally accompanies the shy acknowledgment of love. When it describes the mouth, it is difficult to find a satisfactory translation. It seems to the author to describe the gleam and play of light on the lips, the surface of which reflects better than the surrounding skin. Whatever the exact meaning, it is clear from Sophocles' comment that he "saw" more in πορφύρεος than hue and that he found nothing unattractive in its use in Phrynichus and Simonides. He may have been unable to understand the schoolmaster's difficulty, or he may have thought it not worth his while to explain. His laugh suggests that the latter is more likely the case.[31]

30. H. L. Lorimer "Gold and Ivory in Greek Mythology" in *Greek Poetry and Life* (Oxford 1936) p. 24.

31 Cf. πορφύρω "heave" of the sea, "be troubled" of the mind. Many scholars have

Connected with poetic imagery is the further question of synaesthesia and its implications for our understanding of Greek sense perception. Synaesthesia is the expression of one sense in terms of another, e.g. the ascription of a visual quality to a sound. This is found not infrequently in Greek poetry in such lines as "the trumpet set the shores ablaze," where the trumpet sound seems to be a form of light (Aesch. *Pers.* 395), "unquenchable laughter arose," where the laughter is perceived as a flame (Hom. *Il.* 1.599) and the fine passage in Hesiod where the house of Zeus gleams with the lily-like voice of the Muses (*Theog.* 40-42).[32] For the author who does not see the world as the Greek poets saw it, and in particular, does not feel the unity they felt in the perception of the senses, these lines clearly involve metaphor. Synaesthesia can be a problem when we find sound described as coloured (e.g. a voice can be "white" or "black"), but it may help our understanding if we can find analogies within the range of our own or others' experience (see further Appendix I).

A strong association between colour and music is experienced

attempted to explain the range of meanings in πορφύρεος: N.-P. Bénaky "Des termes qui désignent le violet" *REG* 28 (1915) 16-38; L. Deroy "A propos du nom de la pourpre" *LEC* 16 (1948) 3-10; B. Marzullo "Afrodite porporina?" *Maia* 3 (1950) 132-136; A. Castrignanò "Ancora a proposito di πορφύρω, πορφύρεος" *Maia* 5(1952) 118-121; D'Avino pp. 109-112; H. Gipper "Purpur. Weg und Leistung eines umstrittenen Farbworts" *Glotta* 42 (1964) 39-69. See Index of Greek words s.v. πορφύρεος for further discussion and Boisacq s.v. who argues for the existence of two roots to explain the divergence of meaning.

Compare further Soph. *Ant.* 20 καλχαίνουσ' ἔπος "your words are dark and stormy." On this passage Goheen (*The Imagery of Sophocles Antigone* [Princeton 1951]) remarks "the primary denotation of the verb seems to be one of colour "to be purple" or "make purple" for it is apparently formed from *kalchê* a sea mollusk that was a source of purple dye . . . [It is] influenced by the analogy of *porphyrô*, as used by Homer to express the agitation of the sea and of mind, but also related to *hê porphyra* . . . and *porphyreos* . . . Therefore most editors credit the expression here with a double sensuous burden "to be dark and troublous, like a stormy sea" (pp. 45, 139 n. 16).

32. The interesting feature of these lines in Hesiod is the occurrence in combination of γελάω and λειριόεις; the house of Zeus "gleams" and the cause is the "lily" voice of the Muses. Each word reinforces the other in transferring "sight" sensations to sound. See further M. L. West *Hesiod Theogony*, edited with Prolegomena and Commentary (Oxford 1966) on lines 40, 41; and W. B. Stanford *Greek Metaphor* (Oxford 1936) pp. 114-116. A more recent example of synaesthesia can be found in Goethe, that student of perception: *Roman Elegies* no. 5:

Dann versteh ich den Marmor erst recht; ich denk und vergleich,
Sehe mit fühlendem Aug, fühle mit sehender Hand.

(*Werke* ed. E. Beutler [Zürich 1949], vol. 1, p. 167).

by certain people.[33] Newton compared the seven colours of the spectrum and the seven notes of the diatonic scale and tried to prove a close relationship between them. For others who associate colours with music, the key in which a composition is written brings to mind a colour. One of the author's colleagues, Emmet Robbins formerly of University College at the University of Toronto, has this experience of "seeing" a different colour for each key, and, moreover, of liking or disliking a composition because of its colour association. He suspects that it may be, to some degree, a learned association. One can also find colours associated with particular composers or compositions, and also with timbres of instruments. It is interesting that only in the last instance is there general agreement in the colours matched to each instrument. (Consider German *Klangfarbe* "sound-colour" for "timbre.")

The senses of taste and smell are closely linked in our perception. Taste has only four sensations: sweet, sour, salt, and bitter. Refinements are perceived not by taste but by smell, although we speak as if they were perceived by taste. We claim to "taste" orange juice in a fruit punch, or almond flavouring in icing, when in reality we are smelling them. The texture of food also plays a part in its identification. This relationship between taste and smell is seen in the term "bouquet" as applied to wines and in the approach of the connoisseur who first enjoys the aroma before he tastes. The connection is also seen in the noun "savour" which means in common use "taste" but has a poetic and archaic meaning "smell, perfume, aroma."[34]

Another example of synaesthesia is found in the perception of colour by touch. The blind can be taught to distinguish colours in objects of the same material if they are exposed to the sun. Because colours absorb heat at different rates, some colours are hotter to the touch than others. We acknowledge this connection between colour and heat when we choose light colours for summer

---

33. Cf. P. A. Scholes *The Oxford Companion to Music* (London 1955, 9th ed.) s.v. Colour and Music.

34. The *ONED* finds evidence of the meanings "taste" and "smell" also in Latin *sapor, sapere* (Pliny) and in Old French. The editors note that "savour" translates the Greek ὀσμή "smell" in versions of the Bible from Tindale (1526) onward.

wear because they are "cool" and dark colours for winter because they are "warm." We do, in fact, feel cooler in light colours than in dark ones of the same style and material because light colours reflect heat better. For the same reason interior decorators choose cool colours for rooms which receive bright sunlight, warm colours for rooms which do not.

These few examples show that our senses are not isolated from one another. Our cultural background, our understanding of the way in which our senses function, and associations which we have learned all contribute to the way in which we express ourselves. In this matter the learning process is very important. There is, for example, a scientific basis for the relationship between colour and touch, but even without knowing this, people may still learn to think of red as "warm" (the colour of fire) and green and blue as "cool" (the colours of water and grass).

Studies in the psychology of colour indicate that people find certain colours conducive to work and others distracting; some colours depress and others evoke a cheerful mood. The reason for this is largely the association of the particular colour with some experience. For example, because yellow reminds many people of sunshine, a yellow dress on a rainy day can cheer the wearer. Institutions are experimenting with more pleasant colours for the walls of rooms, because "hospital green" was found depressing.

Different cultures make different associations for colours. For example, in western countries, white is associated with purity and is the traditional colour for the bridal gown, whereas in China white is worn for mourning. The colour which suggests happiness for them is red, often used in the West for danger. We dress boy babies in blue and girls in pink — not exclusively — but most mothers hesitate to put pink on a boy. Climate undoubtedly influences colour preferences; in the tropics where the sun is strongest, strong, bright colours are widely used. At times, cultural and climatic influences work at cross purposes; in southern European countries most older women wear black, as befitting their age, in spite of the fact that black absorbs heat better than lighter colours, thus increasing discomfort in hot weather.[35]

35. Havelock Ellis *The Colour-Sense in Literature* (London, 1931) reprinted from

We must take into account the cultural learning process when we consider Greek colour perception, and particularly in the case of the extremes, black and white, we must be sensitive to Greek associations and not attribute our own to them.

II The Development of the Concept of Colour

When we ask what understanding the Greeks had of colour, we must first recognize that the understanding of the earliest poets differs greatly from that of Aristotle. The Homeric Greeks had not yet learned to think in abstract terms. "What is colour?" is a question they would never have formulated, let alone been able to answer. This condition accounts for the much-lamented vagueness of Homer's use of "colour" terms, in particular his habit of not restricting a term to colour, but using it for other effects. Once one realizes that "colour" is not a Homeric concept, it becomes obvious that one has been asking from Homer something beyond his ken. We may expect to see a change in the use of words as the process of abstraction gradually develops. (On colour terms in primitive languages, see Appendix IV.)

Several of the pre-Socratic philosophers considered the perception and production of colours. Parmenides (fl. ca. 500 B.C.) stated that dualism in the world, i.e. the presence of light and darkness, was responsible for the play of colours (fr. no. B.8. 38-41):

> τῶι πάντ᾽ ὄνομ(α) ἔσται,
> ὅσσα βροτοὶ κατέθεντο πεποιθότες εἶναι ἀληθῆ,
> γίγνεσθαί τε καὶ ὄλλυσθαι, εἶναί τε καὶ οὐχί
> καὶ τόπον ἀλλάσσειν διά τε χρόα φανὸν ἀμείβειν,

"Wherefore, all these are mere names which mortals laid down believing them to be true, coming into being and perishing, being and not being, change of place and variation of bright colour." Here perhaps is the explicit basis of the assumption drawn from Greek colour usage, that black and white are considered colours

Contemporary Review, May 1896, pp. 12, 24; J. Gernet, "Expression de la couleur en chinois" in Problèmes de la Couleur, ed. I. Meyerson (Paris 1957) p. 297.

and other colours are shades between these extremes (see below).[36]

Empedocles, in the middle of the fifth century, posited four elements to account for all the various appearances in the world: earth, water, fire and air. In discussing the nature of perception, he argued that "like perceives like" and that the eye must be constituted of these four elements in order to perceive them in the world. Theophrastus reports Empedocles as saying that white was the colour of fire, and black of water (*De Sens.* 59; Empedocles A. 69a): Ἐμπεδοκλῆς δέ καὶ περὶ πῶν χρωμάτων, καὶ ὅτι τὸ μὲν λευκὸν τοῦ πυρὸς τὸ δὲ μέλαν τοῦ ὕδατος. He also reports that Empedocles thought the inner part of the eye consisted of fire and water, fire perceiving white and water black (*De Sens.* 7, Empedocles A.86). It is true that other commentators attribute four primary colours to Empedocles, the same number as the elements (Stob. *Ecl. Phys.* 1.16 Aët. 1.15.3, A. 92): τέτταρα δέ τοῖς στοιχείοις ἰσάριθμα (χρώματα) λευκὸν μέλαν ἐρυθρὸν ὠχρόν, but it has been argued that this theory of four primary colours belongs properly to Democritus and has been mistakenly attributed to the earlier philosopher.[37] If black is the colour of water and white of fire, it is hard to imagine how the other elements, air and earth, could be paired with red and yellow; earth, in this period, is black or dark and air white. (See the discussion of earth and sky, chapter 5.) It seems likely that Empedocles contented himself with accounting for white and black.[38]

Anaxagoras is said by Aristotle to have been older than Empedocles, but later in philosophical activity (Diels *VS* A.43). It seems he may have regarded black and white as basic colours. Theophrastus, after giving Empedocles' view, says that others

36. See G. S. Kirk and J. E. Raven *The Pre-Socratic Philosophers* (Cambridge 1957) p. 277.

37. H. Diels *Doxographi Graeci* (Berlin 1879) p. 222.

38. For further discussion of Empedocles, see C. Prantl *Aristotles über die Farben* (Munich 1849) pp. 40-48; J. Beare *Greek Theories of Elementary Cognition* (Oxford 1906) pp. 14-23; W. Kranz "Die ältesten Farbenlehren der Griechen" in *Hermes* 47 (1912) 126-129. Empedocles thought that light-coloured eyes had a preponderance of fire and saw better at night, whereas dark eyes contained more water and saw dimly at night, better by day. (Arist. *Generat. Animal.* 779b15ff.) For an attempt to make sense of this theory, see D. O'Brien in *JHS* 88 (1968) 111.

thought that white and black were the "beginnings" and other colours resulted from a mixture of these; he adds that Anaxagoras spoke simply about them (*De Sens.* 59): οἱ δ' ἄλλοι τοσοῦτον μόνον, ὅτι τό τε λευκὸν καὶ τὸ μέλαν ἀρχαί, τὰ δ' ἄλλα μειγνυμένων γίνεται τούτων καὶ γὰρ Ἀναξαγόρας ἁπλῶς εἴρηκε περὶ αὐτῶν. Anaxagoras evidently thought that colours were not separable from coloured things, for he said that "while everything was together, no colour was discernible" (Diels *VS* B.4): πρὶν δὲ ἀποκριθῆναι ταῦτα πάντων ὁμοῦ ἐόντων, οὐδὲ χροιὴ ἔνδηλος ἦν οὐδεμία. The impossibility of separating the colour from its object led to Anaxagoras' famous assertion that snow was black, for since water was black, and snow was frozen water, snow, then, must be black (A.97).[39]

A generation after Anaxagoras, Democritus the atomist was the first philosopher to attempt a detailed theory of colour. According to Theophrastus (*De Sens.* 73-78) he posited four simple (ἁπλᾶ) colours: white, black, red and green (λευκόν, μέλαν, ἐρυθρόν, χλωρόν). He argued that the shape of atoms determined their colour: white atoms were smooth, straight-bored, and translucent; black were rough and uneven; red were like atoms of heat, only larger. With green his explanation faltered somewhat, because he attributed green to a combination of the solid and the void, not to shape. Beginning with these four colours, Democritus attempted to account for others. Some of his mixtures are very odd, if one thinks primarily in terms of spectral hue; they can be better appreciated if one realizes that he intended the four primary colours to account for brightness and saturation as well. Purple (τὸ πορφοροῦν) for example is said to result from a mixture of white, black and red; black and red are apparent to sight, and white gives lustre: ὅτι μὲν οὖν τὸ μέλαν καὶ τὸ ἐρυθρὸν ἐνυπάρχει, φανερὸν εἶναι τῇ ὄψει, διότι δὲ τὸ λευκόν, τὸ λαμπρὸν καὶ διαυγὲς σημαίνειν. His derivation of blue (ἰσάτις) from black and green has caused some consternation (see Schultz *above*); his use of black here suggests that the blue is relatively dark and dull. Having set himself the task of accounting for various colours from a basic

---

39. In support of the view that Anaxagoras held black and white to be primary colours, see Prantl p. 58; Beare p. 40 takes a more cautious interpretation.

group of four, Democritus considered their brightness and intensity ahead of their hue. His attempt was unsatisfactory, but he had begun to work out the implications of his theory.[40]

In the fourth century major works on colour were written by Plato, Aristotle, Theophrastus, and the unknown Peripatetic author of *De Coloribus*. Plato mentioned colour in a number of places in his writings, but in the *Timaeus* 67e-68d he put forward a colour theory in the manner of Democritus, accounting for the variety of colours in the world from four primary ones.[41] His primary colours, white, black, red, and "bright" (λευκόν, μέλαν, ἐρυθρόν, λαμπρόν), differ in only one member from Democritus', but that difference is important. Whereas Democritus used white to produce lustre, Plato replaced white in this function with "bright," not strictly a colour term at all, and used white to produce colours lighter in value. For example, white mixed with bright yellow (ξανθός ὠχρός) gives pale yellow (ὠχρός); mixed with dark blue (κυανοῦς) it gives light blue (γλαυκός). His production of purple (ἀλουργὸς) from red mixed with white and black looks on the surface to be very much like Democritus' account (see above), but Democritus, in using white, was accounting particularly for brightness and it should be noted that his "purple" (τὸ πορφυροῦν) is not the same Greek term as Plato's.[42]

Aristotle (*De Sens.* 439a-440b) stated that colours resulted from a mixture of white and black. Between these extremes there were not, as some thought, an infinite number of colours, but five definite species, making a total of seven counting white and black. These he specified as (*De Sens.* 442a) yellow (ξανθόν), crimson (φοινικοῦν), purple (ἀλουργόν), green (πράσινον) and blue (κυανοῦν). Other shades were mixed from this group. Aristotle's

40. Democritus' colour theory is further discussed in Prantl pp. 48-58, Beare pp. 23-37; see also A. Dyroff *Demokritstudien* (Munich 1899) 176-184 (*Exkurs, Zur Farbenlehre des Demokrit*) as cited in W. K. C. Guthrie *A History of Greek Philosophy* vol. 2, p. 445. (Cambridge, 1965)

41. Cf. *Meno* 76d, e, *Phaedo* 110b-e, *Symp.* 211e, *Rep.* 6.500 c-501c, 507d-509a, 9.585b-586c, 10.601a-602e, *Crat.* 424b-425b, *Theaet.* 153d-154b, 156a-157a, 182a, b, *Phileb.* 51b, d.

42. For a discussion of Plato's theory of colour, see K. Gaiser "Platons Farbenlehre" in *Synusia* (Festschr. Schadewaldt) (Pfüllingen 1965) pp. 173-222; Beare pp. 42-56; Prantl pp. 61-77.

choice of colours corresponds quite closely to the range of the spectrum; if ξανθόν is "yellow," then he lacked a particular term for orange. He was aware that some colours are related closely to one another and could be grouped in families. It is interesting that he still kept the traditional black/white measurement along with the recognition of hue and argued for an origin from a mixture of black and white for the hues.[43]

Theophrastus reported and criticized the work of his predecessors in colour theory (*De Sens.* 73-78). He accepted Aristotle's sevenfold division of colours (*De Caus. Plant.* 6.4.1; cf. Arist. *De Sens.* 442a above), and was very interested in his various works in accounting for the appearance of natural objects. It has been argued that he, or a pupil who followed his master closely, was the author of the treatise *De Coloribus* which was wrongly attributed to Aristotle. This work describes and classifies colours of objects in nature and attempts to assign an immediate cause, in particular where there is a change of colour involved. Primary colours are given as white, black, and yellow (ξανθός, 791a1-12).[44]

Thus we see in the colour theorists that colours are persistently treated as gradations between the extremes of black and white, even after an awareness of colour (hue) family groupings has developed. In the modern view the position on the spectrum is of most importance in classifying colours, and their relative value (light − or darkness) does not influence the general grouping. But we learned through Newton that an object is white because the rays of white light are wholly reflected from its surface, and black because the rays of light are wholly absorbed, so that white and black are in this sense extremes of colour (see *supra* on Newton and *ONED* s.v. colour). The Greeks then, were not so unlike us as they seemed in our first consideration of their primary colours. For both them and us, white and black are the extremes. The

43. For a discussion of Aristotle's colour theory, see Prantl pp. 80-159, Beare pp. 56-92.

44. For a discussion of Theophrastus and his colour theory, see Prantl pp. 181-184, W. Capelle "Farbenbeizeichnungen bei Theophrast" in *RhM* 101 (1958) 1-41. For the attribution of *De Coloribus* to Theophrastus or a pupil see H. B. Gottschalk "The *De Coloribus* and its Author" in *Hermes* 92 (1964) 59-85, esp. 83-85. This article also discusses the *De Coloribus*, its relationship to the genuine works of Aristotle, an analysis of the work with some notes on obscurities. Also on the *De Coloribus*, see C. Prantl *Aristoteles über die Farben* (Munich 1849), commentary, pp. 80-159.

difference is in the arrangement. They seem to have arranged colours from the lightest to the darkest hues, as if one could, by gradually abstracting white, produce the various colours, until at last one had only black left. We arrange colours in the order in which we find them on the spectrum: red, orange, yellow, green, blue, violet; and we recognize the validity of this order in such terms as "complementary" and "contiguous" colours. In spite of the differences between Greek colour theory and Newtonian, it is obvious that the theorists of the fourth century understood the nature of colour as the earlier Greeks did not.

Colour is defined in the *ONED* as "the quality or attribute in virtue of which objects present different appearances to the eye, when considered with regard only to the kind of light reflected from their surfaces." There are two points of importance in this definition: the visual nature of colour and its connection with form. The earliest statement in Greek of the nature of colour is found in Plato's *Meno* (75b): ἔστω γὰρ δὴ ἡμῖν τοῦτο σχῆμα, ὅ μόνον τῶν ὄντων τυγχάνει χρώματι ἀεὶ ἑπόμενον. "Well, then, let this be our definition of shape — the only thing which is always accompanied by colour." Later in the same dialogue (76d) we read that "colour is commensurate with and perceived by sight": χρόα ὄψει σύμμετρος καὶ αἰσθητός. Plato understood the visual nature of colour and its occurrence in conjunction with physical objects, both characteristics mentioned in the *ONED*. The recognition of the nature of the quality "colour" affected descriptive terms. The theorists tried to define these terms within the bounds of colour, even those which quite clearly had a meaning broader than colour. They also attempted to make up the lack in terms for green and blue (see n. 46), thus showing that they wanted to be able to describe all appearances which fell under the general term "colour."

III Problems With Individual Words

There are two aspects of the problem here: first, the meaning of individual words, and secondly, the general picture of colour perception. Certain colour terms are used in contexts where their (supposed) colour is quite unsuitable. We find λειριόεις "lily-white" used of sound in Homer and Hesiod, and if we refuse to call it a "metaphor," we must ask, in the manner of a riddle, "Why is a voice like a lily?" (See Appendix I). The epithet οἶνοψ in Homer's oft-quoted "wine-dark" sea also describes cattle (*Od.* 5.132). We may well wonder what point of comparison exists between wine and water and also between wine and cattle. The author inclines to the view that a dark surface reflecting light is in all cases being described. Wine in the ancient world was seen, not through glass as in modern times, but in an opaque *crater* or cup. It was the surface that caught the eye. Similarly the sea viewed from land or shipboard may, under appropriate weather conditions, appear dark with reflected lights. In the case of cattle, too, the surface, i.e. hide, may be dark and glossy. These, however, are small problems (since the epithets occur seldom) in comparison with πορφύρεος. This epithet describes dyed material and is fixed by its etymological connection with πορφύρα "the purple fish" as appropriate to the famous "purple" of the ancient world. The appearance of the best quality of purple dyed stuff is described by Pliny (*N. H.* 9.135): *laus ei summa in colore sanguinis concreti, nigrans aspectu idemque suspectu refulgens.* "Purple" in the ancient world was a rich brilliant crimson. Yet πορφύρεος which describes this colour also is used for a wave which "sang loudly around the keel of the ship as she went" (*Od.* 2.428); for death (*Il.* 5.83); for the rainbow (*Il.* 17.547); for lips and cheeks of young people (as we saw earlier); for Aphrodite (Anacr. fr.357.3 *PMG*). This word would make an extremely interesting study, and has the added interest that its Latin cognate *purpureus* shows a similar, unusual breadth of meaning.[45]

Another term which seems to vary strangely in meaning is κυάνεος. In the colour theorists it is defined as "blue," specifically "dark blue" (Plato Timaeus 68c, Theophr. *De Sens.* 77). But if we translate it as "blue" in early poetry, we produce effects which are hard to imagine: blue clouds (*Il.* 13.563), hair (*Il.* 22.401-403), earth (*Od.* 12.243); a blue bull (*h. Herm.* 194), a blue-winged grasshopper (Hes. *Sc.* 393), blue men from Ethiopia (Hes. *W.D.* 527). One could go on and on with more delightful fantasies. It

---

45. Some of the more striking uses are found in Vergil *Aen.* 1.590-591 "lumenque iuventae purpureum," 6.640-641 "lumine purpureo" (of the Elysian Fields); and Horace *Od.* 4.1.10 "purpureis ales oloribus."

would have been generally acknowledged long ago that κυάνεος was not "blue" in early poetry, were it not for the presence of a material named kyanos, widely identified as "blue glass paste." The problem of κυάνεος is discussed in chapter three and attempts made to explain what it meant to the poets and also to deal with the matter of kyanos.

Another colour term which has caused puzzlement is χλωρός. It is fixed by the theorists as "green," but it describes in poetry many objects which we would not call green: honey (Il. 11.631), a nightingale (Od. 19.518), dew (Pind. Nem. 8.40), tears (Eur. Med. 906), and blood (Eur. Hec. 127). The colours of these objects vary from colourless to red, and one cannot be blamed for feeling that the poets are stretching credulity too far. A closer examination, however, suggests a surprising point: in the list above all but one object (the nightingale) are liquid. It is hoped that the investigation in chapter two of all the occurrences of χλωρός in the poetry of the period in an attempt to establish its basic meaning will show that this is not mere coincidence.

Let these examples suffice to show that part of the method of dealing with the problem of colour in Greek poetry must involve a discussion of terms which cause difficulty. Such studies will help us to get at the meaning of the term and the way in which the Greeks arranged certain characteristics together in groupings which are not familiar to us.

IV The General Problem

The second, and more general, aspect of the problem is the way in which the Greeks before the sophistic age developed their concept of colour. In the matter of vocabulary it has often been observed that they had a surprising variety of words for "white" and "black" (or "light" and "dark"), a goodly number for "red," "yellow," and "purple," and an inadequate representation for "blue" and "green."[46] They preferred to describe contrast rather

46. It is particularly interesting to observe how they filled in the gaps. In the matter of blue, κυάνεος was fixed as dark blue, γλαυκός as light blue, and ἰσάτις "woad" (a dye) was added to the vocabulary. In green, names were formed from green objects: "grass-green" ποιώδης from ποία "grass"; "frog-green," βατράχειος from βάτραχος "frog"; "leek-green" πράσινος from πράσον "leek" and "emerald-green"

than hue, so that, especially in the earliest poets, blacks and whites predominate. They emphasized a contrast by describing one extreme as "black," the other as "white"; e.g. men were dark, women light, sadness dark, happiness light, death dark, life bright. In chapters four and five some of these contrasts between dark/black and white/light objects are considered. It is interesting to see the influence which this way of looking at the world had on Greek speech patterns.

The author's original plan was to discuss a number of words in individual studies, with due regard for their historical development. Because of the amount of material which it seemed advisable to include, it has been possible to discuss in any depth only three: χλωρός, κυάνεος and λειριόεις. Also to be examined was the general problem of perception, i.e. why the Greeks emphasized dark/light contrasts instead of hue, and why blues and greens are so peculiarly lacking in the early period. The first of these problems is considered here, but remarks on the second have been limited to general observations.

Chapter two contains an examination of χλωρός; chapter three of κυάνεος; chapters four and five of contrasts of dark and light. Although the poets considered in this study are those from Homer to the end of the fifth century, where something of interest in later poetry or in prose writers has been found, it has been introduced. It should be noted that the coverage in this period is uneven, varying at one extreme from the long Homeric epics, Hesiod's didactic works and other poems in this style to the four Athenian dramatists at the other. Between these termini the remains of the lyric poets are comparatively few and fragmentary, so this period is less well represented and two difficulties arise: often the context of a particular word is not sufficient to give any assistance in its interpretation, and we cannot be sure whether such a word occurred only once in a particular usage, or whether it was repeated by other poets. On the second score at least we have some indications from ancient commentators to assist us.

σμαράγδινος from σμάραγδος "emerald." Wallace prefers to derive πράσινος from πρασιά "garden" (p. 16).

$$\boxed{\begin{array}{c} \text{Two} \\ \chi\lambda\omega\rho\acute{o}\varsigma \end{array}}$$

I Introduction

Although χλωρός has a far-ranging meaning, the number of its occurrences within our period is not so great as to make impractical a review of all of them here. *LSJ* define χλωρός as I "greenish-yellow"; "yellow, pale-green"; II generally, "pale"; III without regard to colour, "green," i.e. "fresh"; metaphorical, "fresh, blooming, sparkling"; metaphorical, "unripe." A glance at this definition tempts one to believe that the Greeks could not distinguish between green and yellow; worse, that they used the same word for both these colours and "pale." The "metaphorical" meanings are not so likely to trouble us; they may in fact lull us into believing that χλωρός is like the English "green," which can mean "unripe" as e.g. in "green apple, greenhorn."

It will be instructive to look at some Greek words that are related to χλωρός. Χλόη "vegetation" and its derivative χλόος "young green" compare with the use of χλωρός to describe plants and trees, discussed in section two of this chapter. The relationship of χλωρός to χόλος and χολή "bile" will be better understood in the light of section four, in the discussion of fear and other emotions. Χλωρός is also related to χλιδή "delicacy," χλούνις "virility,"[1] and χλούνης, an epic epithet of the wild boar, of disputed meaning,[2] but perhaps, on the analogy of χλούνις

---

1. Χλούνις occurs only in Aesch. *Eum.* 188, where its meaning is determined by the context: σπέρματός τ'ἀποφθορᾶι / παίδων κακοῦται χλούνις.
2. The ancient commentators were clearly at a loss. Some of their guesses were : "castrated" Arist. *H.A.* 578b1; "solitary" Aristoph. Byz. apud Eust. 772.59; "foaming"

"virile." These words correspond, in some measure, to the appropriateness of χλωρός to life and youth (cf. section five), as does the following example from Pindar. Three times he uses a form of κεχλαδ – (the perfect of *χλήδω), twice of music (*Olymp.* 9.2 and fr. 70b.10) and again in *Pyth.* 4.179 of two of the Argonauts, κεχλάδοντας ἥβαι "swelling with youth" according to the interpretation of the scholiast.[3] One can recognize the similarity of "swelling strains of music" and the swelling of youth. Also in Pindar we find the puzzling word χλαρός used with γελάω in *Pyth.* 9.38 of the centaur's laugh. The scholiast gives its meaning as προσηνὲς καὶ γλυκύ, a reasonable guess in the context. If, as appears to be the case, it belongs to the group we have been discussing, then it signifies a "swelling laugh" (cf. the Homeric ἄσβεστος γέλως).[4]

Χλοερός, cognate to χλωρός, not simply an alternate form, is a synonym, but apparently with a narrower range of meaning. On most of the occasions where it is used, it describes vegetation,[5] but once, in Theocritus (27.67), it means "supple," of the limbs of a pair of lovers. (Theocritus might be assumed to be using the word by analogy with χλωρός.)

According to Boisacq,[6] χλωρός developed from the Indo-European *ĝhlo-, and is related to words which connote brightness, e.g. Icelandic *glóra* "to sparkle," *glór-eygdr* "with sparkling eyes," *glan* "shine of polished objects," Old and Middle High German *gluot* "burning coals," etc. It is also related to colour words, e.g. Old Norse *glámr* "moon" ("with a yellow face"), Latin Germanic *glesum* "amber," and Indo-European *ĝhel(e) "the

Schol. B. *Il.* 9.539; "with its bed in the grass" Apollon. *Lex. AB* 1260, *Etym. Magn.* 812.46. This last suggestion equates χλουνής with χλοεύνης formed from χλόη "grass" and εὐνή "bed." The same etymology gives χλοῦναι as "robbers" who lie in ambush in the grass (Hesychius *et al.*).

3. Πληθύοντας τῆι ἥβηι.

4. Cf. *LSJ* s.v. ὑγρογέλως "softly laughing," Phrynichus, *Praeparatio Sophistica* ed. I. de Borries (Leipzig 1911) p. 117, in the light of the conclusions of this chapter that χλωρός has to do with moisture.

5. On the form of χλοερός cf. D. J. Georgacas, *Glotta* 36 (1957) 191. It occurs in Hes. *Sc.* 393; Eur. *Bacch.* 866 (lyr.), *Ion* 497 (lyr.), *Phoen.* 660 (lyr.), χλοεροτρόφος *Phoen.* 826 (lyr.); Soph. *Ichn.* 215; Sim. Theb. fr. 2.2; Philox. Leucad. 836(b)17 *PMG*; *Batroch.* 162.

6. Boisacq s.v. χλωρός. See also R. D'Avino "La visione del colore" in *Ricerche Linguistica* 4(1958) 122-123.

colour yellow or green, shine." Persson[7] attaches to this group Irish *gle, glae* "gleaming," Old Gaelic *gloiu* "liquid," and Modern Gaelic *gloew* "shining, gleaming." Χλωρός is also related through *ĝhlo- to Anglo-Saxon *zlóm, zlómunz* "twilight," from which we get "gloaming." The etymological sense of gloaming, according to the *Oxford New English Dictionary*, would seem to be the *glow* of sunset or sunrise, again an emphasis of brightness. The *ONED* also notes the root glo- with a double idea of shine and staring gaze, as in the obsolete English *glore*, I "shine, glitter, glisten," II "stare." For the hypothesis set forth in this chapter, the most suggestive word in this etymological maze is the Old Gaelic *gloiu* "liquid," since the aim is to show that the basic meaning of χλωρός is "liquid," moist.[8] Of primary concern is the Greek meaning, not the Indo-European origin, but it would add support if the one coincided with, or overlapped, the other.

Before we turn to an examination of the occurrences of χλωρός, it is necessary to establish the connection which the Greeks felt between life, youth, and moisture on the one hand, and death, old age, and dryness on the other. Only then can we begin to appreciate the range of χλωρός and to understand the common element of meaning the Greeks saw in its various applications.

Twice, in the *Odyssey*, Homer uses διερός apparently in the meaning "active, alive."[9] In *Odyssey* 6.201, Nausicaa proudly asserts that no man alive dares harm the Phaeaceans:

οὐκ ἔσθ᾽ οὗτος ἀνὴρ διερὸς βροτὸς οὐδὲ γένηται
ὅς κε Φαιήκων ἀνδρῶν ἐς γαῖαν ἵκηται
δηϊοτῆτα φέρων·

Eustathius' comment on διερὸς βροτός is well worth repeating, since in it he expounds the Greek association of moisture with life and dryness with death, with several illustrations. Διερὸς δὲ βροτὸς ὁ ζῶν καὶ ἐρρωμένος· τὴν μὲν γὰρ ζωὴν ὑγρότης καὶ θερμότης

---

7. P. Persson, *Beiträge zur indogermanischen Wortforschung* (Uppsala 1912) vol. 2. p. 793.

8. Old Gaelic *gloiu* could be <*gl-oi-w, cf. Greek γλοιός "slippery" and Latin *gluten* "glue," giving a root meaning "wet, slippery."

9. So Aristarchus takes it *Scholia Graeca in Homeri Odysseam* ed. K. W. Dindorf (Oxford 1855) at *Od.* 6.201.

συνέχει. τὸν δὲ θάνατον τὰ ἐναντία ποιεῖ. ὅθεν καὶ νεκροὶ ἀλίβαντες οἱ ζωτικῆς λιβάδος ἄμοιροι. καὶ ὁ κωμικὸς δὲ παίζων αὐαίνου λίθον ἐν ἅιδου εἶναι πλάττει. (This is a reference to Aristophanes *Frogs* 194.) ἀπὸ τοῦ αὐαινωθεὶς τοὔνομα. Πλούταρχος δὲ ἐν τοῖς κατ' αὐτὸν συμποσιακοῖς φησὶν οὕτως· ὑγρότητι καὶ θερμότητι τεθήλασι τὰ ζῶια. ἡ δὲ ψυχρότης καὶ ξηρότης ὀλέθρια. διὸ χαριέντως Ὅμηρος διερὸν Βροτὸν καλεῖ. "A διερὸς mortal is one who is living and in good health. For moisture and warmth maintain life. Their opposites cause death. From this also corpses are called ἀλίβαντες "those who have no share of living moisture." The comic poet playfully pictures the Stone of Drying in Hades. The name comes from "being dried." Plutarch, in his *Symposium*, says this: living creatures thrive on moisture and warmth; but coldness and dryness are deadly. Therefore Homer puts it well when he calls a mortal διερός."

It is quite clear from this line of reasoning that Eustathius takes διερός "alive" to be the same as διερός "moist." Some authorities[10] however, separate these meanings and posit the existence of διερός "active, alive" as distinct from and different in origin from διερός "moist, liquid," the opposite of αὖος (Hes. W. D. 460) and ξηρός (Anaxag. Diels VS B.4.12), both "dry." In the former meaning, it is suggested, διερός is cognate with διέμαι "speed, hasten," in the latter, with διαίνω "wet, moisten." Eustathius offers a reasonable explanation of the combination of ideas in διερός and supports this explanation with other literary evidence, incidentally shedding light there as well. His argument deserves to be considered carefully. He comments further: "ἀλίβας and σκελετός are names for the dead. The ancients reproached[11] them with the name of dryness." ὁ δὲ ἀλίβας καὶ ὁ σκελετὸς ἐπὶ νεκρῶν λέγονται· λοιδορουμένων τῶν παλαιῶν τῶι ὀνόματι τῆς ξηρότητος. Didymus also relates ἀλίβας to the concept of dryness; compare his note quoted by the Scholiast on Aristophanes *Frogs* 186: τὸ δὲ λήθης πεδίον, Δίδυμός φησι, χωρίον ἐν ἅιδου τετύπωκεν

---

10. LSJ and Boisacq s.v. διερός. Frisk (s.v. διερός) also posits two derivations, although he questions the connection with διέμαι. He refers to Schultze's suggestion (F. Bechtel *Lexilogus zu Homer* [Halle 1914] s.v.) that the root is related to δείδω.

11. "Reproached." I am at a loss to explain why the names are considered a reproach.

ὡς καὶ τὸν Αὐαίνου λίθον ἔπλησεν ἀπὸ τοῦ αὐαίνεσθαι τοὺς νεκροὺς καὶ ἀλίβαντας εἶναι. Eustathius also mentions the second occurrence of διερός in the *Odyssey* (9.43), in which Odysseus, relating the story of the pursuit of his crew by the Cicones, says, "Then, indeed, I bade us flee with swift foot." ἔνθ᾽ ἦ τοι μὲν ἐγὼ διερῶι ποδὶ φευγέμεν ἡμέας/ ἠνώγεα. Eustathius comments: τὰ δὲ ῥηθέντα (i.e. his previous argument) ἐνταῦθα εἰς τὸ 'διερὸς βροτός' χρήσιμα καὶ ἐν τοῖς ἑξῆς εἰς τὸ 'διερῶι ποδί' ὅτι δὲ ὁ ὑγιὴς καὶ ἡ ὑγίεια ἐκ τοῦ ὑγροῦ παράγεται ἐν ἄλλοις δεδήλωται. "What has been said here is useful for the interpretation of διερὸς βροτός and for διερῶι ποδί, which occurs later. It has been shown elsewhere that 'healthy' and 'health' come from ὑγρός 'moist.'" Eustathius thus suggests that διερός signifies more than merely "living." It connotes good health and can therefore mean "active" as well.

Ὑγρός which has just been related by Eustathius to ὑγιής and ὑγίεια, is similar to διερός in comprising moisture and movement in its definition. It is "moist" as opposed to ξηρός (cf. Plato *Laws* 746e; Luke 23.31; Xenophon *Oec.* 19.7). It also describes the heaving surface of the sea in Homer, ὑγρὰ κέλευθα (*Il.* 1.312; *Od.* 3.71), the back of the slumbering eagle in Pindar (*Pyth.* 1.9), dancing feet in Bacchylides (16.108), and the supple form of Eros in Plato (*Symp.* 196a). These examples show that the basic meaning of ὑγρός is not wetness but the smooth, continuous line found in wet things like the sea and also in fluid motion.

Using this word, pseudo-Aristotle states the belief that the living are moist and the dead dry. (*De Long. et Brev. Vit.* 466a19ff). τὸ δὲ ζῷόν ἐστι φύσει ὑγρὸν καὶ θερμὸν καὶ τὸ ζῆν τοιοῦτον, τὸ δὲ γῆρας ψυχρὸν καὶ ξηρὸν καὶ τὸ τεθνηκός ... ἀνάγκη τοίνυν γηράσκοντα ξηραίνεσθαι. "The living creature is by nature moist and warm, and to live is to be such, but old age is cold and dry and so is what is dead ... It is inevitable, then, that one who grows old should dry up." Not only, then, are the living distinguished from the dead by their moisture, or lack of it, but also the young from the old. New-born creatures were particularly characterized by moisture in the Greek view. Thus Homer, in describing how the Cyclops, Polyphemus, kept his goats in separate pens, says (*Od.* 9.220-222):

διακεκριμέναι δὲ ἔκασται
ἔρχατο, χωρὶς μὲν πρόγονοι, χωρὶς δὲ μέτασσαι,
χωρὶς δ' αὖθ' ἔρσαι·

"Each group was kept separate, apart the firstlings, apart the middle-born, and apart again the dew-drops." Whatever one's interpretation of the various groups, the "dew-drops" are the youngest.[12] Homer is not the only poet to describe young creatures in this way. Aeschylus (*Ag.* 141-143) has the chorus address Artemis who is "gentle to the dew of fierce lions and the young who love the breast of all wild beasts of the field"[13]

δρόσοις . . . μαλερῶν λεόντων
πάντων τ' ἀγρονόμων φιλομάστοις
θηρῶν ὀβρικάλοισι τερπνά.

Here δρόσοι is used in place of the Homeric ἔρσαι to describe the "dewiness" of young animals. Eustathius in his comment on *Od.* 9.220-222 tells us that ἔρσαι is the same as ψάκαλα, derived from ψακάς "dew." Both these terms are used as names for young animals which are, as it were, dewy because of their softness. He reports that Aristophanes of Byzantium gives ψάκαλα as one of the names for sucklings and new-born creatures. As an illustration of this word he quotes from Sophocles (fr. 725 N.):

ψακαλοῦχοι
μήτέρες αἶγές τ' ἐπιμαστίδιον
γόνον ὀρταλίχων ἀναφαίνοιεν.

"May mothers with young and goats show offspring of young at the breast." In form ψακαλοῦχοι is a compound of ψάκαλον "dew-drop" i.e. "new-born" and ἔχω, on the authority of Hesychius s.v. ψακαλοῦχοι. Pearson suggests that the name

12. Eustathius on *Od.* 9.220 (1625. 28-30) interprets the three groups as first-born, middle-born, and youngest. Giles in *CR* 3(1889) 3-4 argued that the division was rather into rams, ewes, and kids as is mentioned elsewhere in the tale. Eustathius' view is commonly accepted, cf. W. B. Stanford *The Odyssey of Homer* (London 1950) on *Od.* 9.221-222.

13. On ὀβρικάλοισι "young." *LSJ* s.v. ὀβρίκαλα suggest a possible connection with ὄμβρος "rain," perhaps reading ὄμβριον for ὄβριον. This is not even accorded mention in Boisacq and Frisk s.v. ὄβρια. Ὀβρίκαλα occurs only in Aesch. *Ag.* 143; ὄβρια is cited by Aelian *N.A.* 7.47 as occurring in Aesch. (fr. 48) and Euripides (fr. 616). It would be interesting indeed if ὀβρίκαλα and ὄβρια were related to ὄμβρος "rain," giving yet another example of young animals described in terms of moisture.

ψάκαλοι "dew-drops" as used by Aelian *N.A.* 7.47 is not a literary curiosity but an indication of a basic association of moisture and young creatures in Greek.[14] (Aelian says that this name is given to the young of birds, snakes and crocodiles by some). A poet of the 6th century after Christ, Agathias Scholasticus, speaks of "birds, mothers of dewy chicks," ὄρνιθες δροσερῶν μητέρες ὀρταλίχων (*A.P.* 5.291). I think that he, too, is expressing the connection between young animals and moisture. In the light of this association of youth and moisture, the name "dew-drop" for a young animal can be properly appreciated.

Old age and death, as we have seen, are dry. Eustathius states that two names for the dead, ἀλίβαντες and σκελετός, indicate their dryness; Didymus also connects ἀλίβας with the concept of the dryness of the dead; and the Aristotelian treatise agrees that as a man grows older, he dries up (see above). So, when in *Od.* 13.430 Athene ages Odysseus to disguise him, "she dried up the fair skin on his supple limbs": κάρψε μὲν οἱ χρόα καλὸν ἐνὶ γναμπτοῖσι μέλεσσι. The same verb, κάρφω, is used by Archilochus (fr.113.D): οὐκέθ' ὁμῶς θάλλεις ἀπαλὸν χρόα· κάρφεται γὰρ ἤδη "But no longer have you a bloom on your tender skin; for it is already being dried up." As we see from these verbs θάλλεις and κάρφεται people can be described in Greek as if they were plants, in terms of moisture, i.e. in terms of freshness or dryness. Κάρφω gives the noun κάρφος "dry stalk," and θάλλω, θαλλός "young shoot." A few more examples of this people/plant relationship follow. In *Od.* 14.214, Odysseus says of himself to Eumaeus: ἀλλ' ἔμπης καλάμην γέ σ' οἴομαι εἰσορόωντα/ γιγνώσκειν. "Nevertheless, I think, as you look at me, you recognize the stubble," i.e. all that remains of my strength, as the stubble indicates the harvest that has been reaped. Aeschylus (*Ag.* 79-80) speaks of an old man φυλλάδος ἤδη κατακαρφομένης "with foliage now drying up." (Cf. Shakespeare's *Macbeth* "My way of life is fall'n into . . . the yellow leaf" Act 5. Sc. 1). Aristophanes calls Cleon's prisoners from Sphacteria a "harvest of ears of grain" which Cleon is "drying." (*Knights* 392ff). All these examples have

---

14. A. C. Pearson, *The Fragments of Sophocles* (Cambridge 1917) in a note on this fragment (fr. 793 in his edition).

as their point of comparison between people and plants, moisture or lack of it.

The best known parallel between the life of a person and a plant is the concept of the tree nymph who lives while her tree stands and perishes when it dies. (Cf *h. Aphr.* 264-272.) Pindar says concerning these nymphs that they "have for their lot as limit αἰών equal to that of a tree," ἰσοδένδρου τέκμαρ αἰῶνος λαχοῖσαι (fr. 165). We shall discover that αἰών which is possessed by the nymph and her tree also belongs to the general concept of moisture and dryness.

Onians[15] argues that the moisture present in living people which decreases with age, and finally disappears at death, is the Homeric αἰών. Αἰών is generally translated "period of existence" on the assumption that it is cognate with *aevum* and ἀεί. It then supposedly develops from meaning "life-time" to meaning "life." But a careful reading of Homer will reveal that both the αἰών and the ψυχή are vital substances which are necessary for life and leave the body at death:

ἐπὴν δὴ τόν γε λίπηι ψυχή τε καὶ αἰών   (*Il.* 16.453)

ἔπειτά με καὶ λίποι αἰών   (*Il.* 5.685)

αὐτὸς δὲ φίλης αἰῶνος ἀμερθῆις   (*Il.* 22.58)

ἰδόντα με καὶ λίποι αἰών   (*Od.* 7.224)

αἲ γὰρ δὴ ψυχῆς τε καὶ αἰῶνος σε δυναίμην   (*Od.* 9.523-524)
εὖνιν ποιήσας πέμψαι δόμον Ἄϊδος εἴσω

Besides this final parting from the body at death, the αἰών is said to be "wasted" in weeping. In *Od.* 18.203-204, Penelope prays for death "so that no longer I may mourn in my heart and waste my αἰών longing for my dear husband":

ἵνα μηκέτ' ὀδυρομένη κατὰ θυμὸν
αἰῶνα φθινύθω, πόσιος ποθέουσα φίλοιο.

15. R. B. Onians *Origins of European Thought* (2nd ed. Cambridge 1954) pp. 200-228.

More explicit still is the passage where Odysseus on Calypso's isle weeps for his home (*Od.* 5.151-153):

οὐδέ ποτ᾽ ὄσσε
δακρυόφιν τέρσοντο, κατείβετο δὲ γλυκὺς αἰών
νόστον ὀδυρομένωι

"Nor were his eyes ever dry of tears, but the sweet αἰών poured down as he wept for his return." A few lines later, Calypso addresses him:

κάμμορε, μή μοι ἔτ᾽ ἐνθάδ᾽ ὀδύρεο μηδέ τοι αἰών
φθινέτω, ἤδη γάρ σε μάλα πρόφρασσ᾽ ἀποπέμψω.

"Wretched man, let me no longer see you mourn here, nor let your αἰών be wasted; for now I shall willingly send you away." The αἰών then, is wasted when one weeps, and is, in fact, the liquid which flows down as tears (κατείβετο αἰών) only, of course, because it is the liquid in the body.[16]

As an alternative to the commonly accepted etymology (αἰών, *aevum* ἀεί), Onians offers the suggestion that αἰών is related to αἰόλλω, "move rapidly," and αἰόλος, "quick-moving," to which group also belongs the English "soul." Page[17] argues that the primary meaning of αἰόλος is "sparkling" not "waving" (or "quick-moving"). He supports his contention with references to Homeric armour, which he claims was metal and therefore bright when described as αἰόλος. He fails, however, to appreciate the connection between light and movement which the early Greeks saw. The flash of light which plays on surfaces is both bright, "sparkling" and "quick-moving." (See further Appendix II, pp. 214-15).

Of interest to our examination of αἰών as liquid is a series of words relating to liquid given by Onians: αἰονάω "moisten, foment, apply liquid to the flesh"; ἐπαιονάω "bathe"; καταιονάω "pour upon"; αἰόνημα, αἰόνησις medical terms for "fomenta-

16. Onians relates this passage (*Od.* 5.151ff) where the αἰών flows as tears, to the husband/wife relationship as well as the more explicit passage in *Od.* 18.203-204. He would like to establish a connection between these verses and ὑγρός describing the eyes — one of the characteristics of love and passion noted by the Greeks. (Cf. *h. Pan* 33f πόθος ὑγρός, Eur. *Hipp.* 525f. Ἔρως ὁ κατ᾽ ὀμμάτων στάξεις πόθον.)

17. D. L. Page, *History and the Homeric Iliad* (Berkeley and Los Angeles 1959) p. 204 n. 22 and p. 288 n. 93.

tions." Further confirmation is provided by the use of αἰών as "spinal marrow" in later writers, (cf. Hipp. *Epidem.* 7.122, Erotian (*Gloss. Hippocr.*) p. 49 (ed. J. Klein Leipzig 1865), Hesychius and *Etym. Magn.* s.v. αἰών).[18]

The effect of death and the loss of αἰών is the decay of the body. Achilles expects (*Il.* 19.24ff) that Patroclus' body will decay because the αἰών is slain from it. ἐκ δ' αἰὼν πέφαται – κατὰ δὲ χρόα πάντα σαπήηι. Thetis, his mother, promises her help and drips in a mixture of ambrosia and nectar through the nostrils of the corpse. This suggests that the fluid was needed in the cerebro-spinal cavity (cf. above αἰών, spinal marrow):

> Πατρόκλωι δ' αὖτ' ἀμβροσίην καὶ νέκταρ ἐρυθρόν
> στάξε κατὰ ῥινῶν, ἵνα οἱ χρὼς ἔμπεδος εἴη.

Hector's body also experiences a remarkable preservation: Phoebus Apollo brought a dark cloud so that the might of the sun would not shine on the corpse and dry up the flesh, (*Il.* 23.190f, σκήλει ἀμφὶ περὶ χρόα); Aphrodite anointed the corpse with oil so that it would not be lacerated when Achilles dragged it behind his chariot:

> ῥοδόεντι δὲ χρῖεν ἐλαίωι
> ἀμβροσίωι ἵνα μή μιν ἀποδρύφοι ἑλκυστάζων.

Twice we are told that, twelve days after he was slain, his body was dewy ἐερσήεις as if just slain (*Il.* 24.419,757). The scholiast explains ἐερσήεις as ὑγρότητα ἔχων οὐ κατεσκελετευμένος. The preservation of the corpse manifested itself by moisture instead of the expected dryness of death. The preservative measures, anointing with oil, dripping fluid inside, protecting from the sun, all indicate the antithesis of moisture and life to dryness and death.

Homeric funeral practices can be better understood if one is familiar with this antithesis. The Homeric burning of the body was not a complete cremation, i.e. a reduction to ashes, since the bones remained and were gathered up and buried (*Il.* 23.252ff; *Od.* 24.72ff). Onians[19] argues that this burning was thought to complete the drying up of the life-fluid αἰών and the release of the

---

18. Cf. also Pindar fr. 100.4 αἰὼν δὲ δι'ὀστέων ἐραίσθη, quoted by Erotian *loc. cit.*
19. Onians p. 262.

ψυχή.[20] Homer describes fire as κήλεος[21] which seems to mean "drying" (cf. περίκηλος *Od.* 5.240, 18.309 of dry timber and Hesychius s.v. κηλόν·ξηρόν). If this is the meaning and Homer did think of fire as "drying," it tends to confirm our view of the purpose of the Homeric cremation. Onians[22] suggests that Homer's name for the funeral process ταρχύειν indicates "to dry" by the action of fire. He compares ταρρός ταρσός "drying-basket," τέρσομαι "dry, bake," Latin *torreo* "dry by heat, bake, scorch," and Danish tørke "dry, dessicate." Hence ταριχεύειν apparently a variant form of ταρχύειν comes to connote "preserve" and hence "embalm."[23] Among other references he quotes Suda s.v. ταριχεύειν · σημαίνει. .τὸ ξηραίνειν, Aeschylus *Choeph.* 296 (the outcast), κακῶς ταριχευθέντα παμφθάρτωι μόρωι and Herodotus 9.120, Protesilaos, the Greek chieftain of the Trojan war period, dead and τάριχος.

This discussion has, I think, established the association of life and youth with moisture and death and old age with dryness in Greek thought. We can now better understand the importance of water to the early Greeks. For Homer, the stream of Ocean was γένεσις πάντεσσι (*Il.* 14.246); for Pindar, "water is the best thing," ἄριστον . . . ὕδωρ (*Olymp.* 1.1) and εἰδ᾽ἀριστεύει μὲν ὕδωρ (*Olymp.* 3.42) — not the best drink, but best absolutely, as being the life-substance. For Thales, the primary substance was water, and in this he was probably influenced by the view of the earlier poets (A.12,13,14,15 Diels. *VS*). It is my hope that this discussion will provide a foundation for an examination of χλωρός on the

20. Although the ψυχή left the body at death, it did not enter the house of Hades until the fire had done its work. In *Il.* 23.71ff, Patroclus' ψυχή complains to Achilles that the ghosts of the dead are keeping it out of Hades. "Bury me as quickly as possible," it pleads, "for I shall not come again from Hades when you have given me a share of fire." οὐ γὰρ ἔτ᾽ αὖτις/ νίσομαι ἐξ Ἀίδαο ἐπήν με πυρὸς λελάχητε. Here the fire causes the final separation of the ψυχή from the body. Odysseus' mother tells him, when he visits the underworld, (*Od.* 11.218ff), that the might of burning fire destroys the sinews which hold the body together, when the spirit leaves the bones and "the ψυχή has gone flying off like a dream": ψυχὴ δ᾽ἠὐτ᾽ὄνειρος ἀποπταμένη πεπότηται. Here, too, there is a correlation between the departure of the ψυχή and the action of fire.

21. Πυρὶ κηλέωι occurs at the end of a line, *Il.* 8.235, 18.346; *Od.* 8.435; Hes. *Theog.* 865. Κήλεος (with "fire") also occurs in *Il.* 8.217, 15.744.

22. Onians p. 257.

23. J. Whatmough in *CP* 48 (1953) 257 disagrees with this etymology; cf. also C. Pugliese Carratelli in *Archivio glottologico italiano* 39 (1954) 78-82.

assumption that this adjective belongs to life/youth/moisture.

II Wood, Trees, and Growing Things

Homer, in the *Odyssey*, three times describes as χλωρός wood which is freshly cut, i.e. no longer growing, but not yet seasoned. In describing the club of Polyphemus he says:

> Κύκλωπος γὰρ ἔκειτο μέγα ῥόπαλον παρὰ σηκῶι
> χλωρὸν ἐλαίνεον · τὸ μὲν ἔκταμεν, ὄφρα φοροίη
> αὐανθέν.

"For the Cyclops' mighty club lay by the pen, a green one of olive wood. This he cut so that he might carry it when it was dried."[24] Speaking of the same club, the poet relates that when the point which Odysseus and his men made at one end was thrust into the fire, it glowed terribly, "although it was green" χλωρός περ ἐών (9.379). Page[25] suggests that the heating in the fire of the weapon for blinding the Cyclops belongs to a version of the tale in which a metal spit was used instead of the wooden club. Metal, when thrust into the fire, will become red-hot, then white-hot: green wood will smoke and smoulder and may even burst into flame, but it will not *glow*. Χλωρός περ ἐών especially the apologetic περ indicates the poet's consciousness of the difficulty inherent in combining two versions of the tale. One of the features of the story, however, is the provision inside the cave of a weapon for Odysseus' purposes, since he could neither go outside in search of one, nor could he arrive in the cave armed, anticipating trouble. It is easy to explain that the club was available because the Cyclops was seasoning it; therefore Homer chooses the "green club" version, in spite of the inconsistency of its behaviour in the fire.

When, in *Od*. 16.47, Eumaeus, the swineherd, prepares a couch for Telemachus, he lays fleeces over green branches, χλωραὶ ῥῶπαι. It is clear that green branches provide "spring" with sleeping comfort, whereas dry branches would snap under the sleeper's weight. In none of these cases, does χλωρός refer to the presence of leaves or greenery, but only to sap.

---

24. *Od*. 9.319-321.
25. D. L. Page *The Homeric Odyssey* (Oxford 1955) pp. 10-11.

In an expression which originates from this connection of wood with χλωρός, Hesiod (*W.D.* 743) forbids his readers to cut their fingernails on certain days:

μηδ᾽ἀπὸ πεντόζοιο θεῶν ἐν δαιτὶ θαλείηι
αὖον ἀπὸ χλωροῦ τάμνειν αἴθωνι σιδήρωι

"Do not cut off the dry (αὖον) from the living part (χλωρόν) of the "five-branched" with the gleaming iron on the bounteous feast-day of the gods." Hesiod uses πεντόζοιο "the five-branched" (πέντε "five," ὄζος "branch, bough") for "hand" and by this word likens the fingers to branches. The part of the nail to be cut off is like dead wood, since there is no feeling in this part of the nail. Χλωρός and αὖος, which elsewhere[26] describe green and dry wood, fit into this context because of the similarity implied by ὄζος between fingers and branches.

Although, as we have indicated, Homer does not use χλωρός for leafiness of trees and plants, later poets certainly do so. In the *Hymn to the Pythian Apollo* (223), a mountain is χλωρός. Pfeiffer[27] points out the frequent association in Homer of mountains and woods (cf. *Il.* 2.455, 5.554, 10.184; *Od.* 9.191). The Homeric epithet εἰνοσίφυλλος "with quivering leaves" used to describe a mountain (*Il.* 2.632; *Od.* 9.22) focusses attention on the trees which cover it. (Cf. also Pind. *Pyth.* 3.36-37 for forested mountain-sides). Because of this connection between mountains and trees, it is reasonable to take χλωρός as "green with trees," i.e. green because of the covering vegetation.

In the Hesiodic *Shield* (393), there is a juxtaposition, perhaps deliberate, of χλοερός and κυάνεος:

ἦμος δὲ χλοερῶι κυανόπτερος ἠχέτα τέττιξ
ὄζωι ἐφεζόμενος θέρος ἀνθρώποισιν ἀείδειν
ἄρχεται. . . .

"When the shrill, dark-winged cricket, sitting on a green branch, begins to sing of summer to men . . . ." The cricket sings of

---

26. The contrast between αὖος and χλωρός is found in prose in Theophrastus (*H.P.* 4.12.3) between the old withered root of a rush and the new root which is sent down fresh each year; in Pausanias (7.18.11) of wood; and again in Theophrastus (*De Sens.* 75) of wood, τὸν ἄνθρακα τῶν χλωρῶν ξύλων ἢ τῶν αὔων.

27. R. Pfeiffer in *Hermes* 87 (1959) 3-4.

summer and the poet goes on to tell of Sirius scorching the flesh, the millet growing a beard, and the grapes changing colour. The season, therefore, is the height of summer, when the "Dog-Star" marked for the ancients the hottest time of the year. This insect seems most vocal in hot weather, perhaps because the birds are silent, as Keats suggests in "On the Grasshopper and the Cricket":

> The poetry of earth is never dead:
> When all the birds are faint with the hot sun,
> And hide in cooling trees, a voice will run
> From hedge to hedge about the new-mown mead;
> That is the Grasshopper's . . . .[28]

As Keats mentions "cooling trees," so Hesiod's green bough (χλοερῶι ὄξωι) where the cricket is perched, suggests that shade from the heat is sought. The desirability of shade supports the interpretation "leafy" for χλοερός, a change from the Homeric usage.

Among the lyric poets, Alcman describes the reed (κάλαμος fr. 106.5 PLF) as χλωρός but the fragmentary context tells us nothing more. Anacreon (fr. 443 PMG) speaks of the μελαμφύλλωι δάφναι and χλωρᾶι ἐλαίαι. Μελάμφυλλος indicates that it is the leaves of the laurel that are μέλας. It is natural to assume that a contrast is indicated between the darker-leaved laurel and the lighter olive. The leaves of the olive (Olea Europaea) are described by a botanist, Makins,[29] as "dark, dull green above and silvery below," definitely not a light green. The laurel (Laurus nobilis) is described by Makins[30] as "an evergreen with glossy, leathery leaves." It can be agreed that there is a contrast here, enhanced, perhaps, by the lighter reverse side of the olive leaves against the dark sheen of the laurel, but there is no warrant for taking χλωρός as "light green" in the passage. An examination of other trees described as χλωρός will show how mistaken is the translation "light green."

---

28. Τέττιξ is variously translated "grasshopper," "cricket" or "cicada," all similar in respect to their chirping. For Keats' poem, see *The Poems of Keats* ed. E. de Sélincourt (London 1905) p. 38.

29. F. K. Makins: *The Identification of Trees and Shrubs* (2nd ed. London 1948) p. 278.

30. Makins p. 294.

The laurel is itself spoken of as "the green-leaved crown of laurel," χλωρόκομος στέφανος δάφνας (Eur. *I.A.* 759). The compound with κόμη "hair" connects the foliage with χλωρός since κόμη is used for "foliage" of trees as early as Homer (cf. *Od.* 23.195, κόμην . . . ἐλαίης). The fir tree (ἐλάτη) is called χλωρός by Pindar (fr. 167.1-2) and by Euripides (*Bacch.* 38). This tree is either the "silver fir," the Latin *abies*, or the pine, Latin *pinus picea*.[31] In either case, it is an evergreen which we consider *dark*.

The vine is twice called χλωρός by Sophocles: in *Thyestes* fr. 239.4 (κεκλημάτωται χλωρὸν οἰάνθης δέμας) and in *Antigone.* 1132-1133, where the chorus sings of Dionysus:

κισσήρεις ὄχθαι χλωρά τ᾽ ἀκτὰ
πολυστάφυλος πέμπει.

Since the beach is both χλωρά "green" and πολυστάφυλος "vine-covered," it is reasonable to explain the first epithet by the second, "green *because* vine-covered." Ivy-covered banks and a vine-covered beach are a suitable habitat for Dionysus (cf. further n. 96).

It has been suggested by Miss Kober that trees *en masse* are described by μέλας as the equivalent of "dark-green" and that χλωρός is "light green."[32] Such a generalization can be shown to be erroneous. We have already produced examples of "dark" trees, such as evergreens, being described as χλωρός e.g. the laurel in Euripides *I.A.* 759 and the fir in Euripides *Bacchae* 38 and Pindar fr. 167.1-2. Areas of massed growth are also at times χλωρός. Euripides so describes a wood (*Hipp.* 17) χλωρὰν ἀν᾽ ὕλην. In the *Hymn to Apollo*, a mountain is χλωρός presumably because it is covered with trees (cf. the discussion above), and in Sophocles *Ichn.* 215 a mountain is both wooded and χλωρός: χλοερὸν ὑλῶδη πάγον.

When μελάμφυλλος occurs, it emphasizes the darkness of the foliage, whether of tree-covered mountains or a single tree, as in Anacreon.[33] Where it is contrasted with χλωρός it indicates the darker, as χλωρός the lighter green. But we must realize that

---

31. *LSJ* (ed. 8) s.v. ἐλάτη; *LSJ* (ed. 7) s.v. ἐλάτη.
32. Kober *The Use of Color Terms in the Greek Poets* p. 115.
33. Soph. *O.C.* 482; Pind. *Pyth.* 1.27; Aristoph. *Thesm.* 997.

χλωρός alone does not mean "light green," as the examples already quoted show. Since Anacreon's listeners were familiar with the trees, they would grasp the contrast at once. It may be, indeed, that Anacreon was trying out the effect of these two epithets placed side by side. His experiment, if it was that, was not to my knowledge repeated. As χλωρός originally indicated that the tree was "fresh," so μελάμφυλλος originally expressed the contrast between the bright sky and the dark silhouette of a mountain, or land mass. It is to be assumed that Anacreon's contrast was not pleasing to the Greek eye (see further, p. 190).

We find rivers described as χλωρός presumably because they are surrounded by, or overgrown with, plants, grasses, etc. Euripides (*Helen* 349-350) says that the Eurotas river is "green with the watery reed," τὸν ὑδρόεντι δόνακι χλωρὸν Εὐρώταν. It is clear, in this case, that the quality is imparted to the river by the reeds. However, in the *Phoenissae* (660), the chorus sings:

φύλαξ
νάματ᾽ ἔνυδρα καὶ ῥέεθρα
χλοερὰ δεργμάτων κόραισι
πολυπλάνοις ἐπισκοπῶν.

"Guardian, overseeing with darting glance watery streams and green rivers (or river-beds)." The primary meaning of ῥέεθρον is "that which flows" (ῥέω) i.e. a river; as early as the *Iliad*, however, ῥέεθρον is used as "river-channel" (21.382). In conjunction here with νάματα "streams," ῥέεθρον is likely to mean something other than "river," to avoid having synonyms in the same line. The epithet χλωρός on the analogy of the passage from *Helen*, suggests that the poet is thinking of plants covering the river-bed. In summertime the Greek landscape is dry and the vegetation browned except along river-beds where there is enough moisture to support growth. In the passage in question, however, there is no suggestion of the season. A stronger reason in favour of taking χλωρός as "covered with green growth," is that χλωρός is not used elsewhere to describe water, except in a doubtful fragment of Euripides, by a late poet and in pseudo-Aristotle. The poet, Marianus Scholasticus, of the fifth to sixth century after Christ, speaks of fountains in a park as χλωρὸν . . . ὕδωρ (*A.P.*

9.669.3) This is interesting but not particularly enlightening. The fragment of Euripides (fr. 1069 N.) is found in Plutarch (*Mor.* 767F)[34], and is connected by Nauck with two lines of Euripides quoted by Strabo (8.379), because προλιποῦσ᾽ Ἀκροκόρινθον occurs in both contexts. Nauck reports Meineke's conjecture that the words ὕδατι χλωρῶι were a quotation by Plutarch and that they were from the exordium of a parodos sung by a chorus of Corinthian women. Nauck, indeed, does not insist that these are Euripides' words, but his inclusion of the piece from Plutarch and his repetition of Meineke's conjecture suggest that he thought there was a reasonable basis for supposing them to be Euripides'. However, the ascription is not certain, and ὕδατι χλωρῶι cannot be adduced to support the translation "green rivers" for ῥέεθρα χλοερά.

The third example of χλωρός describing water occurs in a puzzling and interesting passage from pseudo-Aristotle (*De Color.* 794b26). There we are told that growing things are green (χλωρός), when moist and black (μέλας) when dry. Rain water, declares the writer, behaves in this way. He then continues "for all water which stands (in one place) for a time at the beginning is green, mingled with the rays of the sun, but little by little it becomes black; again mixed with τὸ χλωρόν, it becomes green": τὰ γὰρ ὕδατα πάντα χρονιζόμενα κατ᾽ ἀρχὰς μὲν γίνεται χλωρά, κεραννύμενα ταῖς τοῦ ἡλίου αὐγαῖς, κατὰ μικρὸν δὲ μελαινόμενα, πάλιν μιγνύμενα τῶι χλωρῶι γίνεται ποώδη. The water is standing (χρονιζόμενα) i.e. stagnant and the sun is the cause of the greenness. These factors suggest the growth of algae, common in stagnant pools. As the water dries up, and the moisture which supports the algae disappears, the algae become black. The final statement, that with the addition of τὸ χλωρόν the water becomes green again, is puzzling. If τὸ χλωρὸν means "fresh water" (as the Loeb translater, W. S. Hett, Aristotle *Minor Works* [London & Cambridge, Mass. 1936] takes it), the epithet χλωρός cannot mean "green with algae," in spite of other indications in the passage. The author is at a loss to know what the writer intended

---

34. The quotation from Plutarch is here given in context. ἐπεὶ δὲ ἔρως ἔθιγεν αὐτῆς Ἱππολόχου τοῦ Θεσσαλοῦ ὕδατι χλωρῶι κατακυζόμενον προλιποῦσ᾽ Ἀκροκόρινθον καὶ ἀποδρᾶσα τῶν ἄλλων ἐραστῶν κρύφα μέγαν στρατὸν ὤιχετο.

by τὸ χλωρόν. None of these passages where χλωρός describes water is sufficiently clear to take as support for the Euripidean passage (*Phoen.* 660), whereas the meaning "covered with green growth" is well substantiated.[35]

Euripides has two further examples of χλωρός in the sense of "covered with growth," although not of rivers in these cases. In *Ion* (497), the stadia before the temple of Pallas are χλοερά; in *Phoenissae* (826), the plain is a "producer of green" χλοερετρόφον πεδίον.

Three startling occurrences remain to be examined, all in Euripides. First, in *Helen* (243-244), Helen herself tells the chorus, in a lyric exchange, that Hermes snatched her away as she was picking flowers which she gathered into her dress:

> ὅς με χλοερὰ δρεπομέναν
> ἔσω πέπλων ῥόδεα πέταλα.

The flowers she was picking were χλοερὰ . . . ῥόδεα πέταλα; unless Helen was making a bouquet of leaves, Euripides is here using χλοερός of a growing thing which is not *green* at all. Does πέταλον give us any assistance in determining the meaning of this passage? Πέταλον is related to πετάννυμι "spread out," and in its root meaning could apply to the spread-out shape of either leaves or petals. The usual meaning is "leaf," according to *LSJ* (who take this passage to be an example of the "usual" meaning), although it can mean "flower" (*A.P.* 7.23), and has given us the English "petal." Moreover, when Pindar calls springs Ὠκεανοῦ πέταλα (fr. 326), he seems to be using πέταλα in its basic sense of "things that spread out," rather than as a metaphor comparing the relationship of springs to Ocean with that of leaves to a tree. I take this fragment as an indication that the root idea is strong and that the Greeks would have no difficulty in describing flowers as πέταλα. We find a combination of πέταλα with a flower again in Euripides' *Ion* (888-889).

> εὖτ᾽ἐς κόλπους
> κρόκεα πέταλα φάρεσιν ἔδρεπον.

Here too πέταλα are being gathered in skirts. I can see no reason

---

35. For a further discussion of this passage, see H. B. Gottschalk "The *de coloribus* and its author" in *Hermes* 92 (1964) 70, 72-73.

to doubt that Euripides meant by χλοερὰ . . . ῥόδεα πέταλα "fresh rose petals," and that he used χλοερός as "fresh" without a hint of "green."

Our second surprise comes in a chorus from *Iphigeneia at Aulis* (1297) which sings of a meadow "blooming with χλωρός flowers, and with roses and hyacinths for goddesses to pluck."

λειμὼν ἄνθεσι
θάλλων χλωροῖς
καὶ ῥοδόεντ᾽
ἄνθε᾽ ὑακίνθινά τε θεαῖς δρέπειν.

First we must consider the problem of whether the manuscript reading ἄνθεσι followed so closely by ἄνθεα is correct. D. L. Page, in *Actors' Interpolations in Greek Tragedy*, (Oxford 1934) has shown by many examples that "the fifth century tragedians did not avoid repetitions of sounds, words, or phrases, in proximity or at a distance, within the same play or in different plays."[36] It is strange, in view of this conclusion, to find that Page rejects ἄνθεσι and reads ἔρνεσι (Hermann's conjecture), "thus avoiding repetition ἄνθεσι 1296, ἄνθεα 1298."[36] Scholars are not always consistent. He is influenced also by χλωροῖς which he pronounces a "strange" adjective for ἄνθεσι either unaware of *Helen* 243-244 or else taking ῥόδεα πέταλα there of leaves. (The question, for Page, is further complicated by his conviction that lines 1276-1335 of *I. A.*, as well as much of the rest of the play, are not by Euripides, but, in this case, by a fourth-century interpolator.)[37] There seems to be no reason for emending to avoid repetition, since Euripides himself did not avoid it. In view of Euripides' use elsewhere of χλωρός, we may accept ἄνθεσι . . . χλωροῖς as an example of the way in which he returns from the developed chromatic meaning "green" to the earlier non-chromatic "fresh, moist." If this passage is by an interpolator, he has simply copied Euripides' language.

---

36. Page, *Actors Interpolations* p. 127. To take repetitions quoted by Page from *Medea*, within 13 lines we find βροτούς (191), βροτῶν (195), βροτούς (200), βροτοῖσιν (203); at the end of the line we find three times ἣ τεχνωμένην (369), καὶ τεχνωμένη (382), καὶ τεχνωμένη (402); θήσω is repeated (375, 383, 399); and in 1188-1189, there is an infelicitous repetition — πέπλοι λεπτοί which feed on λεπτὴν σάρκα (see the discussion in n. 21, chapter 4, p. 118).

37. Page, p. 186, 211.

Our third surprise is the bold phrase sung by the chorus of the *Bacchae* (866):

ὡς νεβρὸς χλοεραῖς ἐμπαί-
ζουσα λείμακος ἡδοναῖς.

"Like a fawn at play in the green joys of the meadow . . . " Dodds, in a note on this passage,[38] remarks: " 'Green joy', a colour-word applied to an abstract noun is bold for a Greek poet." He suggests that the phrase has the effect of a compound "green-meadow-joy." For the construction he refers to Wilamowitz,[39] who gives examples of an adjective agreeing grammatically with one noun, but in sense with another noun (usually a dependent genitive): i.e. Wilamowitz would take χλοεραῖς . . . λείμακος ἡδοναῖς to be "joys of a green meadow." It seems to me that Dodds is mistaken in his assumption that ἡδοναί is an *abstract* noun. Many examples of ἡδοναί can be cited with the meaning "things which give pleasure." Ἡδοναί occurs in apposition to a list of nouns, e.g. in Aristophanes (*Clouds* 1072-1073): ἡδονῶν θ᾽ ὅσων μέλλεις ἀποστερεῖσθαι/ παίδων γυναικῶν κοττάβων ὄψων πότων κιχλισμῶν and in Euripides (Hipp. 383), where ἡδοναί are said to be μακραί τε λέσχαι καὶ σχολή. Cf. also Heraclitus (B.67 Diels), where ἡδονή is the "pleasing scent" given off by various oils of incense when they are poured on the fire.[40] It seems reasonable to assume that here Euripides is using ἡδοναί in a concrete sense "pleasant things." The question then is whether the phrase should be taken as "the pleasant things of the green meadow" or "the pleasant green things of the meadow." The second seems to me to have several points in its favour. It takes the Greek naturally without requiring the transferral of an epithet; and it accords with Euripides' use of χλωρός which we have seen elsewhere, to find χλωρός extended, as it were, to mean "growing."

In this section, we have seen that the basic meaning of χλωρός is "moist" i.e. "full of sap," as opposed to αὖος "dry." Because the presence of sap implies life and growth in trees and plants, "living" and "growing" are included in the meaning. A secondary

38. E. R. Dodds, *Euripides Bacchae* (Oxford 1960) on line 866.
39. U. von Wilamowitz-Moellendorf *Euripides Herakles* (Berlin 1895) on 1.468.
40. Cf. also Anaxagoras B.4. Diels *VS*; Eur. *I.T.* 1184. *El.* 596.

colour meaning, "green" arose, because vegetation, trees and grass described as χλωρός showed this quality in greenness. But Euripides, returning to the root meaning, uses χλωρός in an unexpected way, of growing things which are not green at all. Hereby, he makes the implications of "living" and "growing" dominant.

Pindar Fr. 122.3

In the drinking song for Xenophanes of Corinth, Pindar addressed the "hospitable young women" (i.e. prostitutes) in the temple of Aphrodite in Corinth, as "you who sacrifice golden tears of the χλωρός frankincense, or incense-tree." αἴτε τᾶς χλωρᾶς λιβάνου ξανθὰ δάκρη/ θυμιᾶτε.

Λίβανος, masculine, normally means the incense-tree,[41] (cf. Herod. 4.75; Theophr. H.P. 9.4.2), but it is also used in poetry as the equivalent of λιβανωτός "incense" (cf. Soph. fr. 961 N.). Euripides uses it in the feminine in this sense (Bacch. 144), "smoke of Syrian incense" Συριάς ... λιβάνου καπνόν. Two lexicographers, Zonaras and Phavorinus,[42] take Pindar in this passage to be similarly using the feminine as "incense." (Zonaras was responsible for a lexicon dated about 1150 A.D., which is dependent to a large degree on the Etymologicum Magnum. Phavorinus (Guarino of Favera), also known as Varinus and Camers, published a Greek dictionary in 1523 A.D.). Photius, on the other hand, asserts that Pindar has λίβανος feminine, of the tree: s.v. λίβανον· τὸ δένδρον θηλυκῶς Πίνδαρος.

Now, it is possible to say either "tears (consisting) of incense" or "tears of the incense-tree." The choice in this passage is governed by the presence of χλωρός and ξανθός. If λίβανος means "incense," χλωρός and ξανθός both describe the appearance of the incense and are synonymous. Van Groningen[43] points out that

---

41. Phrynichus distinguishes between the tree λίβανος and the incense λιβανωτός (W. G. Rutherford The New Phrynichus (London 1881) p. 163). The distinction does not always hold.

42. A. Turyn Pindari carmina cum fragmentis (Cambridge, Mass. 1952) fr. 130 gives their variant reading in his apparatus criticus: αἴτε τὰν χλωρὰν λίβανον, the accusative in apposition to δάκρη.

43. B. A. van Groningen, Pindare au Banquet (Leiden, 1960) pp. 24-25.

Pindar is not in the habit of using synonyms, but rather of looking for variety in his descriptions. On these grounds he prefers to take λίβανος of the tree.

The incense-tree (Boswellia carteri) is described by Theophrastus (*H.P.* 9.4.2) as "grass-green," ποώδης, but, he reports that others (*H.P.* 9.4.7) say that the leaf is reddish, ὑπέρυθρον. Since, however, the tree is found in Arabia, Pindar would be unlikely to have seen it, neither would he be likely to concern himself with botanical detail. Enough that it was a tree; for χλωρός can well describe any growing thing, whatever the precise colour of its leaves, as we have seen in section two. There is, therefore, no difficulty in taking λίβανος as the tree, described as χλωρός. Our interpretation of χλωρός as being especially appropriate to growing things confirms van Groningen's conclusion.

III Tears and Dew; Honey; Wine, Figs and Cheese

A. Tears and Dew

Pindar (*Nem.* 8.40) uses an arresting comparison:

αὔξεται δ᾽ἀρετὰ χλωραῖς ἐέρσαις
ὡς ὅτε δένδρεον οἴνας

"Excellence flourishes like the vine when (fed) by fresh dews." The description of dew as χλωρός is appropriate on two counts: in its basic meaning of "moist, fresh," χλωρός applies to dew, itself, and in its secondary meaning of "inducing growth," it strengthens the picture of excellence *flourishing* like the vine.

Sophocles picks up the connection with dew and combines it with tears (*Trach.* 847-848): "surely she sheds a fresh dew of fast-falling tears."

ἦ που ἀδινῶν χλωράν
τέγγει δακρύων ἄχναν.

The similarity of tears to dew is easy to see. We say, in English, that someone "waters" something with (her) tears. Ἄχνη here translated "dew" signifies "anything that comes off the surface" (*LSJ*) and can be applied to the sea "foam, froth," wine "effervescence," fire "smoke," and to solids, grain "chaff," material "shreds, fluff." It is an apt description of tears which roll in drops down the cheeks. It is interesting to observe that Sophocles chose χλωρός to describe the "exudation" of tears, as we shall see that χλωρός frequently describes liquids which appear in drops; compare the discussion below of the appearance of honey oozing from the comb in drops, and its similarity to sap, dew, and tears; χλωραὶ σταγόνες; and the "saffron-dyed drop" which, we argue, is bile. Euripides shows that he is pleased with the combination of tears and χλωρός by using it twice in *Medea* (906,922;) and once in *Helen* (1189).

Although Homer does not use χλωρός to describe tears, he does use two words which will enlighten our discussion, θαλερός and τέρην. θαλερός related to θάλλω "bloom, swell, flourish" provides an interesting comment upon χλωρός. Its root, θάλλω, describes the growth of plants, people, and cities, emphasizing chiefly a flourishing, healthy development (see p. 37). The adjective θαλερός describes people "flourishing, blooming."[44] But why should tears be "flourishing, blooming"? We have seen above that for Homer tears are one form in which αἰών is visible. It is, I believe, the source of tears, i.e. their origin in the vital fluid, that explains the Greek description of them as θαλερός.

Τέρην is generally taken (e.g. by *LSJ* and Boisacq) as "soft, delicate," related to τείρω "rub, wear away" and τέρυ (glossed by Hesychius as ἀσθενές, λεπτόν). Both these authorities compare τέρην to Latin *tener* "tender" (with a reversal of consonants), but fail to mention, as Cunliffe[45] does, Latin *teres* "rounded, smooth, well-turned."[46] Cunliffe gives the meaning of τέρην as (1) of tears, "of spheroidal form, round" (2) of flesh "showing firm, round contours" (3) vegetation "swelling with sap, full of fresh life." He has grasped the unity in Homer's use of τέρην. In a note on *Od.* 12.357ff, Stanford[47] points out that τέρην "involves notions of

---

44. *LSJ* s.v. θάλλω. θαλερός of tears: *Il.* 6.496; 24.9, 794; 2.266. Its chief other association is with people: *Il.* 3.261, 8.190; 6.430; Pind. *Nem.* 1.71.

45. R. J. Cunliffe *A Lexicon of the Homeric Dialect* (London 1924) s.v. τέρην.

46. Τέρην: of trees and flowers, Ibycus fr. 315.2 *PMG, Il.* 13.180, *Od.* 12.357, 9.449, fr. 16.3 *PLF incerti auctoris,* Hes. *Theog.* 988; of flesh, *Il.* 4.237, 13. 553, 14.406; of a girl, Hippon. fr. 79 D. *Teres:* of trees Verg. *Aen.* 6.207, *Ecl.* 8.16, Ov. *Metamorph.* 2.735; of parts of body, Lucr. 1.35, Verg. *Aen.* 8.633, Catullus 61.181, Suet. *Caes.* 45; of a boy Hor. *Epod.* 11.28.

47. W. B. Stanford *The Odyssey of Homer* (London 1950) on *Od.* 12.357ff.

'fresh, full, round, flexible'."He derives this sense in part from the particular passage, where, he argues, the leaves were "fresh, not withered" as is shown also by the participle "plucking" δρεψάμενοι.

This definition "fresh, full, round" allows us to understand better Anacreon's description of flutes as τέρην. Athenaeus, who preserves this fragment (4.177A- 182C, fr. 375 *PMG*) says that Anacreon called half-flutes τέρην because they were used for παιδικά "songs for a beloved boy," and presumably τέρην is a suitable adjective for the boy himself. But it is possible that Anacreon is using the word in the sense of "round, swelling," to describe the music that swelled from the flutes. (The Greeks elsewhere described sound as swelling, cf. Pindar's use of a form of *χλήδω above.)

τέρην again describes sound in Theognis (266), where a girl answers her lover, ἡ δὲ τέρεν φθέγγετ' ἀπὸ στόματος. The poem opens,

οὔ μοι πίνεται οἶνος, ἐπεὶ παρὰ παιδὶ τερείνηι
ἄλλος ἀνὴρ κατέχει πολλὸν ἐμοῦ κακίων.

The speaker's beloved is courted by another man, more pleasing to her parents apparently, but not to the girl. The παῖς τερείνη of line 261 utters a τέρεν sound in line 266. Such a verbal echo could not fail to remind the listeners of the earlier line, thus binding the poem together. If the παῖς τερείνη is a fresh, young girl, then she is presumably speaking in a fresh, young voice and not, apparently, in a lover's whisper. (Cf. English "well-rounded tones.")

This cursory glance at τέρην is intended to show that this word, like χλωρός has to do originally with swelling and fulness in relation to moisture. Leaves and plants are filled out with sap when fresh, but when dry they wrinkle and are no longer smooth. The flesh of warriors (men in their prime) is filled out, but as people grow old and the vital fluid dries, wrinkles come and the figure loses its firmness. So tears, evidence of that vital fluid, are τέρην. Here we depart from Cunliffe who took τέρην to apply to the shape of tears "round." In view of what we have learned about tears, it is better to relate τέρην to the "swelling-up" of the vital fluid in the eyes, and the essential quality of tears.

There are two further occurrences of τέρην to which attention should be called. Empedocles (100.6) so describes blood, τέρεν αἷμα. We shall see below that χλωρός is used by Sophocles and Euripides to describe blood. The second example of τέρην to be discussed here occurs in Euripides' *Medea* 905. Medea, speaking of her children whom she has called on stage (894-895), says:

χρόνωι δὲ νεῖκος πατρὸς ἐξαιρουμένη
ὄψιν τέρειναν τήνδ᾽ ἔπλησα δακρύων.

(Πατρός shows that she is talking to or of the children). Medea says that she "filled this fresh face with tears." The face must be the children's not her own, since she succumbs to tears only in line 922.[48] Τέρην, then, appropriately describes the faces of the children because of their youth and freshness, but it has the extra poetic value of reminding the audience of the way Homer used τέρην of tears. This is a very skilful reminiscence, similar in type to Euripides' treatment of χλωρός which we have observed, e.g. in χλοεραῖς . . . ἡδοναῖς λείμακος (cf. pp. 50-51). Interesting also is the fact that in the next line the chorus burst into χλωρός tears, and in line 922, Jason wonders why Medea is weeping χλωρός tears. It looks as if Euripides associated χλωρός with τέρην.

Eustathius' comment on χλωρός and τέρην in connection with tears follows:[49] ἰστέον ὅτι ἐπεὶ τὰ κυρίως θάλλοντα καὶ ἀπαλά εἰσι, διὰ τοῦτο καὶ τέρεν δάκρυόν που λέγεται τὸ ἀπαλόν. ἐπεὶ δὲ καὶ χλωρά εἰσι τὰ θάλλοντα καὶ ὑγρότητα ἔχει πλείω, διὰ τοῦτο καὶ ὑγρὸν δάκρυον καὶ χλωρὸν ὁ Εὐριπίδης φησί. Σοφοκλῆς δὲ ἐν Τραχινίαις χλωρὰν ἄχναν δακρύων ἔφη. Eustathius understood that tears were called χλωρός because of their moisture, as plants were both χλωρός and ὑγρός. As to τέρην, if our conclusions are right, we have been able to see more clearly than Eustathius, that the appropriateness of τέρην as well as χλωρός to tears is based in moisture, which, as sap, causes plants to be round and smooth, and, as vital fluid, makes flesh smooth and firm. It is this vital fluid, from which tears spring,

48. D. L. Page *Euripides Medea* (Oxford 1952). Page argues (at line 905) that ὄψιν refers to the children, adducing in support πατρός and the dramatic use of ὅδε (τήνδ᾽) to refer to another person present on stage.
49. Eustathius 217.1.

which imparts the quality τέρην to tears.

Τέρην, then, has proved to be a remarkable parallel to χλωρός and has assisted us, I hope, in our comprehension of it. When we see the reason for the Greeks describing tears as χλωρός, we can say that it is better to translate χλωρὸν δάκρυον as "fresh tear," which conveys the positive aspect of the Greek, rather than "pale tear," which connotes an absence of colour, a negative aspect.[50]

Euripides (H.F. 1209) uses an expression which apparently owes its force to this use of χλωρός: πολιόν τε / δάκρυον ἐκβάλλων, "letting fall an old man's (literally "a grey") tear." Πολιός describes the grey of grey hair[51] and therefore conveys the idea of age here, but it acquires a particular meaning in this context, because it is contrasted (by implication) with the more familiar χλωρός. Πολιὸν δάκρυον a tear wept by an old man, lacks the moisture and freshness tears ordinarily have, because the one who weeps is old and drying up. Πολιός occurs elsewhere as "hoary, venerable," indicating age of things, which, unlike people, do not show their age by grey hair (cf. Aesch. Supp. 673 πολιῶι νόμωι; Eur. Elect. 701 πολιαῖσι . . . φήμαις; and Plato Tim. 22b χρόνωι πολιῶι). The indication of age seems in some way to be involved in Pindar Pyth. 4.98, where Pelias asks Jason, τίς σε πολιᾶς ἐξανῆκε γαστρός. The point of this obviously barbed comment is debated widely.

B. Honey

Honey is χλωρός twice in Homer; once in an Homeric Hymn; and once each in Stesichorus and Xenophanes. In both the Homeric examples, a drink is being prepared; by Nestor's captive servant for Patroclus in the Iliad (11.631), and by the enchantress, Circe, for Odysseus' men in the Odyssey (10.234). To wine in each case are added barley, grated cheese, and honey. The honey is for sweetening, just as we use sugar.[52] In its natural liquid state, it is

---

50. Page Medea leaves the choice in translation up to the individual (on line 906): "either meaning (i.e. fresh or pale) is possible and applicable; each reader may choose which he prefers."

51. Πολιός of grey hair: cf. n. 91, chapter five p. 194.

52. Sugar was not introduced to the Old World until the discovery of the New, in the sixteenth century.

easily dissolved and mixed. Only under refrigeration does it crystallize, becoming solid and white.

In the *Hymn to Hermes* (560), the Thriae, three sisters who practise divination, speak the truth when they eat χλωρός honey. This honey is found in the honey-comb, κηρία, on which they feed (559). Stesichorus (fr. 179(a)2 *PMG*) gives among a list of "maiden-gifts," various kinds of cakes and χλωρός honey. Xenophanes says that "if the god had not made χλωρός honey, men would have said that figs were much sweeter." (fr. 34D.):[53]

Εἰ μὴ χλωρὸν ἔφυσε θεὸς μέλι, πολλὸν ἔφασκον
γλύσσονα σῦκα πέλεσθαι.

There is nothing in any of these contexts to suggest that χλωρός is any more than a conventional epithet, inherited from Homeric vocabulary. Simonides' description of honey as ξανθός (fr. 593 *PMG*) is sometimes taken as a correction, a more exact or accurate term than χλωρός.[54] Ξανθός which described blond hair,[55] suits the golden hue of honey admirably. The applicability of χλωρός to honey because of its liquid state may not have been understood or appreciated by the later Greek writers, since it does not recur after Xenophanes, and the compound adjective μελίχλωρος has no hint of "moisture" in it. It was perhaps the appearance of honey in the comb, with drops standing out on the wax, which reminded the early Greeks of tears on the cheeks, sap oozing from the stem of a plant, or dew sitting on a leaf. We see that χλωρός is applied to other liquids: dew and tears (pp. 52-56), wine (p. 60) and blood (p. 74). These vary from colourless to red or dark — a wide range indeed.

The components of μέλι χλωρόν unite to form the compound

53. J. M. Edmonds *Greek Elegiac and Iambic Poets* (London, Cambridge Mass. 1931), suggests that χλωρόν is predicative, translating, "if God had not made honey yellow . . . " But surely it is the existence of honey, not its appearance, that makes men contrast its sweetness to that of figs.

54. E.g., by R. A. Cole "Adjectives of Light and Colour in Greek Lyric Poetry" (unpubl. dissert., Dublin 1952) section two p. 103. "Simonides seems to have been the first to notice the rich colour of honey, while all Homer had noticed was its paleness." He calls attention in a note (335) to Aesch. *Pers.* 611-612 where honey is described as παμφαής "gleaming." Cole comments that translucency is more apparent than colour when the honey is in drops (indicated by σπάγμα). The mention of στάγμα is interesting in the light of our discussion.

55. Ξανθός, cf. Eur. *Med.* 980; *Helen* 1224, *I.T.* 52.

adjective μελίχλωρος "honey-pale" as applied to the complexion. Theocritus (10.26-27) says, "Everyone calls you sunburned, but I alone honey-pale."

καλέοντί τυ πάντες - - -

ἀλιόκαυστον, ἐγὼ δὲ μόνος μελίχλωρον.

Kober[56] argues that since the young woman who is so addressed is very tanned, μελίχλωρος suggested a rather dark shade, a flattering equivalent for ἀλιόκαυστος. Gow,[57] on the other hand, in an exhaustive discussion of this passage, and the practice of hypocorism, points out that the question is not so simply resolved. It is true that when a lover palliates his beloved's faults or shortcomings, he turns them into virtues.[58] Plato (Rep. 474d,e) in reference to hypocorism, gives examples of such flattery: the dark-complexioned (μέλας) are called manly, the fair (λευκός) "children of the gods." "Do you think" asks Socrates, "that 'honey-pale' is an invention of another than a lover, calling pallor by an endearing name and bearing it readily if it is in youth?" μελιχλώρους δὲ καὶ τοὔνομα οἴει τινὸς ἄλλου ποίημα εἶναι ἢ ἐραστοῦ ὑποκοριζομένου τε καὶ εὐχερῶς φέροντος τὴν ὠχρότητα ἐὰν ἐπὶ ὥραι ἦι; For Plato μελίχλωρος is obviously a hypocorism for a pale complexion.

Plutarch (Mor. 45A) paraphrases Plato, using μελίχρους as a synonym for μελίχλωρος: τὸν δ'ὠχρὸν ὑποκοριζόμενος μελίχρουν ἀσπάζεται. Aristaenetus, the letter-writer, also quotes Plato (1.18) substituting μελίχρωτος for μελίχλωρος. We can regard these three words as synonyms.

Pseudo-Aristotle, in expounding the way in which appearance indicates character (Physiogn. 812a19), says that people who are μελίχλωρος are cold and so move slowly. Unlike Plato and Theocritus, he seems to be using μελίχλωρος in an uncomplimentary way.

Gow argues, in view of the way μελίχλωρος is used elsewhere, that it may be a synonym for ὠχρός, and that Theocritus is here

56. Kober, The Use of Color Terms in the Greek Poets p. 67.
57. A. S. F. Gow Theocritus (2nd ed. Cambridge 1952) on 10.26-27.
58. Examples of hypocorism: Hor. Serm. 1.3.38ff, Ov. A.A. 2.657ff; Lucr. 4.1153ff, Ov. Rem. Am. 327.

not flattering the girl but describing her as opposite to what she was. Although she was dark, to her lover she seemed fair, as suited an attractive girl. He cites in support of μελίχλωρος ("pale") Plato and the fact that μελίχρους (a synonym for μελίχλωρος) is the regular word for "fair-skinned" in Egyptian legal documents.[59] But Gow also introduces evidence that μελίχλωρος meant "dark" to some writers. Meleager (*A.P.* 12.165ff) contrasts two boys as λευκανθής and μελίχροος; in the fourth line of the poem, they are λευκός and μέλας, corresponding apparently to the two parts (μέλας and ἀργός) of his name.

> λευκανθὴς Κλεόβουλος, ὁ δ᾽ἀντία τοῦδε μελίχρους
> Σώπολις, οἱ δισσοὶ Κύπριδος ἀνθοφόροι
> τοὖνεκά μοι παίδων ἔπεται πόθος· οἱ γὰρ Ἔρωτες
> πλέξειν ἐκ λευκοῦ φασί μς καὶ μέλανος.

Lucretius (4.1160), in speaking of men ascribing to women excellencies they do not possess, gives as the flattering equivalent of *nigra*, *melichrus*. It is possible, according to Gow, that for Theocritus, too, μελίχλωρος suggested "dark," and he was using it as a synonym for ἀλιόκαυστος. Gow, then, leaves the question open. Professor L. Woodbury of the University of Toronto has pointed out to the author that the two extremes of pale and dark need not present a contradiction. From Plato we know that μελίχλωρος is not the lightest complexion (represented by λευκός). Presumably it lies somewhere between λευκός and μέλας, and as a medium shade was capable of being applied to either extreme. Theocritus used it hypocoristically for "sun-burned"; for him it was a complimentary expression, lightening the girl's colouring somewhat. So, with the other passages, if we take μελίχλωρος as a medium complexion, it can be used as a hypocorism for someone who is either too pale or too dark.

For these writers (with the possible exception of pseudo-Aristotle) μελίχλωρος was an attractive expression particularly suited to the complexion, whereas χλωρός alone indicated a sickly pallor (see p. 64 f.). Although for the early poets, μέλι χλωρόν ought to have meant "liquid honey," no trace of this meaning remains in the adjective. Perhaps the fact which we remarked earlier, that μέλι χλωρόν disappeared from poetic vocabulary explains why the transition to the adjective could be made with a loss of the original force. One would suppose that the epic tag applied mistakenly to the hue of honey led to the coining of μελίχλωρος.

C. Wine, Figs, and Cheese

In Euripides' satyr-play, Cyclops (67), the chorus comes in bewailing the absence of Dionysus and his companions, the revels, and οἴνου χλωραὶ σταγόνες. Most wine in the ancient world was dark; certainly the wine with which Odysseus made Polyphemus drunk was so described in Od. 9.196 (μέλανος οἴνοιο). This play is a reworking by Euripides of the Homeric tale of Odysseus and the Cyclops as told in the Odyssey. White wine was, of course, known to the Greeks, as we see from Cratinus fr. 183 (K,) where ὡς ἀπαλὸς καὶ λευκός is applied to Mendian wine. But in this context, the epithet χλωρός appears to be applicable to wine in general, not to a specific type. The point of the complaint, the absence of all wine, would be lost, if "white" wine were specified.[60]

Since it is the σταγόνες "drops" that are χλωραί, I suggest that the connection here is with moisture, and that to the chorus, χλωραί emphasizes the refreshment of wine, as dew refreshes plants.[61] It is somehow appropriate that drops are singled out as χλωραί by Euripides. Dew and tears, also described as χλωρός, are found as drops on leaves and flowers and on the face respectively. Honey, also χλωρός, oozes from the comb in drops, and stands on the wax. It is possible that Euripides mentions "drops" because they do not appear as *dark* as larger quantities of the same liquid. This explanation would keep the general association of χλωρός with light-coloured (pale) objects. But one

60. Wine is described by the ancients as μέλας, λευκός or ἀργής, ἐρυθρός and αἶθοψ (λευκός, ἀργής are late, the others Homeric). On wine color cf. A. D. Fitton-Brown in CR N.S. 12 (1962) 192-195.

61. Regarding "the refreshment of wine," see Onians, pp. 215-221, where he discusses the views of the ancient world on wine, and in particular, the idea "wine is life."

cannot be sure that this is the intention, especially in view of the description of blood as χλωρός (p. 74).

Euripides (fr. 907) says that Heracles ate χλωρός figs along with beef: κρέασι βοείοις χλωρὰ σῦκ᾽ἐπήσθιεν. Χλωρός has been taken to mean "unripe" when applied to figs,[62] but, while Heracles' tastes undoubtedly left something to be desired, it seems far more likely that the χλωρὰ σῦκα he ate were fresh figs right off the tree, i.e. undried, rather than unripe.[63] This is confirmed by Pollux (Onomast. 1.242): ἰσχὰς νέα, χλωρὰ, καὶ ἀρχαία, ξηρά. A fig is new and fresh, or old and dried. Again at 6.48, Pollux reports: σῦκα τῶν χλωρῶν· τυροῦ τροφαλὶς τυρὸς χλωρός. "Syca" is said of fresh figs; of cheese "trophalis" is fresh cheese. According to Pollux, then, cheese can be χλωρός. We find this epithet also in Aristophanes (Frogs 559). At this point, the hostess of the inn in Hades takes Dionysus with his lion's skin to be Heracles, and complains that on his previous visit, he ate the χλωρός cheese, crates and all.

οὐδὲ τὸν τυρόν γε τὸν χλωρόν, τάλαν,
ὃν οὗτος αὐτοῖς τοῖς ταλάροις κατήσθιεν.

These crates (τάλαροι) which Heracles devoured are elsewhere mentioned as the containers into which the milk or curds are poured, so that the whey can drain off, leaving the cheese (cf. Od. 9.446; Theocritus 5.86; and Pollux 7.175 τὸν τάλαρον ὧι ὁ χλωρὸς τυρὸς ἐμπήγνυται). The resultant cheese could be marketed without further processing, as we learn from Lysias (23.6) who speaks of entering the fresh cheese market, ἔλθοντα εἰς τὸν

62. LSJ, cf. our discussion in Introduction to this chapter.
63. A further note on "unripe" as a translation for χλωρός. LSJ so translate χλωρός in a fragment of Gorgias (Diels V.S. vol. 2 p. 235) reported by Aristotle (Rhet. 1406b5). The reading of A, the best and oldest manuscript, is χλωρὰ καὶ ἔναιμα πράγματα, but others read ἄναιμα for ἔναιμα; this second reading is preferred by the editors of the Oxford text, although Diels prefers ἔναιμα. The natural interpretation, if one reads ἄναιμα "bloodless," would be to associate it with pallor, translating "pale and bloodless deeds." One might wonder what deeds were pale and bloodless, and it was perhaps this difficulty in meaning that led LSJ to suggest "unripe" here. Presumably the thought was that since no blood had been shed the deeds were not ripe for doing. Since we have shown that LSJ were mistaken in translating χλωρὰ σῦκα "unripe figs," and there is no other warrant for this translation, we ought to read ἔναιμα and take χλωρά as "fresh." Thus Gorgias is describing deeds as "fresh and bloody" — a vivid phrase, borrowed from freshly killed meat, with the blood still in it, or (taking αἷμα figuratively for sap), from stalks of grain just mowed down in a field.

χλωρὸν τυρὸν. Χλωρός cheese, then, is freshly made, and still moist. Χλωρός figs are fresh, just picked. These two examples, found in prose as well as poetry, show how strong and persistent was the association of moisture with χλωρός.

IV Fear and Other Emotions

Homer most commonly used χλωρός to describe fearful people or fear itself. Twice in the *Iliad* (10.376; 15.4), people are χλωροὶ ὑπαὶ δείους i.e. fear is the cause of their being χλωροί. Elsewhere in Homer,[64] it is not the people themselves, but fear which is χλωρός, and which seizes a person (αἱρέω in some form). Whereas χλωρός is not specifically related to the complexion in these cases, ὦχρος "pallor," is connected with the cheeks (*Il.* 3.35) ὦχρός τέ μιν εἷλε παρείας, and the skin (*Od.* 11.529) οὔτ᾽ὠχρήσαντα χρόα κάλλιμον.

Twice in tragedy χλωρός is used to describe fear. Aeschylus makes the chorus in the *Supplices* (566-567) say that those who saw Io in her animal shape "shook at heart with pale fear at the strange sight":

χλωρῶι δείματι θυμόν
πάλλοντ᾽ὄψιν ἀήθη.

Similarly, Euripides, in the *Supplices* (598-599), has the mothers of the dead heroes who await word of the outcome of the battle say, "So pale fear perturbs me beneath my liver."

ὥς μοι ὑφ᾽ ἥπατι
δεῖμα χλοερὸν ταράσσει.

It is to be noted that in both these cases, the fear affects an internal part (the heart or the liver), not the face. It is particularly suggestive that Euripides should mention the liver, because it secretes bile, (χόλος and χολή), which the ancients thought flowed to various organs under emotional stress. We noted at the beginning of this chapter the etymological relationship of χλωρός to χόλος and χολή. Onians[65] discusses the action of bile,

---

64. *Il.* 7.479, 8.77, 17.67; *Od.* 11.43, 633, 12.343, 22.42, 24.450, 533; *h. Demeter* 190.

65. Onians, pp. 84-89, esp. p. 84.

particularly as a result of love or anger, without, however noting or commenting on χλωρὸν δέος. He does draw attention to the famous passage (Aesch. Ag. 1121) where the puzzling κροκοβαφὴς σταγών runs to the καρδία of 'the chorus, and argues for interpreting this drop as bile.[66] As an analogy, he quotes Choeph. 183-184, spoken by Electra when she sees the lock of Orestes' hair. κἀμοὶ προσέστη καρδίαι κλυδώνιον / χολῆς. The "little wave of bile" roused by her emotion goes to the *heart*, like the "saffron-dyed drop." It is worth quoting the context in which the "saffron-dyed drop" appears.

> ἐπὶ δὲ καρδίαν ἔδραμε κροκοβαφὴς
> σταγών, ἅτε καὶ δορὶ πτωσίμοις
> ξυνανύτει βίου δύντος αὐγαῖς.

"To my heart there ran a saffron-dyed drop, the very one which, to warriors mortally wounded, coincides with the sunset of life." The meaning of this passage has been debated. The scholiast took the drop to be blood, and he is followed in this by Fraenkel[67] and Denniston and Page[68] among others. Both these commentaries quote Aristotle (fr. 243), in which it is said that, in moments of great terror, blood runs to the heart. "Why do those who are frightened grow pale (ὠχριῶσιν)? Because blood runs to their heart and leaves the other parts of the body." Fraenkel says that the yellow colour is applied by Aeschylus to blood by "an easy transference," because yellow is the colour of fear. But Aristotle accounts for pallor (yellowness) as the absence of blood, and should not be quoted in support of making blood yellow. We find in Theocritus that pallor is caused by the action of the bile (23.13): τᾶι δὲ χολᾶι τὸ πρόσωπον ἀμείβετο, φεῦγε δ' ἀπὸ χρώς. Here is evidence that bile was thought to be responsible for the change of colour in a frightened person. Since bile is greenish-yellow, the colour of the complexion results from the activity (or

---

66. The use of "drop" in this context is interesting, since it lends support to a connection with χλωρός. Cf. our earlier discussion of the association of χλωρός with drops.

67. E. Fraenkel *Aeschylus Agamemnon* (Oxford 1950) vol. 3 on line 1122. Fraenkel also has an excellent discussion of the variant reading of 1122.

68. J. D. Denniston and D. L. Page *Aeschylus Agamemnon* (Oxford 1957) on line 1121.

over-activity) of bile. If one takes the "saffron-dyed drop" as bile, one has much less difficulty in explaining the yellow hue. It is, in fact, the colour of bile.

I suggest that this passage in the *Agamemnon* lends support to an association of fear with bile and the liver (and other internal organs) and explains the Homeric χλωρὸν δέος. Χλωρός originally described the "bile-stirred" condition of the frightened man (recall the etymological connection between χλωρός and χόλος, χολή). Then, because of the characteristic blanching accompanying fear, χλωρός came to describe pallor. This becomes the common prose usage, although it also appears in poetry.

In the Hesiodic *Shield* (264-265), Achlys, a figure personifying the privations of war, appears on the battle scene of the shield, "mournful, and dread, pale, shrivelled, shrunk with hunger."

> ἐπισμυγερή τε καὶ αἰνή
> χλωρὴ αὐσταλέη λιμῶι καταπεπτηυῖα.

The adjectives applied to her also describe her victims, except for αἰνή. Sophocles used χλωρανθείς in the sense of "having become pale," as reported by the Suda with the gloss: ἀντὶ τοῦ χλωρὸς γενηθεὶς οὕτως Σοφοκλῆς (fr. 1114). It is impossible to tell without the context whether there was an association with fear. Medical writers use χλωρός to denote pallor, e.g. Hippocrates (*Progn.* 2.24) and Thucydides, in his account of the plague (2.49). The latter relates that the body of the victim "was neither too hot nor pale, but reddish, livid" οὔτε ἄγαν θερμὸν ἦν οὔτε χλωρόν, ἀλλ᾿ὑπέρυθρον, πελιδνόν. Page points out that χλωρός, ὑπέρυθρος (or ἐρυθρός) and πελιδνός are used by the Hippocratic school of medical writers, Thucydides' contemporaries,[69] as clinical descriptions of their patients.[70] Χλωρός, which Page translates "yellowish," describes the colour of the skin in jaundice in the Hippocratic corpus. Now jaundice, or more properly hepatitis, is a disease of the liver, the organ which secretes bile. The choice of χλωρός and not e.g. ὠχρός to describe the effect of jaundice on the complexion confirms the connection between χλωρός and bile. It is to be observed in this connection, that χλωρός describes

69. D. L. Page CQ N.S. 3 (1953) 103.
70. *Morb*² 46; *Progn.* 24.64; *Art.* 86.17.

a sickly pallor, not the "fair skin" admired in women (who ideally avoided exposure to the sun) and censured in men because it betokened effeminacy. For this, λευκός is employed, bespeaking quality as well as colour. (See further chapter four, pp. 112-121).

An echo of the Homeric χλωρὸν δέος is found in Theocritus (25.220) in a poem in epic dialect on the story of Heracles. There we read that "pale fear held each one," χλωρὸν δέος εἶχεν ἕκαστον. This is a simple imitation, but it is of interest as the only instance known to the author in later poetry.

We have seen that χλωρός is related to χόλος, χολή "bile" and the action of bile is associated with strong emotion (cf. Electra's reaction to Orestes' hair (Choeph. 183-84, above). With this in mind, we come to Sappho's famous poem quoted by Longinus, describing herself under strong emotion. Using a type of comparison for which she was famed in antiquity, the "exemplary" comparison,[71] she speaks of herself as χλωροτέρα ποίας when she sees the girl to whom the poem is addressed. Her other symptoms, buzzing in the ears, loss of speech and vision, indicate her great emotion. Her comparison might be expressed as "more grassy than grass" i.e. in this type of comparison, the essential quality is stressed (cf., e.g., γάλακτος λευκοτέρα, χρυσοτέρα χρύσω). One would take this essential to be a positive rather than a negative characteristic, in the light of our understanding of χλωρός.

This passage is imitated by Longus Pastor, a poet of the third century after Christ (1.17.4):

χλωρότερον τὸ πρόσωπον ἦν πόας θερινῆς

Two additions have been made to the Sapphic original, the mention of the face and of the season of summer. The latter, if the reading is correct,[72] shows that Longus plainly takes χλωρός as typical of grass dried by the summer's heat, and so no longer green, but pale. The mention of the face indicates that he is specifying that χλωρός describes the complexion. He interprets the Sapphic χλωροτέρα ποίας as "paler than grass." Longinus,

71. For Sapphic comparisons of this type, cf. Demetrius Eloc. 127 and 162 and Gregorius ad Hermogenem Rhet. Graec. 7.2236.

72. Πόας θερινῆς is Courier's conjecture for the ms. χλόα ἠς 'ς καθε'ιρινῆς as reported by G. Dalmeyda Longus (Paris 1934) pp. xlviii-xlix.

also, in his comments upon the poem, says that Sappho described among other parts of herself, her complexion, τὴν χρόαν, by which he must be referring to χλωροτέρα. It is not, of course, surprising, that both of these men, educated Greeks of the imperial period, as well as many commentators after them,[73] should take χλωροτέρα to mean "paler," as part of Sappho's feeling that she is approaching death, as she says specifically in the line following: τεθνάκην δ᾽ ὀλίγω 'πιδεύης. The chief difficulty with this interpretation is that χλωρός ought to describe fresh grass, as we have seen that it properly describes the presence of life and moisture in trees and plants. It seems doubtful that Sappho could so ignore these associations as to describe *dried* grass as χλωρός as Longus did. Moreover it is characteristic of grass in Greek poetry to be soft and tender, inviting for animals to eat (*Od.* 6.90 ἄγρωστιν μελιήδεα), often close to water (*Od.* 6.124 καὶ πηγὰς ποταμῶν καὶ πίσεα ποιήεντα), and given epithets to emphasize its tenderness (*h. Hom.* 30.15 κατ᾽ ἄνθεα μάλακα ποίης and Inc. Auct. fr. 16 (b) *L.P.* πόας τέρεν ἄνθος μάλακον μάτεισαι). The growth of grass was linked in the minds of the Greek poets with sexual love. For example, fresh grass and flowers spring up during the ἱερὸς γάμος of Zeus and Hera (*Il.* 14. 347): τοῖσι δ᾽ ὑπὸ χθὼν δῖα φύεν νεοθηλέα ποίην and grass grows beneath the feet of Aphrodite, goddess of sexual love, as she steps ashore on Cyprus (Hes. *Theog.* 194-195): ἀφφὶ δὲ ποίη / ποσσὶν ὑπὸ ῥαδινοῖσιν ἀέξετο. If Sappho was thinking of this association in comparing herself to grass, she certainly would intend fresh grass.[74]

In the context of the poem we have a clear indication of the presence of moisture, for Sappho says that sweat pours down her (fr. 31.13 *L.P.*). The connection between love and moisture appearing as sweat is hinted at in Hesiod (*W.D.* 582-588) where the heat of the dogstar burns head and knees and the flesh is dry, and at this season women are most wanton and men most feeble. Did Hesiod think that heat dried up the seminal fluid making men less able to respond to the women? Alcaeus, Sappho's contem-

73. Supported by the "pathological" use of χλωρός exemplified in this section.
74. See further M. L. West *Hesiod Theogony* (Oxford 1966) on l. 194; also his comment on the use of sex by men to make things grow on l. 971.

porary and also a poet of Lesbos, imitated Hesiod's passage (fr. 347. *L.P.*) similarly linking heat, dryness and lack of power in men. One cannot draw too much from these passages, especially since women were not thought to be affected in this way by heat. If any conclusion can be drawn, it is that love and moisture flourish together.[75]

The meaning of χλωρός, then, combined with the intention of the "exemplary" comparison, namely a violent intensification, a stressing of the essential quality, as Thesleff[76] explains, suggests that Sappho is here comparing a reaction within herself to the moisture which is characteristic of plants. What this moisture within her was, we can only guess. It may be bile, stirred by her strong emotion, since the liver is affected by the "yearning pain of love."[77] It may be the moisture which is associated with love in such expressions as ὑγρὸς πόθος (cf. n. 16 and references in ancient literature to the "swimming eyes of passion"[78]). I suggest these as possible explanations, which seem to me to make more sense than the common interpretation of pallor. Χλωροτέρα ποίας is taken not as a symptom of exhaustion, but of excitement. This is not inconsistent with her feeling the approach of death in the following line; one can die, or nearly die, of excitement. One advantage of this interpretation is that the poem reaches a climax, rather than falling back limply in the last two lines. The other advantage is that χλωρός retains a positive meaning, in line with the poetic precedents, as one would expect from a sensitive poet.

In summing up this section, we conclude that χλωρός is applied to fear and frightened people because bile was stirred by fear. We find confirmation in the use of χλωρός by medical writers to describe the complexion in jaundice (a disease of the liver), as well as in the evidence that bile was thought to behave in this way. This fits into the general picture of χλωρός as basically

75. See Onians pp. 191-192. There is a contrast between unseasonable love which comes with parching madness (ἀζαλέαις μανίαισιν) and a well-watered spring (Ibycus fr. 286 *PMG*).

76. H. Thesleff: *Studies on Intensification in Early and Classical Greek* (Helsingfors 1954) (in *Commentationes humanarum litterarum* vol. 21, no. 1) pp. 127-128.

77. Cf. Onians pp. 85, 87-88, on the association of the liver with the pangs of love. Cf. also the reaction of bile, e.g. Aesch. *Choeph.* 183-184, given above.

78. E.g. Eur. *Hipp.* 525-526; Catullus 45.11; *Anacreont.* 28.21; *A.P.* 7.27; Polemon. *Physiogn.* See further Onians p. 203.

"moist." From this use of χλωρός, the wider meaning "pale" developed, as the colour of a frightened man's complexion.

V Homer's Nightingale, Deianeira, Life and Blood

In *Odyssey* 19.518ff, a Homeric simile describes the nightingale as χλωρηΐς. The connection between this simile and the situation to which Homer compares it, is, as in many Homeric similes, rather tenuous. Penelope, addressing her as-yet-unrecognized husband Odysseus, relates how she grieves day and night. During the day, she is involved in household duties, "but when night comes and sleep falls on everyone, I lie in bed and throngs of sharp cares disquiet my beating heart as I grieve. But as when the daughter of Pandarus, the χλωρηΐς nightingale, sings beautifully just at the beginning of spring, sitting among the thick leaves of the trees, and at the same time, with trills, she pours forth her many-toned voice, mourning her own child, Itylus, whom once she slew with the sword through folly, ... so also is my heart divided this way and that, whether to remain by my son ... or to go with the best wooer ... ":

αὐτὰρ ἐπεὶ νὺξ ἔλθηι, ἕληισί τε κοῖτος ἅπαντας,
κεῖμαι ἐνὶ λέκτρωι, πυκιναὶ δέ μοι ἀμφ'ἁδινὸν κῆρ
ὀξεῖαι μελεδῶναι ὀδυρομένην ἐρέθουσιν.
ὡς δ'ὅτε Πανδαρέου κούρη, χλωρηῒς ἀηδών,
καλὸν ἀείδηισιν ἔαρος νέον ἱσταμένοιο,
δενδρέων ἐν πετάλοισι καθεζομένη πυκινοῖσιν,
ἥ τε θαμὰ τρωπῶσα χέει πολυηχέα φωνήν,
παῖδ' ὀλοφυρομένη Ἴτυλον φίλον, ὅν ποτε χαλκῶι
κτεῖνε δι'ἀφραδίας κοῦρον Ζήθοιο ἄνακτος,
ὡς καὶ ἐμοὶ δίχα θυμὸς ὀρώρεται ἔνθα καὶ ἔνθα,
ἠὲ μένω παρὰ παιδὶ .... ἦ ἤδη ἅμ' ἕπωμαι. ...

The nightingale is the symbol of the consuming grief Penelope felt. The variations in her song seem to mirror the various problems Penelope faced. The myth to which Homer refers is not the common Attic one of Philomela, Procne, and Tereus but rather of Aedon who had one son, Itylus.[79] Jealous because of her

79. J. Lemprière *Classical Dictionary* (London 1949, new ed. rev. F. A. Wright) s.v. Aedon.

sister-in-law Niobe's large family, Aedon planned to kill Niobe's eldest son. By mistake she killed her own son instead. Transformed by Zeus into a nightingale, she continues to mourn.

That this bird is a nightingale and not some other song-bird, the characteristics given in this passage attest. The bird's habitat is the woods; it appears in early spring; it is a noted singer, whose song is characterized by trills and variations in tone. From the fact that Penelope is speaking of her grief at night, one might infer that the bird is a night singer. All these points are typical of the nightingale. In addition, the name, ἀηδών, and the legend of her lament, guarantee the identification. D'Arcy Thompson devotes several pages to the identification of this bird and the characteristics mentioned in ancient literature, agreeing that Homer's ἀηδών is indeed the nightingale.[80] Since the bird is brownish in colour, χλωρηίς cannot be intended to describe its plumage.

Demetrius (*Eloc.* 133, 164) cites the phrase χλωρηίς ἀηδών as an example of the way in which beautiful words embellish poetry and add to its charm. He apparently thought of χλωρηίς as a poetic variant for χλωρή. Grube,[81] in a note on this section, refers to Demetrius' discussion of lengthened words (ch. 70) for an explanation. In that chapter Demetrius observes that the placing of clashing vowels side by side is productive of charm; e.g. ἠέλιος (for ἥλιος) and ὀρέων (for ὀρῶν).

In a note on *Od.* 19.518, Munro[82] suggests that the relationship of χλωρηίς to χλωρός is analogous with that of νηρηίς and νηίς "water nymph" to *νηρόν. Now *νηρόν does not exist in classical Greek, although it is attested in late inscriptions (sixth century after Christ) and gives the Modern Greek νερό "water." (The adjective ναρός "flowing, liquid" does occur in tragedy.) Munro argues that *νηρόν is a possible form for Homer's time. Νηρηίς, however, is not simply a water-dwelling nymph, but one of the fifty daughters of Nereus, the old man of the sea. In form,

---

80. D'Arcy W. Thompson *A Glossary of Greek Birds* (2nd ed., Oxford 1936) s.v. ἀηδών pp. 16-22; also pp. 331-333 on various birds related in name to χλωρός: χλωρεύς unknown species, enemy of turtle-doves; χλωρίς greenfinch, or green linnet; χλωρίων golden oriole. None of these birds could be Homer's ἀηδών.

81. G. M. A. Grube *A Greek Critic: Demetrius on Style* (Toronto 1961) p. 93 n. 133.

82. D. B. Munro *Homer's Odyssey* (Oxford 1901) vol. 2 on *Od.* 19.518.

it is treated as a feminine patronymic from Νηρεύς as Βρισηίς is from Βρισεύς. Both names and other words for "nymph" are related to νάω, etc. The other examples put forward by Munro are found only in late writers: ὀρειάς "mountain-nymph" from ὄρος and δρυάς "tree-spirit" from δρῦς. Munro's theory assumes the existence of τὸ χλωρόν "the green-wood," so that χλωρηίς can mean "green-wood-dwelling." But Homer nowhere describes the woods as χλωρός though the word is so used by later poets (see discussion above). For example, Sophocles (O.C. 673) places the nightingale in a χλωρός habitation: ἀηδὼν χλωραῖς ὑπὸ βάσσαις. It is possible to argue that this line is Sophocles' comment on the Homeric epithet.[83]

We have mentioned that χλωρηίς may be a poetic variant for χλωρή or that the -ίς ending may signify "belonging to." A third

___

83. Cf. also Aesch. Supp. 63, ἄτοπο χώρων ποταμῶν τ'ἐργομένα (of the nightingale), emended by G. Hermann (Aeschyli Tragoediae [Leipzig 1852] on Supp 1. 59) to read ἄτ' ἀπὸ χλωρῶν πετάλων ἐγρομένα. This would give a combination of the χλωρός habitation with the nightingale. Let us look at the passage in context.

κιρκηλάτου τ'ἀηδόνης
ἄτ' ἀπὸ...
πενθεῖ μὲν οἶκτον ἠθέων

"the hawk-pursued nightingale, who ... mourns in lament for her haunts ... " The haunts are mentioned in the middle line. The ms. reading ἄτοπο χώρων ποταμῶν τ'ἐργομένα must be emended to read as Greek. Victorius' emendation is widely accepted: ἄτ'ἀπὸ χώρων ποταμῶν τ'εἰργομένα. It makes the jumble at the beginning of the line translatable, and it replaces the Epic form ἐργομένα with the Attic εἰργομένα. The difficulty with this version is in understanding χώρων without an epithet. The line is supposed to mean "kept away from places and rivers." Hermann is justified in asking "A quibusnam locis? et num aquatilis avis est luscinia?" Having in mind, as he himself says, the Homeric description of the nightingale, he emends: ἄτ'ἀπὸ χλωρῶν πετάλων ἐγρομένα; ἐγρομένα from ἔγρω (a later form of ἐγείρω) "roused" replaces ἐργομένα, avoiding the problem of an Epic form, and suiting better than ἐργομένα the scholiast's comment διωκομένη i.e. "pursued by the hawk." (Ἔγρω occurs rarely: twice in Eur. Rhes. 532 [of doubtful authenticity] and in fr. 773.29). T. G. Tucker The Supplices of Aeschylus (London 1889) has carried emendation a step further to ἄθ'ὑπὸ χλωρῶν πετάλων τεγγομένα "who weeping beneath green leaves ... " He argues that ΤΕΓΓΟΜΕΝΑ for ΤΕΡΓΟΜΕΝΑ explains the presence in the text of τ' as Hermann's conjecture does not. But Tucker has lost the sense of "pursuing" seen by the scholiast, and the ἠθέων (of the next line) is unexplained in this version.

Hermann's conjecture seems to be a felicitous suggestion for a passage in need of correction. The objections to Victorius' reading, the fact that χώρων without a clarifying epithet is weak and vague and that rivers in themselves are not associated with the nightingale, are well taken. If, indeed, Hermann is right, then here too we find an association of the nightingale with χλωρός. Since Hermann confesses that he was influenced by the Homeric passage, Aeschylus may have been also.

suggestion has been put forward, that χλωρηίς is formed from χλωρός and ἀείδω "sing," (cf. καλάις, the cock "who sings clearly").[84] The nightingale is noted for its song, more than for anything else, and in the Homeric passage, the bird is said to sing beautifully (1.519). Since colour epithets or other visual qualities may be applied to sound it is possible for χλωρός to be used in this way. But if χλωρηίς derives its ending from ἀείδω, it is strange to find καλὸν ἀείδῃσιν at the beginning of the next line with no indication that this phrase explains or clarifies the adjective. If Homer sets out to explain a word he has used, he does so explicitly (cf. the explanation of Astyanax, *Il.* 6.402-403 and of Lotophagoi, *Od.* 9.84). In both these cases, the word in question is defined by other words, not its component parts.[85] It does not seem likely, then, that καλὸν ἀείδῃσιν is an explanation of χλωρηίς or that Homer would repeat himself, saying that the χλωρόν-singing bird sings beautifully.

The scholiasts and commentators offer us a wide choice of educated guesses as to the meaning of the word.[86] For the most part they assume that χλωρός has to do with leaves and greenery in such interpretations as "the one who delights in, lives in, greenery" or "who appears in spring when everything is green." Some offer "because of the colour of the plumage," but if this were reasonable, it would have been adopted long ago and no problem would have been thought to exist. Now, we have seen that χλωρός is used by poets later than Homer to describe trees and woods. We have also seen that a river, mountain, shore, or other area can be described as χλωρός because it is covered with vegetation. But even if we were to allow that Homer might comprehend τὸ χλωρόν, it would require an extension of meaning to make χλωρηίς mean "living in a χλωρός place." It is one thing to describe places where vegetation is actually growing as χλωρός; it is quite another to describe the nightingale as such simply because she *lives in*, or *frequents* the woods. There is a possible

---

84. Boisacq s.v. χλωρηίς. Καλάις (*LSJ* s.v.) occurs in an inscription of the fifth century B.C. (*IG* 4.914.3). It occurs elsewhere meaning "turquoise" (the stone).

85. On Homer's method of explaining neologisms, cf. Stanford, *Greek Metaphor* (Oxford 1936) p. 125.

86. E.g. *Etym. Magn.* 813.8; Stephanus vol. 8, 1534, s.v. χλωρηίς and Hesychius s.v. χλωρηίς.

parallel for this extension of meaning in Theocritus (28.4), where the poet says: Κύπριδος ἷρον καλάμῳ χλῶρον ὑπ'ἀπάλῳ. The ἷρον is said to be "green from the surrounding reeds." Gow[87] takes ἷρον as "precinct," and, if he is right, this example is like the others to which we have referred, where a surface is covered with growth and, as a result, χλωρός. If, however, ἷρον is a temple building, then the building itself takes its colour from the marsh around it. But this is an easier extension of meaning, because of the specific mention that the reeds make the temple χλῶρον. Moreover, the reflexion of green on a presumably white temple can be seen, whereas the bird does not become *coloured* by the woods.

Other suggestions have been raised for χλωρηΐς; one possibility is that since Homer uses χλωρός chiefly of the pallor of fear, the epithet here means "pale."[88] The nightingale, like Penelope whom she typifies, is overcome with emotion and grief. Now, although the bird is Aedon, she is in the form of a nightingale. In the flesh, Aedon might well be pale with grief, but in her altered shape, she conforms to the appearance of a bird. To describe a bird as "pale with grief" strikes me as more suitable to the comic opera than to epic![89]

Twice in subsequent Greek poetry, the nightingale is described as χλωρ-. A melic fragment, attributed by some authorities to Sappho, (Adesp. 964(b) *PMG*) repeats the Homeric phrase, χλωρηΐς ἀηδών, but the context has not been preserved. Simonides (fr. 586.2 *PMG*) describes nightingales by the compound adjective χλωραύχην, and thus specifies that the necks or throats of the birds are χλωρός. It is to the scholia on the Homeric passage that we owe this fragment, an indication that it was thought to be an imitation of Homer and to shed light on him. Indeed, it would be surprising if Simonides did not know the Homeric original. There is nothing noteworthy about the plumage on the neck of the nightingale to cause Simonides to mention the colour of their necks. The neck or throat is only noteworthy as

---

87. *Theocritus* on 28.4.
88. J. M. Boraston "The Birds of Homer" *JHS* 31 (1911) 216-250, esp. p. 246.
89. Cf. W. S. Gilbert's "tit willow." Also Aristoph. *Birds* 667-668, where the nightingale is represented as an attractive girl (ὥσπερ παρθένος): ὡς καλὸν τοὐρνίθιον/ ὡς δ'ἀπαλόν, 'ὡς δὲ λευκόν. The adjectives clearly describe the actor, not the bird.

the source of the music the nightingale sings. If one observes a song-bird, one can see the throbbing of the throat as he pours forth his song. I suggest, then, that in this context, χλωρ- means "throbbing." As a parallel to this use of χλωρός, I put forward Pindar's description of the back of Zeus' eagle (*Pyth.* 1.9) as ὑγρός. This word, which connotes a fluid continuity (like the surface of the sea), here portrays the "heaving" of the great bird's back in sleep (cf. p. 35).[90]

When we next encounter χλωραύχην it is in quite a different context. Bacchylides relates how in Hades, Meleager arranged for Heracles, who had come to fetch Cerberus, to marry his sister, Deianeira, who was as yet unmarried in her father's house. Deianeira is described as χλωραύχην (5.172). The term is certainly to be taken as complimentary, and not an indication of an unhealthy pallor. As Simonides' nephew, Bacchylides must have known his uncle's works and have been borrowing with purpose. One would expect him to use the word in the same sense, since he could hardly avoid recalling Simonides' poem to his hearers. (These are the only two occurrences of the word that are preserved.) The translation "pale-throated," indicating the beauty of a pale (or fair) complexion, ought to be rejected, because it would not be suitable for the earlier passage, and also, because the regular word for beauty of complexion is λευκός (cf. pp. 112-121).[91] If, as we assume, χλωραύχην expresses Simonides' observation of the bird's throat throbbing in song, it ought here to bear some relationship to Deianeira's voice. It may be simply that Bacchylides is drawing attention to the musical quality of her voice, or that he is contrasting the dead and the living in terms of their speaking. We know that Homeric ghosts were unable to speak until they had drunk blood (*Od.* 11.96, 146ff). Otherwise they squeaked and gibbered like bats in a cave (*Il.* 23.101; *Od.* 24.7). Although

---

90. Cf. further G. E. Marindin in *CR* 4 (1890) 231, who suggests "living, gushing" as a translation for χλωρηίς, and W. W. Fowler *ibid.* p. 50 who argues for a connection with trees and shadow.

91. Cf. R. C. Jebb, *Bacchylides* (Cambridge 1905) on 5.172f in his appendix pp. 473-474. J. Stern "The Imagery of Bacchylides' *Ode* 5" in *GRBS* 8 (1967) 41-42 calls attention to the plant imagery in the poem and interprets the epithet χλωραύχην in these terms. "Deianeira like a beautiful plant blooms for a moment before the disaster, vividly brought to mind by the myth's abrupt end, strikes."

Bacchylides says nothing directly about the voices of the living and dead, it is possible, in view of the Homeric account, that this would be easily supplied by the reader. Here then, it makes sense to call Deianeira χλωραύχην when she is alive and in the upper world, while the conversation is taking place in Hades.

There is more literary evidence connecting χλωρός with life and living people. Hesychius quotes a tragic fragment χλωρόν τε καὶ βλέποντα with the gloss, ἀντὶ τοῦ ζῶντα. This comment must refer to χλωρόν, since the equivalence of ζάω and βλέπω is too common in tragedy to be remarkable. (This fragment is restored by Toup to Aesch. Ag. 677, and replaces the manuscript reading ζῶντα καὶ βλέποντα.)[92]

From Hesychius also we obtain the gloss χλωρόν: ὑγρόν. We have already noted the frequency with which χλωρός and moisture are associated: in plants and trees; in cheese and figs; in tears, dew, bile and other liquids. Like sap which indicates life in growing things, blood is the liquid which, in a sense, represents life in people, and it is twice described as χλωρός. In Sophocles (Trach. 1055), poison is destroying Heracles, drinking his blood: ἐκ δὲ χλωρὸν αἷμά μου/ πέπωκεν. Here, his blood has not been spilled as by a weapon, but is unshed. In translating this passage, Cicero (Tusc. 2.20) renders χλωρὸν αἷμα by decolorem sanguinem, showing that he took χλωρόν as an unnatural colour, the blood affected in appearance by poison. This is made unlikely by the second occurrence of χλωρὸν αἷμα in Euripides (Hec. 126-127). The Greeks are threatening to "crown Achilles' tomb with Polyxena's blood":

> τὸν Ἀχίλλειον τύμβον στεφανοῦν
> αἵματι χλωρῶι.

Here there is no question of discoloration from poison or any other cause. Like Heracles, Polyxena's blood is as yet unshed,

92. This restoration is given primarily as a matter of interest. Fraenkel (Aeschylus Agamemnon [Oxford 1950]) reports Verrall's support: "It is not certain that the gloss relates to this passage, but it is highly probable, and the improvement is great." Fraenkel gives a word of caution on the principle of replacing ms. readings with Hesychian glosses (in his note on Aesch. Ag. 639): "We should be put on our guard against blind faith in the excellence of our mss ... and on the other hand, against blind Ἡσυχιασμός (CR 51 51[1937] 60) by the many horrors which haunt the textual criticism of the past." Very sound advice!

because the deed is only contemplated. The adjective adds pathos, by stressing the life and youth of the victim. These three examples show a definite association of χλωρός and life. The tragic fragment is unambiguous; the association with blood in these two instances, provides further support for the meaning "living," which has its origin in the Greek association of moisture and life.

Two further examples are given in this vein by Theocritus (14.70) γόνυ χλωρόν and (27.67) χλοεροῖσιν ἰαινόμενοι μελέεσσιν. Evidently one's limbs are χλωρός while one is young, as shown by ease of movement. As one becomes older, the joints become stiff and less supple, due to a drying up of the fluid in the joints.

In this section we have seen the same association of χλωρός and moisture that we found in earlier sections. If one keeps the idea of moisture in mind, with all the Greeks felt about moisture, χλωρός presents a remarkably unified picture.

VI Three Less Tractable Examples

Three rather odd occurrences remain to be discussed. In the Hesiodic *Shield* (231) adamant is χλωρός; in Xenophanes, the rainbow is a cloud, with three bands of colour, one of which is χλωρός; and in Sophocles, the sand where Menelaus threatens to leave Ajax's body (*Ajax* 1064) is χλωρός.

In the Sophoclean passage, ἀλλ' ἀμφὶ χλωρὰν ψάμαθον ἐκβεβλημένος, the word, it seems, presents three choices. First, we may take it as a general epithet of sand "pale" with stress on the desolate nature of the shore, as Jebb[93] does, and we might extend it further to represent the desolate future of the unburied. In this sense, compare Vergil (*Aen.* 5.374) where sand and a dead body are also brought together: *fulva moribundum extendit harena.* Stanford[94] makes the perceptive observation that in *Ajax* 1064 "the preposition is contemptuously vague, the epithet poetically vivid." He takes χλωράν as a colour epithet "yellow" and suggests that "perhaps Sophocles wishes to indicate Menelaos' heartlessness here: the colour of the sand means more to him than the abandoned corpse." Although I cannot agree in the translation

93. R. C. Jebb *The Ajax of Sophocles* (London 1898) on line 1064.
94. W. B. Stanford *Sophocles Ajax* (London and New York 1963) on line 1064.

"yellow" (which results from a mistaken translation of χλωρὸν μέλι), I think the general comment on the vividness of the epithet is enlightening. If we do not take χλωράν in a general sense "pale," there are two other suggestions. We might take it as "green with vegetation" as we did in Soph. *Ant.* 1132. There, however, the χλωρὰ · · · ἀκτά is further defined by πολυστάφυλος "with many vines," and somehow, ἀκτά is less forbiddingly barren than ψάμαθος. A third suggestion, put forward by Campbell,[95] is the only one which takes into account the basic meaning "moist" in χλωρός. He proposes to translate χλωρὰν ψάμαθον as "that part of the sands which the sea has moistened." Here, however, and only here, so far as I can discover, the "moistness" of the object is not an integral part of it, as with tears, dew, etc., but something added from without. There is nothing in the passage to confirm this possibility. Moreover, it seems to me to emphasize a physical discomfort, i.e. dampness, which would be of no concern to the corpse, at the expense of the greater concern, denial of burial. Since sand, in itself, tends to be barren and desolate, it seems impossible to interpret χλωράν in its original sense of "moist" or the extension of this "fresh, living." For the present, I think the first proposal is preferable, i.e. "pale."

In the second occurrence, Xenophanes is explaining to his hearers what a rainbow really is (fr. 28D.):

> ἥν τ' Ἶριν καλέουσι νέφος καὶ τοῦτο πέφυκε
> πορφύρεον καὶ φοινίκεον καὶ χλωρὸν ἰδέσθαι.

"This which they call Iris is also a cloud, purple and red and yellow-green to behold." Xenophanes is obviously attempting to describe the bands of colour in the rainbow. For the pale band between the brighter extremes of red-orange and blue-violet he chooses χλωρός. This is the earliest definitely chromatic use of χλωρός and what better occasion!

Finally, we turn to the Hesiodic passage, where "adamant" is certainly metal, as it clanged when the pursuing Gorgons trod on it yet is described as χλωρός. Adamant "the unconquerable substance," probably steel, is elsewhere described as grey, πολιός

---

95. L. Campbell, *Sophocles* (Oxford 1881) on *Ajax* 1064.

(*Theog.* 161). Here, (*Shield* 231) then, χλωρός must mean simply "pale."

VII An Historical Survey

We remarked that χλωρός is most frequently used in Homer for fear and people who are afraid. After Homer, this association is rare, being found twice in tragedy (Aesch. *Supp.* 566, Eur. *Supp.* 599) and once in an epic imitation (Theocr. 25.220). This change leads us to suppose that the force of this early use may not have been fully understood by later writers. It is from this association with fear that the common prose meaning "pale" developed. We saw that Homer also describes as χλωρός wood and honey. The epithet of the nightingale (χλωρηίς) is not easy to understand, and was perhaps only half-understood by the poet himself. Hesiod (*W.D.* 743) contrasts χλωρός with αὖος "dry" showing clearly the basic meaning "moist." The Hesiodic *Shield* shows less sensitivity; two of the three occurrences seem to mean simply "pale" and the third "green" of a branch (see above).

We saw earlier how examples from the lyric poets repeat an association previously found in epic, as with honey, trees and plants, and even the nightingale. Bacchylides describes Deianeira as χλωραύχην repeating the epithet used by his uncle Simonides for the nightingale. Sappho's description of herself as χλωροτέρα ποίας seems to be related to the Greek view of strong emotion as having marked physical effects. Xenophanes is the first to use χλωρός in a purely chromatic sense, to describe the pale, yellow-green band of the rainbow, between the red-orange and blue-purple bands. Pindar achieves a delicate balance in meaning by placing χλωρός so that it describes "dew," but contributes also to the picture of flourishing growth.

Among the dramatists, Euripides uses χλωρός most often and makes the most of its range of meaning. He models himself at times on his predecessors, as in the case of fear (*Supp.* 599), tears (*Med.* 906, 922, *Helen* 1189), blood (*Hec.* 127, cf. Soph. *Trach.* 1055), and vegetation of all kinds. But even in borrowing he does the unexpected, as e.g. "fresh rose petals" (*Helen* 243-244), and the "green pleasant things of the meadow" (*Bacch.* 866). He obviously understands the basic meaning of χλωρός and is able to remind his hearers of this basis in his use of it. It is interesting that it appears twice in several plays (*Bacch.*, *I.A.*, *Phoen.*, *Med.*) and three times in one (*Helen*). Perhaps he liked the cumulative effect of repetition. At any rate, it is certain that he used χλωρός with its general Greek associations with moisture, youth, and life.[96]

96. It is interesting in this connection to note the cult titles of Dionysus given by E. R. Dodds *Eur. Bacch.* (2nd ed. Oxford 1960) pp. xi − xii: Δενδρίτης or Ἔνδενδρος power in the tree; Ἄνθιος blossom-bringer; κάρπιος fruit-bringer; Φλεύς or Φλέως the abundance of life; (Plut. *Is. et Os.* 35.365A, Pind. fr. 140 Bowra). "His domain is, in Plutarch's words, the whole of the ὑγρὰ φύσις − not only the liquid fire in the grape, but the sap thrusting in a young tree, the blood pounding in the veins of a young animal, all the mysterious and uncontrollable tides that ebb and flow in the life of nature."

Three
κυάνεος

I Introduction

To Homer, it seems, κυάνεος meant simply "dark," with no trace
of "blue." This primary meaning becomes clear when we consider
Homer's descriptions of the material κύανος (from which the
adjective κυάνεος is derived). It is not until we turn to the later
poets that an element of "blueness" becomes associated with
κυάνεος.

Before our examination of κυάνεος in the early poets, let us
consider what Plato and Theophrastus have to say about the
composition of τὸ κυανοῦν in their discussions of colour theory.
Plato (*Tim.* 68c) says that κυανοῦν is composed of "bright"
(λαμπρόν), "white" (λευκόν) and "deeply saturated black" (μέλαν
κατακορές). We learn from this that for Plato κυανοῦν was dark,
since the black was "deeply saturated," but also highly lustrous,
since λαμπρόν was one of its component parts. The addition of
more white to κυανοῦν produced γλαυκόν "light blue," so we
surmise that Plato thought white lightened black to dark blue and
more white lightened it further to light blue, and that κυανοῦν is
dark blue. Theophrastus' account of κυανοῦν is, at first sight, quite
unlike Plato's since he derives it from a combination of woad
(ἰσάτις) which gives blueness and fiery-red (πυρώδης), "with
round figures and needle-shaped figures to give a gleam to the
colour's darkness" (*De Sens.* 77). Although the component parts
differ from Plato's, the results are the same: τὸ κυανοῦν is dark but
it has a gleam or lustre. It may seem strange that it differs from
woad, a blue dye, by the addition of fiery-red, but apparently

Theophrastus thought fire added a gleam (cf. *De Sens.* 75 for things which have the most and finest fire in them and are λαμπρότατα) as did the sharp figures which he says specifically produced a gleam (cf. also *De Sens.* 74). This definite association of lustre or gleam with κυάνεος perhaps explains Euripides' compound "dark-gleaming" (κυαναυγής *Alc.* 261). Moreover, it gives particular relevance to the description of various birds as κυάνεος (Simon. fr. 597 *PMG*, the swallow; Eur. *Andr.* 862, an unidentified bird, sometimes assumed to be the raven;[1] [Arist.] *H.A.* 616a15, the halcyon). The swallow and the kingfisher are noted for the metallic lustre of their feathers.[2] It seems likely, too, that there is a reference to the glossiness of the porpoise in κυάνεος (*H.A.* 566b12) rather than to a specific shade of blue, since the porpoise is dark with a lighter greyish belly.[3] Hence it will be well to bear in mind its association with lustre.

In his treatise, *De Lapidibus*, Theophrastus mentions several varieties of the material *kyanos* (we shall for convenience transliterate κύανος). Caley and Richards identify these as (a) lapis lazuli, a blue precious stone, (b) azurite, dark blue basic copper carbonate, and (c) an artificial blue pigment.[4] We note that all these substances are blue, although the actual shade varies from pale to dark. In the light of Theophrastus' identification, it is natural that commentators have taken Homer's *kyanos* as "blue-glass paste" i.e. category (c).[5] Sir Arthur Evans pronounced the "brilliant cobalt hue" in the frescoes of the Palace of Minos to be of the classical *kyanos*.[6] Blue-glass paste in the form of beads, ornaments, and inlays has been found in the remains of the Mycenaean period, although the material (presumably wood) in

1. *LSJ* assume that the bird is the raven, although this is not specified in the passage.
2. Lacking a classical authority, we quote from *A New Dictionary of Birds* ed. Sir A. Landsborough Thomson (London 1964) s.v. Kingfisher p. 413: "The plumage is commonly of bright colours, often of metallic brilliance"; and s.v. Swallow p. 791: "The plumage, especially on the upper parts, tends to be dark — black, brown, green, or blue, often with a metallic lustre."
3. *ONED* s.v. porpoise.
4. E. R. Caley and J. F. C. Richards *Theophrastus On Stones* (Columbus, 1956) pp. 126-127, 143-144, 175, 183-184.
5. E.g. Wallace *Color in Homer and in Ancient Art* pp. 5, 10-12, 38.
6. Sir Arthur Evans *The Palace of Minos* 5 vols. in 7 (London 1921 - 1936) vol. 2, p. 534.

which the decorations were inlaid has perished.[7] Several tablets from Pylos give evidence of inlaid furniture, and on the basis of this and the form of the paste decorations, the assumption is made that these were originally inlaid. Blue-glass paste is also known from contemporary Egyptian furnishings and from the frieze of the Great Megaron at Tiryns.[8]

Homer, however, calls kyanos "dark" (μέλανος κυάνοιο Il. 11.24,35), and I suggest that when he uses the adjective κυάνεος he means either "made of kyanos" or simply "dark." This might be considered strange if kyanos is blue-glass paste. What do we know about the use of kyanos from Homer, and even earlier, from the Pylos tablets? Κύανος is thought to be a loan word from some non-Indo-European language.[9] It occurs first in Greek in the Pylos tablets (PY 239,244) in association with silver and gold. In PY 239, a stone table is inlaid with aquamarines, kyanos, silver, and gold.[10] In PY 244, a chair and a footstool are decorated with kyanos, silver, and gold, and the chair is inlaid "with men's figures in gold and with a pair of gold finials and with golden griffins and with griffins of kyanos." Wace disagreed with the common identification of kyanos as "blue-glass paste" and preferred to take it as niello, the black amalgam used in the Enkomi bowl and the dagger blades and silver cups from Mycenae.[11] Stubbings also made

7. E. T. Vermeule Greece in the Bronze Age (Chicago & London 1964) p. 208 beads; p. 131 ornaments; p. 175 inlays.

8. M. Ventris and J. Chadwick Documents in Mycenaean Greek (Cambridge 1959) p. 340.

9. Boisacq s.v. κύανος concludes that it is a loan word, etymology unknown. Frisk s.v. κύανος compares Mycenaean ku-wa-no and Hittite kuuanna(n)- "blue stone." O. J. L. Szemerenýi claims that an "Asianic source is visible" for κύανος (CR N.S. 8 [1958] 61) because A. Götze showed that Hittite kuwana meant "lapis lazuli, copper" (Journal of Cuneiform Studies 1 [1947] 307f). In this article, Götze argues in part from κύανος to conclude that ku(wa)nnan- could mean (1) copper, (2) azurite i.e. carbonate of copper, (3) azurite bead — a far different matter from proving that kuwana was "lapis lazuli, copper." Gladstone would have been glad of this "evidence" when he argued that κύανος was copper (Nineteenth Century 2[1877] 378-379). Ventris and Chadwick Documents p. 399 cite Ugaritic iqnu, Akkadian uqnu "lapis lazuli"? and ku-wa-an-na-še, an unknown Hurrian term describing furniture. They challenge Wace in his identification of kyanos with niello (p. 240), while admitting that a substance like niello might be more plausible for Agamemnon's breastplate (Il. 11.24).

10. The word translated "inlaid" is a-ja-me-no, with no equivalent in later Greek. Cf. Ventris and Chadwick p. 386 s.v. a-ja-me-no.

11. A. J. B. Wace quoted without reference by Ventris and Chadwick p. 340; possibly his opinion was expressed privately to the authors.

this suggestion,[12] and the identification of *kyanos* as *niello* accords better with the evidence of the Homeric poems, as we shall see.

Kyanos is one of the decorative substances on the breastplate which Cinyras of Crete gave to Agamemnon (*Il.* 11.24-27):

> δέκα οἶμοι ἔσαν μέλανος κυάνοιο
> δώδεκα δὲ χρυσοῖο καὶ εἴκοσι κασσιτέροιο·
> κυάνεοι δὲ δράκοντες ὀρωρέχατο προτὶ δειρήν
> τρεῖς ἑκάτερθ' ἴρισσιν ἐοικότες·

"There were ten bands of dark *kyanos*, twelve of gold, and twenty of tin. Three snakes stretched towards his [Agamemnon's] neck on either side, like rainbows [i.e. curved]."[13] Agamemnon's shield was also decorated with *kyanos* (*Il.* 11.34-35):

> ἐν δὲ οἱ ὀμφαλοὶ ἦσαν ἐείκοσι κασσιτέροιο
> λευκοί, ἐν δὲ μέσιοσιν ἔην μέλανος κυάνοιο

"On it there were twenty white bosses of tin, and in the middle there was (one) of dark *kyanos*." Further, on the silver strap by which he supported his shield "a snake of *kyanos* twisted" (11.39): κυάνεος ἐλέλικτο δράκων. On the shield of Achilles, in the vineyard scene, Hephaestus used silver, gold, tin and *kyanos* (*Il.* 18.561-565).

> ἐν δὲ τίθει σταφυλῆισι μέγα βρίθουσαν ἀλωήν
> καλὴν χρυσείην· μέλανες δ' ἀνὰ βότρυες ἦσαν,
> ἑστήκει δὲ κάμαξι διαμπερὲς ἀργυρέηισιν.
> ἀμφὶ δὲ κυανέην κάπετον, περὶ δ' ἕρκος ἔλασσε
> κασσιτέρου·

"On it he made a beautiful, golden vineyard, heavily weighed down with grapes. The grapes were dark and they were supported on silver poles. Around it he put a trench of *kyanos* and a fence of tin."

The work on these pieces of armour is similar to the work of the Mycenaean period in which various metals and *niello* are inlaid

---

12. F. H. Stubbings in *A Companion to Homer*, ed. A. J. B. Wace and F. H. Stubbings (London 1962) pp. 509, 535.

13. For those who like to work out details, Walter Leaf *Homeri Ilias* (London 1895) suggests an arrangement of five bands of *kyanos* (k), six of gold (g), and ten of tin (t) on the front of the breastplate and the same on the back, giving the required number in this order: g t k t g t k t g t k t g t k t g t k t g.

on a metal background. According to Ventris and Chadwick, "*niello* is applied in powdered form into incised patterns cut in silver or gold, fused under heat, and then scraped and polished level with the metal surface."[14] They argue that, although the *niello* technique is suitable for Agamemnon's armour and Achilles' shield, it does not suit the description in the Pylos tablets, since there *kyanos* was apparently applied directly to wood, whereas *niello* is applied to metal. However we find that *kyanos* is always grouped with metals (gold and silver) in the tablets, and the *kyanos* may very well have been applied first to a metal base and then to the (wooden) furniture. In an inventory, such a detail might well be assumed.

So far, there is no obstacle to the identification of *kyanos* as *niello*. Let us look at the other two occurrences of *kyanos* in Homer. The table which Nestor has set before Patroclus (*Il.* 11.629) is κυανόπεζα which is usually translated "with feet of *kyanos*." Ventris and Chadwick agree that "with feet of blue paste" (as they interpret *kyanos*) "is admittedly improbable if taken quite literally."[15] Blue-glass paste is presumably too soft for such a purpose. Chadwick has suggested a possible alternative meaning for -πεζα "border," but evidence for this meaning is mostly late and infrequent.[16] On this interpretation, Nestor's table would have a border of *kyanos* instead of feet of *kyanos*, and it might seem slightly more likely that *kyanos* was inlaid on a table-top both because it would be more easily seen and because of the impracticality of doing inlaid work on feet. The choice of location for the ornamentation, however, has no bearing on the identification of *kyanos*. *Niello* might be used in either place as reasonably

14. Ventris and Chadwick p. 340.
15. *Ibid.* p. 340.
16. The discussion arises in connection with tablets PY 239-241, where tables are described as *e-ne-wo pe-za* or *we-pe-za*, tentatively translated "with nine feet" or "with six feet" (*e-ne-wo* corresponding to ἐννέα "nine " and *we-*(^{h}we^k) to ἕξ "six" in later Greek). Since tables do not normally have six or nine feet, Chadwick suggests alternatives, among them, "with a nine-fold border," taking πέζα in the rare sense "border" (cf. *Il.* 24.272 πέζηι ἔπι πρώτηι, Ap. Rh. 4.46 πέζαν χιτῶνος, 4.1258 πέζα ἠπείροιο). The only frequent compound in Homer in - πεζα is ἀργυρόπεζα an epithet of Thetis, usually translated "silver-footed" (see C. D. Buck and W. Petersen *A Reverse Index of Greek Nouns and Adjectives* [Oxford 1945] p. 745.) This epithet, together with the difficulty of substantiating this rare use of πέζα tends to support the meaning "*kyanos*-footed" or "dark-footed" for κυανόπεζα rather than "*kyanos*-bordered."

as blue-glass paste. There is an alternative to the translation "with feet of *kyanos*," and that is "with dark feet," taking κυανό- as appearance rather than material. This avoids the problem of imagining how *kyanos*, whatever it was, was used on table legs. In spite of our uncertainty over Nestor's table, we have found no obstacle in the *Iliad* to interpreting *kyanos* as *niello*. On the contrary, it makes much better sense to think of armour as decorated with black amalgam which is fused on to metal, than with the rather soft blue-glass paste.

The only mention of *kyanos* in the *Odyssey* occurs in the description of Alcinous' palace, where, we are told, there was a frieze of *kyanos* (*Od.* 7.87). Ventris and Chadwick draw attention to the frieze in the Great Megaron at Tiryns in which blue-glass paste was used, combined with alabaster.[17] It is tempting to take Alcinous' frieze as an "echo" of the frieze at Tiryns,[18] but the fact that an object in Homer is similar to an archaeological "find" does not mean that it is identical with it (cf. "the cup of Nestor"). The finding of a frieze in blue paste does not rule out the possibility that Alcinous' frieze was done in *niello*.

To sum up: *kyanos* inlaid on metal may be *niello*, since we know the Mycenaeans had this technique. Homer's description of *kyanos* as "dark" suits *niello*. On the other hand, we know the Mycenaeans also used blue-glass paste, and, in particular, its use in a frieze corresponds to Homer's description of Alcinous' frieze. The Pylos tablets enumerating tables inlaid with *kyanos* do not settle the identification either way. It is interesting to note the possibility of identifying *kyanos* as *niello*, but the important point is that for Homer, κυάνεος was "dark" whatever κύανος may be. We have called attention above to the phrase μέλανος κυάνοιο, and we can demonstrate that κυάνεος meant "dark" in other examples of Homer's usage.

II The Evidence Of Homer

At *Iliad* 24.93-94, the poet portrays Thetis, surrounded by the other sea-nymphs, mourning because Achilles must soon die, now

---

17. Ventris and Chadwick p. 340. For a description see Vermeule pp. 168-169.
18. As Wallace does p. 5.

that he has slain Hector. On hearing that Zeus has summoned her, she agrees to go.

ὡς ἄρα φωνήσασα κάλυμμ' ἕλε δῖα θεάων
κυάνεον, τοῦ δ' οὔ τι μελάντερον ἔπλετο ἔσθος

"Thus speaking, the fair goddess took a κυάνεον veil; there was no garment darker than it." Notice that the poet does not say "she had no garment darker than it" (using a dative of interest), as if poor Thetis had to "make do" with a (dark) blue veil, not having access to a black one. This would be ridiculous at such a point in the story, as it would detract from the pathos of the occasion. I cannot accept Wallace's suggestion that black dye was of poor quality in Homer's day, and cloth dyed black was really only dark blue.[19] If this were the case, why introduce μελάντερον? Such a comparison is incongruous and unnecessary. Surely Homer means that a κυάνεος veil is very dark.[20]

Κυάνεος is associated with μέλας again in the *Iliad* (4.275-282):

ὡς δ' ὅτ' ἀπὸ σκοπιῆς εἶδεν νέφος αἰπόλος ἀνήρ
ἐρχόμενον κατὰ πόντον ὑπὸ Ζεφύροιο ἰωῆς·
τῶι δέ τ' ἄνευθεν ἐόντι μελάντερον ἠύτε πίσσα
φαίνετ' ἰὸν κατὰ πόντον, ἄγει δέ τε λαίλαπα πολλήν,
ῥίγησέν τε ἰδών, ὑπό τε σπέος ἤλασε μῆλα·
τοῖαι ἅμ' Αἰάντεσσι διοτρεφέων αἰζηῶν
δήϊον ἐς πόλεμον πυκιναὶ κίνυντο φάλαγγες
κυάνεαι, σάκεσίν τε καὶ ἔγχεσι πεφρικυῖαι.

"But as when from a height a shepherd sees a cloud coming in from the sea driven by the roaring blast of Zephyrus, and to anyone at a distance it seems blacker than pitch as it comes from the sea, and it brings a great storm; seeing it he shudders and drives the sheep into a cave; so moved thick phalanxes of Zeus-reared, lusty men into ruinous war with the two Ajaxes — dark phalanxes, bristling with shields and spears." This description of the battle-line as κυάνεαι and the comparison of it to a cloud "blacker

19. *Ibid.* pp. 11-12.
20. Moreover, it would credit Homer with a high degree of sophistication to suppose that he is differentiating between κυάνεος the actual and μέλας the desired colour. See further the discussion on metrical position later in this chapter.

than pitch" has caused some difficulty, since in a number of passages in Homer metal armour gleams (*Il.* 2.455-458, 13.340-343, 19.359-361, 20.156). In later poetry armour is dark (cf. Pindar *Nem.* 10.84; Soph. *Trach.* 856, *Ant.* 231; Eur. *Bacch.* 628). We find no mention of Homeric warriors polishing their armour, so perhaps the gleaming surfaces were dulled and darkened by use (recall the evidence of a gleam in κυάνεος). Webster allows the description "like *kyanos*" to be apt as a point of comparison with the cloud "if the sun is behind them."[21] Kober supposes the explanation to be "darkness caused by density" and compares Pindar *Olympian* 6.40 λόχμας κυανέας (cf. p. 104).[22]

It seems to me that there are two similarities between a crowd of men and a cloud, either of which Homer may intend, and that there are two good reasons for stressing the darkness of the warriors. We find other examples of a "cloud of men": *Iliad* 16.66 κυάνεον Τρώων νέφος; Herodotus 9.109 νέφος τοσοῦτον ἀνθρώπων; Epistle to the Hebrews 12.1 τοσοῦτον νέφος μαρτύρων. In the last two cases, the stress is apparently on the size (τοσοῦτον). It may be that Homer, too, is depicting a crowd so large that one cannot distinguish the individuals, one in which faces blur with the general effect of cloud-like fuzziness. (Cf. English "a sea of faces.") The second possible similarity, between the battle-line and a cloud, seems less likely, although Homer mentions elsewhere the dust which rises as the army advances (*Il.* 3.13-14), and it is possible that dust swirling around the troops gave them a cloudy appearance.

More important, however, is the connection between the warriors and darkness. I think it is perfectly simple to explain the darkness as a contrast with their background, especially if one thinks of the poet observing from a distance (as the shepherd in the simile). This is the darkness of the caravan crossing the desert, the wagon-train travelling across the prairies. It is also possible that Homer describes the warriors as dark because, like the dark storm cloud, they bring destruction (4.278). This would be an emotional

21. T. B. L. Webster *From Mycenae to Homer* (2nd ed. London 1964) p. 219.
22. Kober *Color Terms in the Greek Poets* p. 74.

rather than descriptive use of κυάνεος and while I do not think that this is impossible or even unlikely, I suggest that the natural explanation is that the crowd of warriors appeared dark against the (dusty) plain.

Besides these two comparisons of men and dark clouds, clouds are κυάνεος several other times in Homer. The death of Polydorus is recounted (Il. 20.417-418): γνὺξ δ᾽ ἔριπ᾽ οἰμώξας, νεφέλη δέ μιν ἀμφεκάλυψε/ κυανέη "With a cry he fell on his knees and a dark cloud covered him." This is the cloud of death, elsewhere described as μέλας (e.g. in Il. 16.350).[23] Twice in the Iliad Phoebus Apollo protects someone with a dark cloud. In Iliad 5.344-345, he guards Aeneas from the weapons of the Greeks, presumably by making him invisible to them, as a cloud in itself offers no substantial protection.[24]

καὶ τὸν μὲν μετὰ χερσὶν ἐρύσατο Φοῖβος Ἀπόλλων
κυανέηι νεφέληι μή τις Δαναῶν ταχυπώλων
χαλκὸν ἐνὶ στήθεσσι βαλὼν ἐκ θυμὸν ἕλοιτο.

"And Phoebus Apollo protected him with his hands by means of a dark cloud so that none of the swift-horsed Greeks should cast a spear in his chest and take his life away." In Iliad 23.188-191, Apollo covers Hector's body with a cloud to protect it from the drying effects of exposure to the sun. In this case the darkness seems to refer to the shade given by the cloud.

τῶι δ᾽ ἐπὶ κυάνεον νέφος ἤγαγε Φοῖβος Ἀπόλλων
οὐρανόθεν πεδίονδε, κάλυψε δὲ χῶρον ἅπαντα
ὅσσον ἐπεῖχε νέκυς, μὴ πρὶν μένος ἠελίοιο
σκήλει᾽ ἀμφὶ περὶ χρόα ἴνεσιν ἠδὲ μέλεσσιν

"Phoebus Apollo brought a dark cloud for him from heaven to the plain and he covered all the place where the corpse lay so that the might of the sun might not dry up his flesh around his sinews and limbs."

In the Odyssey, the crag in which Scylla has her cave is cloud-topped (Od. 12.73-76):

---

23. Cf. Pindar's description of sleep as "dark-eyed" (Pyth. 1.7) κελαινῶπις νεφέλη. The epithet indicates that darkness comes on the eyes of the sleeper.
24. Cf. Odysseus hidden by "mist" in Od. 7.15. Presumably he was invisible, not a "walking cloud."

οἱ δὲ δύω σκόπελοι, ὁ μὲν οὐρανὸν εὐρὺν ἱκάνει
ὀξείηι κορυφῆι, νεφέλη δέ μιν ἀμφιβέβηκε
κυανέη· τὸ μὲν οὔ ποτ᾽ ἐρωεῖ, οὐδέ ποτ᾽ αἴθρη
κείνου ἔχει κορυφὴν οὔτ᾽ ἐν θέρει οὔτ᾽ εν ὀπώρηι.

"Of the two crags, one reaches high heaven with its sharp peak and a dark cloud covers it. Nor does the cloud ever leave it, nor is there ever clear air around its peak in summer or harvest-time." Scylla's crag is utterly unlike Olympus, where the air is always clear and cloudless (*Od.* 6.44-45; cf. p. 163). Zeus covers Odysseus' ship with a dark cloud, obviously mist, before a storm (*Od.* 12.405-406, 14.303-304):

δὴ τότε κυανέην νεφέλην ἔστησε Κρονίων
νηὸς ὕπερ γλαφυρῆς, ἤχλυσε δὲ πόντος ὑπ᾽ αὐτῆς.

"Then the son of Cronus set a dark cloud over the hollow ship and the sea grew misty beneath it."

It should be clear that when Homer uses κυάνεος for clouds, he is doing so as a synonym for μέλας and that there is no hint of "blue" in the darkness of clouds. This point becomes clearer when we analyse the position in the Homeric hexameter of κυάνεος and μέλας. It is interesting to observe that of eighteen occurrences of κυάνεος in the *Iliad* and *Odyssey*, it occupies the first foot nine times,[25] the second foot eight times,[26] and on the remaining occasion the last two feet (*Il.* 15.103 κυανέηισιν). This analysis suggests that its presence in the text was strongly influenced by metrical considerations.

This impression is reinforced by an examination of the Homeric formulae for expressing "a dark cloud covered him" with μέλας for "dark." We find two slightly different metrical patterns:

μέλαν νέφος ἀμφεκάλυψε   (*Il.* 16.350, *Od.* 4.180)
νεφέλη ἐκάλυψε μέλαινα   (*Il.* 17.591, 18.22)

Two of the occasions on which a cloud is described as κυάνεος follow these formulae in part; but μέλαν or μέλαινα is crowded out by the addition of other words, and is replaced by κυανέη which conveniently occupies the first foot of the next line:

25. In *Il.* 4.282, 5.345; 11.26, 39, 20.418, 22.402, 24.94; *Od.* 12.75, 16.176.
26. In *Il.* 1.528, 17.209, 16.66, 18.564, 23.188; *Od.* 12.243, 405; 14.303.

νεφέλη δέ μιν ἀμφεκάλυψε/ κυανέη   (Il. 20.417-418)
νεφέλη δέ μιν ἀμφιβέβηκε / κυανέη.   (Od. 12.74-75)

It is a strong argument for the synonymity of μέλας and κυάνεος that the one can substitute for the other in formulae.

Metrical analysis also sheds light on the two passages in which the comparative μελάντερον appears in close association with κυάνεος, since in each case a form of κυάνεος appears in the first foot and μελάντερον in the last syllable of the third and the fourth foot (Il. 24.94, and Il. 4.277, 282). This comparison makes it clearer that Homer regarded μέλας and κυάνεος as synonyms, and more examples appear as we proceed.

Poseidon is given the epithet κυανοχαίτης five times in the Iliad and three times in the Odyssey. Leaf and Bayfield reflect a general belief in their comment "Poseidon is 'blue-haired' because he is the god of the blue sea."[27] This sounds very plausible until one realizes that Homer uses many epithets for the sea, e.g. οἶνοψ "wine-like," γλαυκός, πολιός "grey," πορφύρεος "disturbed," ἠεροειδής "misty," ἰοειδής "violet," μέλας "dark,"[28] but not once does he employ κυάνεος. If Poseidon had had οἶνοψ hair, Leaf and Bayfield could have supported their theory with references to the οἴνοπα πόντον (Od. 2.421). But, in fact, the earliest poet we know who described the sea as κυάνεος is Simonides (fr. 567.3-5 PMG, see below). Moreover, we cannot overlook the fact that other immortals (not sea-deities) and even mortals possess κυάνεος hair. Zeus and Hera both have κυάνεος eyebrows (Il. 1.528, 17.209, 15.101-103). The description of Zeus as he nodded to Thetis is said to have inspired Pheidias for his great statue of Zeus at Olympia (Il. 1.528-530):[29]

ἦ καὶ κυανέηισιν ἐπ' ὀφρύσι νεῦσε Κρονίων·
ἀμβρόσιαι δ' ἄρα χαῖται ἐπερρώσαντο ἄνακτος
κρατὸς ἀπ' ἀθανάτοιο· μέγαν δ' ἐλέλιξεν Ὄλυμπον.

27. W. Leaf and M. A. Bayfield The Iliad of Homer (London 1895, 1898) on Il. 20. 144.

28. To give one reference for each epithet: οἶνοψ Il. 2.613; πορφύρεος Il. 16.391; γλαυκός Il. 16.34; πολιός Il. 4.248; ἠεροειδής Il. 23.744; ἰοειδής Od. 5.56; μέλας Il. 24.79.

29. Strabo 8.3.30 as quoted by J. A. Overbeck Die Antike Schriftquellen zur Geschichte der bildenden Künste bei den Griechen (Leipzig 1868) p. 128 n. 698.

"The son of Cronus spoke and nodded agreement with his dark brows, and down flowed the lord's ambrosial locks from his immortal head; and great Olympus shook." By κυανέῃσιν ὀφρύσι, Homer focuses attention on one detail of Zeus' face, his dark brows. The epithet indicates that his hair is dark, but more than that it may suggest a severity or solemnity of expression as the importance of the occasion demands. It may be worth noting that the two occasions on which Zeus' dark brows are mentioned are those when he nods in solemn agreement to a prayer. Hera is said to have κυάνεος brows once when she is displeased (Il. 15.100-103):

> ἡ μὲν ἄρ' ὣς εἰποῦσα καθέζετο πότνια Ἥρη,
> ὄχθησαν δ' ἀνὰ δῶμα Διὸς θεοί· ἡ δὲ γέλασσε
> χείλεσιν, οὐδὲ μέτωπον ἐπ' ὀφρύσι κυανέῃσιν
> ἰάνθη·

"Thus then spoke the lady Hera and sat down, and throughout the house of Zeus the gods were vexed. But she smiled with her lips and her forehead did not relax over her dark brows." Here, I submit, the darkness of her brows is mentioned to reinforce the picture of her annoyance. The fact that κυανέῃσιν occupies the last two feet of the line rather than the first or second foot, as we have shown it does elsewhere in Homer, suggests that this description of Hera is individual and that κυανέῃσιν is not simply a stock epithet but has a poetic purpose.

Among mortals Hector, the Trojan champion, had κυάνεος hair. When his corpse was dragged behind Achilles' chariot, "his dark hair spread out around and all his head, once comely, lay in the dust" (Il. 22.401-403):

> ἀμφὶ δὲ χαῖται
> κυάνεαι πίτναντο, κάρη δ' ἅπαν ἐν κονίῃσι
> κεῖτο πάρος χαρίεν·

Odysseus, restored again to his prime by Athene, undergoes certain physical changes, among them a darkening of the beard (Od. 16.176): κυάνεαι δ' ἐγένοντο γενειάδες ἀμφὶ γένειον. "His beard grew dark around his chin." Many commentators feel puzzled that Odysseus should have a κυάνεος beard, when we are told elsewhere that his hair was ξανθός "fair" (*Od.* 13.399).[30] I suggest that the adjective indicates a change from grey or white hair to its original colour: even a blond beard would be dark by contrast. Hence the phrase need not mean that the beard was dark rather than fair, only that it regained pigment from white to ξανθός. One might properly object that Homer was not too skilful in describing this transformation, as the passage is open to misinterpretation. Still if his audience knew perfectly well that Odysseus was ξανθός (and one supposes that such a detail was firmly established), this line would be understood in context.[31]

Because Homer can use κυάνεος of Hector's hair and Odysseus' beard, it seems certain that the colour was not unearthly, as for instance a blue suited to sea-deities. The suggestion that κυανοχαίτης is not naturalistic but hieratic or derived from representations in art is seen to be incorrect for the same reason.[32] But we have also to contend with the suggestion that κυάνεος represented "black hair with blue highlights" or "black hair with an absence of all red tones."[33] This supposition attempts to justify Homer's use of "blue" for hair, and, of course, it ignores the possibility that κυάνεος means simply "dark." In the case of Odysseus' rejuvenated beard, κυάνεος can hardly be "blue-black" if his hair was blond. Beards may indeed differ from hair in colour: a blond man may sport a red beard or a grey-haired man a black beard, but no one yet has grown a blue-black beard and fair hair. It is genetically impossible! One can counter that "even Homer nods," but surely a preferable explanation is to interpret κυάνεος as a dark tone and not the colour "blue." I suggest moreover, that the darkness of Zeus' and Hera's brows is

---

30. E.g. Cole "Adjectives of Light and Colour" vol. 1 pp. 85-86, p. 38 n. 88.

31. Hera is blonde in Bacch. 10.51 (Argive setting). On hair colour, cf. Cole vol. I, pp. 84-86; C. G. Brouzas in *Proceedings, West Virginia Academy of Science* 12 (1938) 153-160.

32. Κυανοχαίτης is used of Boreas, the north wind, when he takes the form of a horse in an amorous adventure with some mares (*Il.* 20.223-224). Cole suggests that Poseidon and not Boreas was originally involved and that the epithet was, so to speak, left behind when Poseidon was replaced (vol. 1 p. 24). It seems better to take it as "dark-maned" — a natural description for a horse (cf. *h. Herm.* 194 where a bull is κυάνεος). Since Hades is κυανοχαίτης in the *Hymn to Demeter* (347), we cannot insist that it belongs exclusively to Poseidon.

33. Wallace p. 20.

particularly suited to the context, and relates to their emotions as well as to their hair colour (on darkness and emotion, see pp. 135-155). Although Homer describes hair as κυάνεος, he never uses μέλας (elsewhere a synonym for κυάνεος) as a hair colour, and even the later poets use it infrequently and usually in contrast to the white (λευκός) hair of old age (see pp. 194-196). The compound μελαγχαίτης is also found (Hes. Sc. 186, Soph. Trach. 837, Eur. Alc. 439).

Ships in Homer are κυανόπρωιρος (three times in the Iliad, nine in the Odyssey) or κυανοπρώιρεως (Od. 3.299). Here κυανό- may indicate material "of kyanos" or colour "dark"; and -πρωιρος either "prow" or by metonymy "the whole ship."

For example, it has been suggested that the prows of the Homeric ships were sheathed in copper,[34] or painted with copper-blue wax paint,[35] or decorated in some way with kyanos. Wallace argues that κυανόπρωιρος is too specific to be a synonym for μέλας, the most common description of ships in Homer.[36] Then too other epithets for ships suggest a decoration of the prow. In Homer ships are μιλτοπάρηιος "vermilion-cheeked" (Il. 2.637, Od. 9.125) and φοινικοπάρηιος "crimson-cheeked" (Od. 11.124, 23.271); these adjectives suggest that the ship's sides are painted like cheeks, since redness is the colour of cheeks. However, "cheek" may be simply the side of the ship, rather than a naturalistic representation of features, or "cheek/side" may stand for the whole ship. There are more definite suggestions in the later poets of a decoration of the prow: Bacchylides (13.160) calls ships κυανῶπις "dark-eyed"; Aeschylus uses the same adjective (Pers.

---

34. Gladstone (Nineteenth Century II [1877] 378-379) suggested that κυάνεος in Homer was "(1) made of (2) in hue like to, bronze." His general point that κυάνεος was "dark" was quite correct. Wallace points out (p. 11) that ships "sheathed in bronze" or copper would acquire a greenish-blue patina from the dampness of the sea-air, a fact which Gladstone failed to take into account. She thinks it quite possible that Homer's ships were sheathed in bronze or copper and were "greenish-blue prowed."

35. Wallace p. 11.

36. Ships are μέλας over eighty times in Homer: Il. 1.14, 300, 329, 433, 485, 2.170, 358, 524, 534, 545, 556, 568, 630, 644, 652, 710, 737, 747, 759, 5.550, 700, 8.222, 528, 9.235, 654, 10.74, 11.5, 824, 828, 12.107, 126, 13.267, 15.387, 423, 16.304, 17.383, 639, 19.331, 24.780; Od. 2.430, 3.61, 360, 365, 423, 4.646, 731, 781, 6.268, 8.34, 51, 52, 445, 9.322, 10.95, 169, 244, 272, 332, 502, 571, 11.3, 58, 12.186, 264, 276, 418, 13.425, 14.308, 15.218, 258, 269, 416, 503, 16.325, 348, 359, 17.249, 18.84, 21.39, 307, 23.320, 24.152.

559, *Supp.* 743); Euripides introduces a variation κυανέμβολος (*Elect.* 436) "dark-beaked," and this epithet is picked up by Aristophanes (*Knights* 554, *Frogs* 1318). Sidgwick thought that Aeschylus was referring to eyes painted on the bows of ships (cf. *Supp.* 716 καὶ πρῷρα πρόσθεν ὄμμασιν βλέπουσ᾽ ὁδόν),[37] but Broadhead understands κυανώπιδες as an Aeschylean variation of the Homeric κυανόπρωρος.[38] Whatever the interpretation of Aeschylus, there is evidence that the Greeks decorated the prows of their ships, and Euripides' epithet κυανέμβολος suggests that the beak particularly was κυάνεος.

We cannot, however, ignore the fact that Homer described ships as "dark" (μέλας) and "dark-prowed" (κυανόπρωρος) without differentiation. Moreover, a metrical analysis of the occurrences of κυανόπρωιρος reveals an interesting fact: the epithet always occurs in the genitive singular and always at the end of the line. A certain flexibility is gained by a variation in the form of the genitive singular of ναῦς "ship" between νηὸς and νεὸς so that the first syllable can complete a spondee or a dactyl as required. Three times the line ending appears this way:

$$-|- \quad \cup\cup|- \quad -\,|\,-\cup$$
νηὸς κυανοπρῴροιο

(*Il.* 23.852, 878, *Od.* 14.311; and nine times this way:

$$\cup\,|- \quad \cup\cup|- \quad -\,| \quad -\cup$$
νεὸς κυανοπρῴροιο

(*Il.* 15.693, *Od.* 9.482, 539, 10.127, 11.6, 12.100, 148, 354, 22.465). Although this rhythm, with a spondee in the fifth foot, is unusual in the hexameter, Homer does not avoid it as studiously as Vergil. The epithet appears once in a slightly different form in the plural but still at the line's end (*Od.* 3.299): νέας κυανοπρῳρείους. On the other hand ναῦς μέλαινα can occupy several positions in the line.[39] Since Odysseus' ship is described as

37. A. Sidgwick *Aeschylus Persae* (Oxford 1903) on 559.
38. H. D. Broadhead *The Persae of Aeschylus* (Cambridge 1960) on 558-563; he gives as an argument against Sidgwick the fact that "eyes were usually painted in bright colours to contrast with the dark colour in which they were set."
39. E.g. second and third feet, *Il.* 1.141; fifth and sixth, *Il.* 1.300; part of the third, fourth, and fifth *Il.* 2.524.

μέλας (Od. 2.430) and κυανόπρωιρος, it is reasonable to assume that the two epithets are synonymous, that κυανό- should be translated "dark" rather than "of kyanos" and that -πρωιρος stands by metonymy for "ship."

In Od. 12.243, Odysseus and his crew are passing between Scylla and Charybdis and see the ocean floor laid bare by the whirlpool:

ἀλλ ὅτ᾽ ἀναβρόξειε θαλάσσης ἁλμυρὸν ὕδωρ
πᾶσ᾽ ἔντοσθε φάνεσκε κυκωμένη, ἀμφὶ δὲ πέτρη
δεινὸν βεβρύχει, ὑπένερθε δὲ γαῖα φάνεσκε
ψάμμωι κυανέη·

"But when Charybdis sucked down the salt water of the sea again, all within appeared stirred up, and the rock around rang terribly and beneath the dark earth appeared with sand." Cole quotes with approval the note of the Scholiast: "the κυανέη earth, as elsewhere the μέλαινα earth. Therefore the adjective is not particular but belonging to all earth."[40] His opinion, then, is that κυανέη here is a poetic variant for μέλαινα. Stanford, on the other hand, translates "dark-blue with sand": "the poet imagines that in such depths the sand will be tinted by the pervading submarine blue."[41] We saw earlier, however, that Homer never described the sea as κυάνεος, and we cited instances of κυάνεος used as a synonym of μέλας. It is best to follow the Scholiast here. A metrical analysis of the position of κυάνεος and the formula γαῖα μέλαινα will confirm us in our decision. We remarked above that, with one exception, κυάνεος occupies the first or second foot of the line, here the second. In five of its seven occurrences, γαῖα μέλαινα occupies the fifth and sixth feet (Il. 2.699, 15.715, 17.416, 20.494; Od. 19.111); once the first and second feet (Od. 11.587); and once the second and third (Od. 11.365). Its rhythm −∪∪|−∪ makes γαῖα μέλαινα a unit as γαῖα κυανέη could not be. One of these passages is of particular interest because its meaning is approximately the same although the vocabulary differs slightly. Odysseus sees Tantalus in the underworld, standing in a pool up to his chin, but unable to take a drink, "for as often as the old man stooped,

40. Cole vol. 1 p. 23.
41. W. B. Stanford Homer's Odyssey on Od. 12.243.

desiring to drink, the water vanished being sucked down, and around his feet dark earth appeared and a god dried it up" (*Od.* 11.585-587):

ὁσσάκι γὰρ κύψει᾽ ὁ γέρων πιέειν μενεαίνων,
τοσσάχ᾽ ὕδωρ ἀπολέσκετ᾽ ἀναβροχέν, ἀμφὶ δὲ ποσσὶ
γαῖα μέλαινα φάνεσκε, καταξήνασκε δὲ δαίμων.

The passage seems to describe a situation similar to Charybdis' whirlpool, since in both cases the water was sucked down (ἀναβρόχω) and the earth beneath was laid bare. The fact that in the one case the earth is κυανέη and in the other μέλαινα suggests that the two are synonymous. (For another instance of κυάνεος as an epithet of earth, see Pind. fr. 33b.6, below).

In *Od.* 12.60, Amphitrite, wife of Poseidon, is described as κυανῶπις:

προτὶ δ᾽ αὐτὰς
κῦμα μέγα ῥοχθεῖ κυανώπιδος Ἀμφιτρίτης.

"Against them [the Clashing Rocks] a great wave of dark-eyed Amphitrite dashes." It has been argued that Amphitrite is here a personification for "ocean" and therefore, the epithet κυανῶπις is particularly appropriate as reflecting the colour of the sea. Recalling that Homer nowhere uses κυάνεος for the sea, we can appreciate that the special appropriateness of the adjective is imagined here. Since this epithet κυανῶπις is popular with later poets, where it often describes beings other than sea-deities or nymphs, we conclude that it had no special appropriateness to the sea (see below). It is interesting to note that the epithet ἑλίκωψ, ἑλικῶπις occurs in the *Iliad* but not in the *Odyssey*, whereas the reverse is true of κυανῶπις. Page argues for the meaning "dark-eyed" for ἑλίκωψ.[42] If he is right, these epithets are synonyms, with the more archaic ἑλίκωψ being replaced except in a few passages modelled on epic.

In Homer, then, we find no support for translating κυάνεος

42. D. L. Page *History and the Homeric Iliad* pp. 244-245. His arguments are convincing, although much of the evidence for the meaning "black" comes from the Alexandrian period, far removed from Homer in time. He argues very successfully against the possibility of deriving ἑλίκωψ from ἕλιξ "helix, spiral" on the grounds of logic, for since a helix is not just "curved," but "curly," ἑλίκωψ ought to mean "curly-eyed."

"blue" or even "dark blue," but much for translating "dark."
Kyanos is dark (μέλας) and objects which are κυάνεος are also
μέλας in the same passage. We saw that the same objects are on
different occasions described as κυάνεος and μέλας: clouds, ships,
the earth. We suggested that this variation between κυάνεος and
μέλας is influenced not by meaning but by metrical considera-
tions. Hair and eyes are κυάνεος, never μέλας, in Homer. Since
mortals and immortals alike have κυάνεος hair and it is not the
property of sea deities alone, we argued that there was no
connection between Poseidon's title κυανοχαίτης and the sea. The
same was true of the description of Amphitrite as κυανῶπις. Not
until Simonides is the sea described as κυάνεος. We conclude, then,
that for Homer κυάνεος was a synonym for μέλας and meant
"dark."

III The Evidence of Other Epic Writers

A. Homeric Hymns

In the *Homeric Hymns*, κυάνεος apparently retains its early
meaning "dark." In the *Hymn to Demeter* reference is made six
times to Demeter's κυάνεος clothing (42, 182-183, 319, 360, 374,
442). This wearing of dark clothing is surely related to her
mourning as she searches for her daughter, just as in *Il.* 24.93-94,
Thetis took a κυάνεος veil because of her grief for her son's
approaching death. The objection might be raised that Demeter is
wearing a κυάνεος robe before she hears of Persephone's disappear-
ance (in line 42) and therefore did not choose it as the garb of
mourning. As this *Hymn* is full of details connected with the cult
at Eleusis, let us assume that the dark clothing of Demeter may
have been one of these details, i.e. Demeter was the "sorrowing
mother." Κυανόπεπλος occurs elsewhere only in Hesiod (*Theog.*
406).

The epithet κυανοχαίτης is applied to Poseidon (*Hymn* 22.6),
and to Hades, who is god of the underworld and appropriately
"dark-haired" (*h. Dem.* 347). Dionysus has κυάνεος hair and eyes
(*Hymn* 7.5,15). The fact that Hades and Dionysus who have no
marine associations have κυάνεος hair supports our conclusion that
the epithet signifies dark, not blue.

The *Hymn to Apollo* (405-406) throws interesting light on the epithet of ships κυανόπρωιρος since the same ship is κυανό-πρωιρος and μέλας:

> οὐδ' οἵ γ' ὅπλ' ἔλυον κοίλην ἀνὰ νῆα μέλαιναν
> οὐδ' ἔλυον λαῖφος νηὸς κυανοπρώιροιο.

"Nor did they loose the sheets through the black, hollow ship, nor lower the sail of their dark-prowed vessel."

B. Hesiod and Hesiodica

The shield of Heracles, like Achilles' shield in *Iliad* 18, was decorated with scenes wrought in metals and *kyanos* (Hes. *Sc.* 139-143). Of interest to us are the lines which describe snakes, for these are κυάνεοι just like the snakes on Agamemnon's breastplate (*Il.* 11.26). "It was as though there were spots on the dreadful snakes; their backs were dark and their jaws black" (166-167):

> στίγματα δ' ὡς ἐπέφαντο ἰδεῖν δεινοῖσι δράκουσι·
> κυάνεοι κατὰ νῶτα, μελάνθησαν δὲ γένεια.

We must allow that a contrast may be intended here between κυάνεοι and μελαίνω.

Several Hesiodic heroines are "dark-eyed" κυανῶπις: Themis-tonoe (*Sc.* 356), Helen (fr. 196.8), Electra, one of the Pleiades, (fr. 169.1), Clytemnestra (fr. 23(a) 14, *27) and Althea (fr. 25.14). Alcmene also has dark eyes: βλεφάρων κυανεάων (*Sc.* 7). Some translators take κυανῶπις as "blue-eyed" on the assumption that κυάνεος is "blue." Later in this chapter we shall see that just as we classify eye-colour generally as "blue" and "brown" (although within these two classes there are more exact descriptions, e.g. "hazel," "grey," "green"), the Greeks generally classified eye-colour as "dark" (in prose μέλας, in poetry κυάνεος) and "light" γλαυκός. In terms of value, κυάνεος was dark and γλαυκός light. We conclude, therefore, that κυάνεος described dark eyes (our "brown") and γλαυκός light eyes (our "blue").

Leto is "dark-robed" κυανόπεπλος (*Theog.* 406), but not in reference to mourning, as we argued was present in the case of Thetis (*Il.* 24.93-94) and Demeter (*h. Dem. passim*). In the *Theogony* we read that Phoebe "bore Leto of the dark robe who is always gentle and kind to mortals and the immortal gods":

Λητὼ κυανόπεπλον ἐγείνατο μείλιχον αἰεί
ἤπιον ἀνθρώποισι καὶ ἀθανάτοισι θεοῖσιν.

The description "dark-robed" is strange in the context of her birth unless there is some cult significance. It has been suggested that the name Leto is related to λήθη "forgetfulness" and Latin *lateo* "hide," and signifies "the obscure," "the concealed."[43] From this darkness issued the divinity in all his splendour and brilliancy – Apollo. If Leto is "the obscure," we can understand why she is "dark-robed," as the Greeks connected obscurity with darkness (cf. Bacch. 3.13-14, Pind. fr. 94a.2-10, cf. chapter five).

The grasshopper, perched on a green (χλοερῶι) branch is "dark-winged" κυανόπτερος (*Sc.* 393 see above, p. 43). We argued in our discussion of χλωρός that χλοερῶι referred to the leafiness of the branch, i.e. its greenness, because of the stress on the heat of the season in this context. The epithet "dark-winged" seems to be the poet's attempt to contrast the insect with his background.

Hesiod uses κυάνεος of dark-skinned people (*W.D.* 527-528):

ἀλλ᾽ ἐπὶ κυανέων ἀνδρῶν δῆμόν τε πόλιν τε
στρωφᾶται, βράδιον δὲ Πανελλήνεσσι φαείνει.

"But [the sun in winter] goes to and fro over the land and city of the dark men, and shines more sluggishly on the Pan-Hellenes." By κυανέων ἀνδρῶν he means apparently the inhabitants of Africa, likely the Ethiopians, since from the Greek view, the winter sun travelled low in the Greek sky and provided less warmth and light than it did in summer (βράδιον φαείνει), but it was still overhead for the Africans. Xenophanes implies that the Ethiopians were dark when he says that they picture their gods as "snub-nosed and dark" (fr. 14D.):

Αἰθίοπές τε (θεοὺς σφετέρους) σιμοὺς μέλανάς τε.

Waern argues that κυάνεοι ἄνδρες is a kenning, using "blue men" in a way similar to our "red men" for North American Indians,[44]

---

43. *Harper's Dictionary of Classical Literature and Antiquities* ed. H. T. Peck (New York 1965) s.v. Leto p. 938.
44. I. Waern Γῆς Ὀστέα: *The Kenning in Pre-Christian Greek Poetry* (Uppsala 1951) pp. 39, 46, 111, 118.

but her argument depends on the establishment of κυάνεος as "blue" at this date and this she has failed to do (see further discussion below).

An examination of κυάνεος in the *Homeric Hymns* shows nothing without precedent in Homer; we conclude, then, that the meaning of κυάνεος remains "dark." In Hesiod and the *Hesiodica* we find new uses introduced: men, probably Ethiopians, are κυάνεοι, a reference to their dark skin (*W.D.* 527); the Furies are κυάνεαι (*Sc.* 249) and since they are chthonic, it is appropriate that they should be dark (see chapter five); the grasshopper is dark-winged (*Sc.* 393) in contrast to his leafy background. In none of these examples is there any evidence of a trend towards "blueness" in κυάνεος. The only hint of change is the contrast implied between κυάνεος and μελαίνω in the description of Heracles' breastplate.

IV The Evidence of The Lyric Poets

Many of the examples of κυάνεος in the lyric poets follow the epic usage, but an indication of blue appears in Simonides and Bacchylides. Anacreon follows Homer (*Od.* 12.60) and Hesiod (*Sc.* 356, and elsewhere) when he calls the Nymphs "dark-eyed" (fr. 357. 2-3 *PMG*): Νύμφαι κυανώπιδες / πορφυρῆ τ᾽ Ἀφροδίτη. "The dark-eyed Nymphs and blushing Aphrodite." He speaks of the men of Ialysos in Rhodes "with shields of *kyanos*" κυανάσπιδας (fr. 349 *PMG*): Bowra thinks that Anacreon is referring to a material rather than a colour; he comments that κυάνασπις is "too rare to be a stock epithet," and suggests that "Anacreon knew something about the Rhodian art of decorating metal with blue enamel, of which some evidences have survived."[45] The words which interest us here are "blue enamel": "enamel" because it would resemble the Mycenaean *niello* technique, and "blue" because this would give us an indication that for Anacreon *kyanos* was definitely blue. Unfortunately, Bowra neglected to give references for the surviving evidences, and the author has been unable to find any information about blue Rhodian enamel.[46]

45. C. M. Bowra *CJ* 29 (1934) 377.
46. When this passage was discussed with Prof. F. E. Winter of the Department of

Ibycus sings of the power of Love even in old age (fr. 287.1-4 PMG):

Ἔρος αὖτέ με κυανέοισιν ὑπό
βλεφάροις τακέρ᾽ ὄμμασι δερκόμενος
κηλήμασι παντοδαποῖς ἐς ἄπει-
ρα δίκτυα Κύπριδος ἐσβάλλει.

(With this fragment, cf. Eur. *Alc.* 261, discussed below and n. 69). "Love again looks at me meltingly with dark eyes beneath his lids and draws me with all kinds of wiles into the nets without outlet of the Cyprian." In this translation κυανέοισιν is taken with ὄμμασι but it would be possible grammatically to take it with βλεφάροις and, in fact, there are at least two instances in which this is done. In one case βλέφαρον is translated "eyebrow"[47] and in the other "eyelash,"[48] with κυάνεος indicating dark hair colour. *LSJ* give no examples of βλέφαρον in either of these meanings; according to them it can only mean "eyelid" or "eye." Since "eye" ὄμμασι appears in the same line, one would expect βλέφαρον to be "eyelid." Common sense suggests that eyes rather than eyelids are dark, and so we construe κυανέοισι with ὄμμασι "dark eyes." The ambiguity of two nouns in the dative plural and an adjective agreeing grammatically with either one is awkward. Page's *apparatus criticus* to this fragment shows how this difficulty might be avoided. He questions whether βλεφάρων might not be read for βλεφάροις, comparing *Il.* 19.17 ὄσσε ὑπὸ βλεφάρων.[49] What picture is Ibycus presenting by "Love looks meltingly at me with dark eyes beneath his lids"? This is not the coquette who looks "beneath dark lashes," nor the severe lad who gazes "beneath dark brows." Could it be an early Greek parallel to the sultry, heavy-lidded look which Hollywood considers attractive?[50]

Κυάνεος, then, describes eyes elsewhere in poetry, but in

Fine Art, University of Toronto, he was unable to recall having seen any information about "Rhodian blue enamel."

47. J. M. Edmonds *Lyra Graeca* (London 1931) vol. 2 p. 87.

48. H. Fränkel *Dichtung und Philosophie des frühen Griechentums* (Munich 1962) p. 323: "unter blauschwartzen Wimpern." He says that "dark-blue" hair is given to Love as a symbol of his power.

49. D. L. Page *PMG* fr. 287.

50. Cf. the half-shut eyes of an actress such as Marilyn Monroe.

prose, it is replaced by μέλας. We saw (chapter one, n. 38) that Empedocles thought that people with γλαυκός eye-colour see badly by day whereas people with μέλας eye-colour see badly by night (Arist. De Gen. An. 779b15ff); the range of eye-colour is given in the same Aristotelian work (779a34ff) as γλαυκοί, χαροποί, (both apparently in the blue-grey group) and μελανόφθαλμοί. It is worth remarking, however, that μέλας occurs as a description of eyes only twice in Greek poetry, once in Bacchylides (17.17-18) where it seems to have a definite emotional tone (cf. pp. 155) and once in the Anacreontea (16.12). The rarity of μέλας as a poetic epithet for eyes contrasted with the frequency of κυάνεος and the opposite situation in prose suggests strongly that κυάνεος is the poetic and μέλας the prose term for "dark" as applied to eyes.

If κυάνεος is the poetic equivalent of μέλας, Ibycus' "dark-eyed" Love may refer to a black-eyed lad who inspired emotion in the poet. We find the word used in a different and grimmer sense by Aeschylus of the glare of the serpent (Pers. 81-82):

κυάνεον δ᾽ ὄμμασι λεύσσων
φονίου δέργμα δράκοντος

"Gazing with the dark glare of the murderous serpent." Here, I think, κυάνεον indicates not the colour but the quality of the gaze; the serpent's basilisk glare was noted frequently by ancient writers (Pindar Olymp. 6. 45-46, Pyth. 4.249, cf. also Olymp. 8.37; Eur. Ion 1262-1263, Orest. 479-480; and Homer Il. 22.93-95). Most of these refer to the brightness of the glare, but Aeschylus stresses the gloom and death threatened by the serpent and by Xerxes who is likened to the serpent. In chapter five we will encounter Aeschylus' use of "dark" as "sad, gloomy," or "fatal."

Of the four occasions when Simonides uses κυάνεος, one is as the stock epithet of ships κυανοπρῴρα (fr. 625 PMG) preserved in the Etymologicum Magnum because it differs from the Homeric form κυανόπρωρα; the others describe darkness, sea-water and a swallow which Simonides addresses as κυανέα χελιδοῖ (fr. 597 PMG); D'Arcy Thompson does not include a description of the swallow in his article Χελιδών,[51] but other authorities inform us

51. D'Arcy Thompson A Glossary of Greek Birds (London 1936) pp. 314-325, esp.

that the colour varies according to species from brown to dark blue and many are characterized by a metallic lustre. According to Thompson none of the later poets repeats the epithet κυάνεος in describing the swallow.[52] In the *Rhodian Swallow-Song*, for instance, the bird is "white on the belly and black [μέλαινα] on the back" (fr. 848.4-5 *PMG*). The Aristotelian treatise on animals describes as κυάνεος the halcyon (*H.A.* 616a15), the porpoise (566b12), and an unidentified small bird (617a23).[53] It is worth noting that the halcyon, our kingfisher, has a metallic lustre on his feathers like the swallow (cf. n. 2), and that the skin of the porpoise would gleam as he emerged from the water. In the light of the colour theorists' inclusion of "brightness" in the composition of κυάνεος it is possible that Simonides was depicting the dark, lustrous plumage of the swallow when he called it κυανέα χελιδοῖ.

Simonides puts into the mouth of Danae a lament in the form of a lullaby for herself and her babe, Perseus, cast adrift in a chest (fr. 543.8-12 *PMG*):

> σὺ δ᾽ ἀωτεῖς, γαλαθηνῶι
> δ᾽ ἤθεϊ κνοώσσεις
> ἐν ἀτερπέι δούρατι χαλκεογόμφωι
> τῶι δε νυκτιλαμπεῖ,
> κυανέωι δνόφωι ταθείς.

"But you sleep and slumber in your baby way in this joyless, brassbound vessel that gleams in the night, stretched out in the dark gloom." If νυκτιλαμπεῖ is right,[54] and the chest gleams in the night, κυανέωι must surely describe the contrasting darkness around them. Does it indicate any blueness in the darkness of night and the night sky? Compare for example, later occurrences: νὺξ κυαναυγής (*Orph. Hymn* 3.3) and Timotheus (fr. 803.1-2

---

p. 315; for the swallow, see above n. 2.

52. *Ibid.* p. 315.

53. *Ibid.* p. 178: Thompson suggests that it may be the Syrian nuthatch *Sitta syriaca*, but he is not happy about the identification.

54. For a discussion of the text and the establishment of the reading given here, see D. L. Page in *JHS* 71 (1951) 137-138. H. W. Smyth (*Greek Melic Poets* [London 1900] p. 323) has a slightly different reading: νυκτιλαμπεῖ κυανέωι τε δνόφωι, which he interprets as "the dark gloom in which only night shines," i.e. as an oxymoron. Cf. Milton's "darkness visible."

PMG): διὰ κυάνεον πόλον ἄστρων.[55] It is possible that Simonides chose κυάνεος to represent the dark blue of the night sky, but more likely that he simply meant "dark."

V The Element of Blue

Simonides was the first, so far as we know, to describe the sea as κυάνεος (fr. 567. 3-5 *PMG*):

> ἀνὰ δ' ἰχθύες ὀρθοί
> κυανέου 'ξ ὕδατος ἄλ-
> λοντο καλᾶι σὺν ἀοιδᾶι.

"Fish leaped straight up from the dark (blue) sea at the beautiful song." He is followed in this by later poets, among them his nephew Bacchylides and Euripides. As the adjective continues to be considered suitable for the sea, Simonides may well have associated it with blueness, although he obviously felt a strong element of darkness.[56] Pindar, on the other hand, keeps entirely to the more basic meaning "dark," although some commentators have argued for a blue content. In *Paean* 6, he speaks of Achilles as the "mighty son of dark-haired Thetis of the sea" (83-84):

> κυανοπλόκοιο παῖδα ποντίας
> Θέτιος βιατάν.

Because he specifies "of the sea," it might be argued that he intended Thetis' hair colour to reflect the colour of the sea. However, we established earlier that for Homer κυάνεος was not an epithet of the sea, and that it described the hair of immortals who were not sea-gods and even of mortals, and was therefore not especially appropriate to sea-deities. Although Pindar may have known of Simonides' description of the sea as κυάνεος, he himself did not use it this way. I assume, therefore, that κυανόπλοκος means "dark-haired." Similarly in fr. 29.3, the nymph Thebes is described as κυανάμπυξ "with a dark headband," a phrase in which no indication of blueness need be inferred. In *Olympian.* 13.70, Pallas Athene is κυάναιγις, which the Scholiast explains as the

---

55. Note that for κυάνεον (Plutarch's reading), Macrobius (*Sat.* 7.16. 28) reads λαμπρόν.

56. Cf. Hesychius s.v. κύανος for "sea-water."

equivalent of "having a dark and terrible aegis": ἀντὶ τοῦ μέλαιναν καὶ φοβερὰν αἰγίδα ἔχουσα. His interpretation is supported by the general context which favours "dark" rather than a specific hue. In *Olympian* 6.39-41, we find an unusual concentration of "colour" words:

> ἁ δὲ φοινικόκροκον ζώναν καταθηκαμένα
> κάλπιδά τ' ἀργυρέαν λόχμας ὑπὸ κυανέας
> τίκτε θεόφρονα κοῦρον.

"She laid aside her girdle with crimson woof and her silver pitcher and she bore a boy with a god-like mind beneath a dark thicket." The suggestion has been made that Pindar is describing by κυανέας the blueness of daylight shadows, and a comparison is made with artists who mix blue pigment with dark when they paint shadows.[57] This seems an overly subtle interpretation in view of the long history of κυάνεος as simply "dark." Kober sees density implied both here and in *Iliad* 4.282 and 16.66, arguing that "a *dense* crowd of human beings seems *dark* at a distance."[58] But the Pindaric epithet is more simply taken as descriptive of the darkness of the shade, synonymous with μέλας but perhaps slightly more poetic.

Finally we have a fascinating apostophe to Delos (fr. 33b3-6):

> πόντου θύγατερ, χθονὸς εὐρείας ἀκί-
> νητον τέρας, ἄν τε βροτοί
> Δᾶλον κικλήσκοισιν, μάκαρες δ' ἐν Ὀλύμπωι
> τηλέφαντον κυανέας χθονὸς ἄστρον.

"Daughter of the sea, unmoved marvel of the broad earth, whom mortals call Delos, but the blessed ones on Olympus the far-seen star of the dark earth." Wilamowitz argued that Pindar meant that the earth appeared to the gods as the sky appears to us. "Wie grossartig ist die Vorstellung, dass die Erde für den Blick der Götter eine blaue Fläche ist, wie ihr Himmel für uns, auf dem ihnen dann Delos, so klein sie ist, als ein heller Stern lieblich aufleuchtet."[59] It is essential to this interpretation that κυάνεος be

57. Wallace p. 27: "subjective, poetical use of color comparable with the use of blue shadows in modern painting."
58. Kober p. 74.
59. U. von Wilamowitz-Moellendorff *Sappho und Simonides: Untersuchungen über*

"blue" in order to establish a comparison between our sky (which is blue) and the earth which the gods regard as their sky. We have seen in this study that κυάνεος meant "dark" for Homer and the early poets and that even for Pindar the element of "blueness" was doubtful. Moreover, although Simonides described the darkness of night as κυάνεος and two later poets called night or the night sky κυάνεος (fr. 803.1-2 PMG, Orph. Hymn. 3.3), there is certainly no long tradition linking the sky with this epithet, as one would expect as background for Wilamowitz' reversal. Moreover such a reversal of sky and earth, us and the gods is too sophisticated a concept for this period. It gives the impression of being a fourth-century idea, akin to Plato's famous epigram (fr. 4D):

$$\text{ἀστέρας εἰσαθρεῖς ἀστὴρ ἐμός · εἴθε γενοίμην}$$
$$\text{οὐρανὸς ὡς πολλοῖς ὄμμασιν εἰς σὲ βλέπω.}$$

"You gaze at stars, my star. Would that I were the heaven, so that I might look on you with my many eyes." Aristides, a rhetorician of the second century after Christ, compares stars in heaven to islands in the sea; Snell argues that "he probably had in mind the invocation of Delos in (Pindar's) Hymn to Zeus,"[60] but I would suggest that Aristides has developed the idea far beyond Pindar's intention, although Pindar may have been his inspiration.

Waern, however, explains the phrase κυανέας χθονὸς ἄστρον as a kenning.[61] Her working definition of a kenning is "an expression consisting of two or more words for a person or thing which could be rendered by a single word, but which for reasons of effect, metrics, and so on, is described periphrastically."[62] Some simple

---

griechische Lyriker (Berlin 1913) p. 131.

60. B. Snell The Discovery of the Mind (Oxford 1953) p. 81 accepts the reversal suggested by Wilamowitz. He quotes Aristides (fr. 145.13): κοσμήσας μὲν ἄστροις τὸν πάντα οὐρανὸν ὥσπερ ταῖς νήσοις τὴν θάλατταν. Similarly, Oratio 44.14, p. 350 Keil (Berlin 1898): ὥσπερ δὲ οὐρανὸς τοῖς ἄστροις κεκόσμηται, οὕτω καὶ τὸν Αἰγαῖον πέλαγος ταῖς νήσοις κεκόσμηται.

Snell also says "it is of course quite true that under the southern sky the earth gleams brightly while the sea reposes in livid darkness." This is quite mistaken from the Greek point of view. The Greeks always thought of the earth as "dark" (γαῖα μέλαινα), whereas the epithets given to the sea suggest a constantly changing surface, whatever their exact meanings may be. Certainly "wine-like" hardly suggests "livid darkness." It is possible that the Greeks saw a contrast between the dark, inert earth and the lighter, active sea.

61. Waern pp. 84-85.
62. Ibid. p. 7.

kennings are: "day-sleeper" for thief, since he works at night and rests during the day, "house-carrier" for snail, a creature who carries his house with him, "to put on a stone shirt" meaning "to be stoned." Aristotle called such a figure a "metaphor based on proportion" (*Poet.* 1457b9, *Rhet.* 1411a2, 1412b35). He explained that the cup is to Dionysus as the shield is to Ares, therefore the shield is the cup of Ares, or the wineless cup. The apparent contradiction in the second example "the wineless cup" is a characteristic of the kenning.

Waern argues that the description of Delos as "the star of the blue earth" is a series-kenning.[63] Taking χθών as mainland as opposed to sea and κυάνεος as blue, she concludes that κυανέα χθών "blue land" is an impossibility, as land is not blue, and that it must be a kenning for "sea."[64] Delos is a star set in the sea (probably a reference to one of its earlier names "Asteria;" see *Paean* 5.41-42). Since Delos lies, in fact, in the middle of the Aegean, Waern's explanation is quite tempting. However, we have shown that Pindar (like the earlier poets, with the possible exception of Simonides) uses κυάνεος to mean "dark," not "blue." Moreover, κυάνεος is not a regular epithet for the sea, being so used for the first time by Simonides (fr. 567.3-5). Half Waern's argument collapses if κυάνεος is not definitely blue, since she must establish that it is an impossible epithet for the mainland. Then, it is by no means certain that χθών is mainland in Pindar. Radt has examined the uses of χθονὸς and γῆς with ὀμφαλός and concluded that both refer to the whole earth, the totality of land and sea.[65] When in the earlier lines of this same fragment (fr. 33b3-4), Pindar addressed Delos as "daughter of the sea, unmoved marvel of the broad earth [χθονός]," he is clearly referring to the whole earth, not the mainland. (To say "unmoved marvel of the mainland" would be ridiculous!)

It would seem, then, that the meanings Waern requires for her interpretation of this phrase are not supported by the evidence. Recalling that κυάνεος is often a poetic equivalent for μέλας, and

---

63. *Ibid.* pp. 54-55.
64. *Ibid.* p. 85.
65. S. L. Radt *Pindars zweiter und sechster Paian* (Amsterdam 1958) pp. 118-120; cf. also G. J. de Vries *REG* 69 (1956) 445.

that χθών, like γῆ, may refer to the whole earth, it seems best to take the phrase κυανέα χθών as a lyric elaboration of the epic formula γαῖα μέλαινα. This explanation was put forward by Harvey in a discussion of the way lyric poets varied Homeric epithets,[66] and it seems the simplest and most natural interpretation of the Greek. Finally, the Scholiast's comment on *Od.* 12.243, given above, that the adjective κυανέη, like μέλαινα, when describing earth, "is not particular but belonging to all earth" strengthens the case for concluding that for Pindar κυάνεος is "dark."

Bacchylides' uses of κυάνεος are unremarkable for the most part. He describes a ship as "dark-prowed" κυανόπρωιρα (17.1) and "dark-eyed" κυανῶπις (13.160); the cloud of death as κυάνεος (13.64, cf. *Il.* 20.417-418); several women as "dark-haired" κυανοπλόκαμος (Victory 5.33; Thebes 9.53; the daughters of Proetus 11.83); and possibly Night as κυανάμπυξ (25.15).[67] It might be argued that this epithet for Night shows evidence of blueness in κυάνεος as a reflection of the blueness of the night sky (recall Pindar's epithet for Thetis "of the sea" κυανόπλοκος *Paean* 6.83-84). But since the earlier meaning "dark" is just as appropriate for night, we cannot take this as certain evidence. The most interesting of Bacchylides' uses is the modification he has made of Simonides' phrase (fr. 567.3-5 *PMG*). Whereas the uncle was describing a pleasant scene — in which the phrase κυανέου 'ξ ὕδατος could reasonably be translated "out of the blue (sea-) water," the nephew is apparently describing a storm (13.124-125):

ἐν κυανανθέϊ Θ[ρακὶ / πόντωι·

Jebb takes κυανανθής (which occurs only here) as "of dark hue," comparing it with μελανθής: "for -ανθής in this compound could not refer to the white crests of the waves."[68] The sea is buffeted by the north wind (Βορέας ὑπὸ κύμασιν δαΐζει) and the picture suggested is that of the dark surface of the sea roughened

---

66. Harvey CQ N.S 7 (1957) 216ff.

67. Snell deciphers from the papyrus this reading: κ] υανάμπυκα νυ[on which he comments "Νυ [κτα pot. qu. νυ [μφαν nam inferior pars litt. φ appareret." While the reading Νύκτα seems likely, it is not certain.

68. R. C. Jebb *Bacchylides The Poems and Fragments* (Cambridge 1905), on 12.124.

by winds. Just such a roughening of the sea, a "cats-paw," is described by Homer as dark (μέλας *Il.* 7.63-64, 21.126-127, *Od.* 4.402, see chapter five) and one would suppose that Bacchylides, too, has in mind the darkness of the sea in κυανανθής. The other possibility, which seems to follow Simonides more closely, is to take κυανανθής as a general epithet of the sea "blue-surfaced." In this case, -ανθής would have a particular force, indicating the surface of the sea, the "bloom" of colour, and would have the effect of localizing κυάνεος. It seems less likely in the context than the earlier explanation.

VI Conclusion

In Simonides and Bacchylides κυάνεος begins to change in meaning from "dark" to "blue." The fact that Bacchylides picks up the association of κυάνεος with both sea and night from Simonides, and that these associations are found in later poetry, suggests the gradual inclusion of a colour element. A brief glance at the dramatists shows that sometimes κυάνεος means "dark" and other times, apparently, "blue." Aeschylus, for example, describes ships as "dark-eyed" (κυανῶπις *Pers.* 559, *Supp.* 743) as Bacchylides had done before him − probably in a variation on the Homeric κυανόπρωιρα. He calls Fate (Moira) κυανέη (fr. 2.1-2D), clearly a synonym for μέλαινα. The glare of the serpent is κυάνεον (*Pers.* 81-82); it was suggested above that the glare is dark in the sense of deadly. For Aeschylus it seems that κυάνεος was a synonym for μέλας.

Euripides presents a more complex picture. He confirms the association of κυάνεος with the sea (*I.T.* 7, *Helen* 179, 1501-1502); his description of Poseidon's horses as κυάνεος (*Andr.* 1010-1011) was probably chosen because of his position as a sea-deity. He also calls ships κυάνεος (*T.W.* 1094) and κυανέμβολος (*Elect.* 436), an association dating back to Homer. We remarked above on his description of a bird as κυανόπτερος (*Andr.* 862), commenting that the kingfisher (halcyon) and swallow, both described as κυάνεος have a metallic lustre to their feathers. It may be that Euripides is depicting a gloss on this bird's feathers. We find evidence of lustre in his description of Hades as "looking with

dark-gleaming brows" (*Alc.* 261 ὑπ' ὀφρύσι κυαναυγέσι βλέπων).[69]
The last two examples suggest that the meaning "dark" is still
strong as does the unusual phrase, κυανόχρωτα χαίτας πλόκαμὸν
"a dark-hued lock of hair" (*Phoen.* 308). We suppose that because
Euripides describes the Sea as κυάνεος, he feels the "blueness"
which the colour theorists find in it; he also feels, apparently, the
lustre or gloss they noted; but he can still use it to mean "dark."
One might question whether any difference between μέλας and
κυάνεος was evident to the sensitive ear of the Greek poet. We saw
that Homer distinguished between them on a metrical basis, but in
the later poets, the metre is not so restricting. Kober tried rather
unconvincingly to show a connotation of density in κυάνεος.[70] A
scanning of the related articles in *LSJ* suggests that except when
κυάνεος means "blue" (e.g. in the discussions of the colour
theorists) or in the geographical term Κυάνεαι for the
Symplegades,[71] κυάνεος is confined to poetry. We conclude, then,
that κυάνεος is more poetic than μέλας, having in Greek much the
same effect as using "sable" as a synonym for black in English.
While in prose κυάνεος definitely developed towards "blue," in

---

69. A. M. Dale *The Alcestis of Euripides* (Oxford 1954) 261 comments: "Possibly
the epithet "dark-gleaming" is more naturally used of the eyes than the brows, but even
so this might be no more than a 'transferred epithet,' not overbold in lyric diction."

70. Kober p. 74.

71. Κυάνεαι (νῆσοι or πέτραι) are two small islands at the entrance of the Euxine:
Herod. 4.85, Demos. 19.273, Strabo 7.6.1 (cf. *LSJ* s.v. Κυάνεαι). In the dramatists they
occur with this epithet at: Soph. *Ant.* 966 (uncertain text), Eur. *Med.* 2,1263, *I.T.* 241,
392, 746, 889-890, *Andr.* 864. M. L. Earle *The Medea of Euripides* (London 1904)
pp. 36-37 says that they are not the *Planctae* "Wandering Rocks" of *Od.* 12.59ff, which
he takes as the Lipari Islands — formed by a marine volcano. The Symplegades (Κυάνεαι
νῆσοι or πέτραι or Κυάνεαι by itself) he takes as the shores of the Bosporus, and the
explanation of their behaviour (clashing together) is that the channel seems to open as
one approaches and to close behind. (This is the explanation of Pliny, who follows
Eratosthenes). What interests us here is the epithet Κυάνεαι which has become so firmly
fixed in this application that it appears in prose, although otherwise κυάνεος is rare in
prose until it becomes definitely "blue." Here one supposes that the islands or shores
were described as κυάνεαι because they were dark in contrast with the sky (cf. γαῖα
μέλαινα), or perhaps because they symbolized death and destruction. The epithet must
have been adopted early as a proper name. J. Lindsay *The Clashing Rocks: A study of
Early Greek Religion and Culture and the Origins of Drama* (London 1965) pp. 5-14
discusses the clashing rocks. He sees magical and chthonic significance in κυάνεος pp.
47-60. He remarks (p. 13) on the link between the dark bird and the dark rocks in Eur.
Andr. 854ff. He concludes (p. 52) that "kyanos-dark is not a dead black. It glitters and
shimmers like snake scales and the many-hued rainbow set against storm-clouds; it
involves a movement of lustres on a dark surface."

poetry the older meaning of "dark" persisted, side by side apparently with the newer prose meaning; hence the appearance of both meanings in some poets.

Four
Dark and Light Contrasts, Part One

I Introduction

In chapter one our consideration of Greek colour theory revealed
that the Greeks included black and white in discussions of colour.
They seem, indeed, to have pictured a gradation of colour from
white at one extreme through light hues to darker ones and finally
to black at the other extreme. Moreover, they were very sensitive
to contrasts of light and dark, more so, apparently, than to
differences in hue. They tended to describe as "light" and "dark"
things which were contrasted or opposed for other reasons, but
which we would not consider definitely "black" or "white." For
example, in chapter four we shall discover that men and women,
who, to our eyes, do not differ extremely in skin colour are
described as "dark" ($\mu\acute{\epsilon}\lambda\alpha\varsigma$) and "light" ($\lambda\epsilon\upsilon\kappa\acute{o}\varsigma$) respectively. The
differentiation between the sexes was very clearly marked,
whereas in our culture, one can be sorely perplexed as to the sex
of a trousered, long-haired adolescent. We assume, then, that the
dark and light contrast in Greek poetry reflects a contrast
between men and women with regard to their social status and
functions. Men worked outdoors, women in the house; men were
tough and hardy, women soft and vulnerable; men's work was
physically demanding, whereas women were occupied with house-
hold tasks. We shall explore this contrast, considering the history
of the division between fair women and dark men and the changes
which we see in the period from Homer to the end of the fifth
century.

111

Dark and light contrasts are found in poetic descriptions of the emotions. The Homeric formula φρένες μέλαιναι which was apparently descriptive of the normal state of the inner man, finds its antithesis in Pindar *Pythian* 4.109: λευκαῖς φρασίν (see below). A good example of polarity is found in the Greek distinction between two species of eagle: the "blackrumped" (μελάμπυγος) was "brave and strong" and typified men, such as Heracles, who behaved in this way; the "whiterumped" (πύγαργος) was cowardly, rapacious, and shameful and gave his name to men who were like him in disposition (see fuller discussion below, pp. 139-144). Apparently the natural way for the Greeks to emphasize contrast (i.e. in behaviour or function) was to describe the one extreme as dark and the other as light.

II White Women and Dark Men in Ancient Art and Homer

An interesting artistic convention is found in the ancient world by which the artist distinguishes women from men by painting women's flesh white (or light-coloured) in contrast to reddish-brown or black for men. This is found in Mycenaean wall-paintings and many archaic vases, e.g. Corinthian early sixth-century vases and Attic black-figure vases.[1] The same convention is parallelled in poetry throughout the period under study. In the *Iliad* one of the commonest formular expressions for Hera is θεὰ λευκώλενος Ἥρη "the white-armed goddess Hera."[2] Mortal women are also white-armed (λευκώλενος) in Homer: Andromache (*Il.* 6.371, 377, 24.723), Helen (*Il.* 3.121, *Od.* 22.227), Arete, queen of the Phaeaceans (*Od.* 7.233, 335, 11.335), and her daughter, Nausicaa (*Od.* 6.101, 186, 251, 7.12), as well as less royal personages, Nausicaa's companions (*Od.* 6.239) and Penelope's servants (*Od.* 18.198, 19.60). The reference in the epithet to "arms" is not

---

1. Originally this was apparently an Egyptian convention; see Wallace p. 33, where she says that the flesh tones of men were painted terracotta and of women yellow, and p. 36, where she states, "Egyptian conventional color of skin prevails" i.e. in Mycenaean wall-painting. On pottery, cf. J. D. Beazley and B. Ashmole *Greek Sculpture and Painting to the End of the Hellenistic Period* (Cambridge 1932), on eighth and seventh-century pottery, pp. 6-7, Corinthian, p. 23. Cf. also, J. D. Beazley *The Development of Attic Black-Figure* (Berkeley, 1951), on the use of white paint for female flesh, p. 1.

2. For occurrences in Homer, see *Index*, s.v.

surprising since women's dress in ancient Greece was arranged to leave the arms bare, so that their beauty (or lack of it) would be conspicuous.[3] It may surprise the reader, however, to find Nausicaa and her companions described as "white-armed" when they are spending a day outdoors in the sun, washing clothes by the river and playing ball. It is much easier to understand how the matrons, Andromache, Helen, and Arete, were "white-armed" since they led more sedate lives weaving and spinning within the house.[4] The epithet, however, is obviously conventional, a general indication of beauty. Moreover, we shall find reason later to believe that λευκός refers as much to the texture of skin as to its fairness, and that it can imply a contrast between men's skin and women's.

There are other indications of women's fair skin in Homer. In Il. 5.314, Aphrodite throws her white arms (πήχεε λευκώ) around her son Aeneas, to protect him. In Od. 23.239-240, Penelope clung to Odysseus, and did not let go her white arms (πήχεε λευκώ) from his neck. The most obvious connection of λευκός with womanly beauty is found in Od. 18.195-196 where Athene made Penelope "taller[5] and fuller to behold and she made her whiter than sawn ivory."[6]

καί μιν μακροτέρην καὶ πάσσονα θῆκεν ἰδέσθαι,
λευκοτέρην δ᾽ ἄρα μιν θῆκε πριστοῦ ἐλέφαντος.

In contrast (almost certainly deliberate)[7] to Penelope's whiteness is Odysseus' dark skin when Athene restores him from an old beggar to his prime for Telemachus to admire (Od. 16.174-176).

3. In the Mycenaean period, women wore short-sleeved dresses, with arms bare from above the elbow; the Doric *chiton* was fastened with brooches at each shoulder, leaving the arms completely bare; the Ionic *chiton* had a short sleeve, but it too left the lower arm uncovered.

4. In Il. 3.125 Helen is weaving, in Od. 4.121ff she is preparing to spin. Nausicaa expects that her mother will be in the megaron spinning (Od. 6.305-306). Cf. also Od. 21.350-353.

5. Height is also a mark of beauty for the Greeks in both men and women; see Od. 6.107-108, where Nausicaa is taller than her companions, Od. 23.157, where Odysseus is made taller, and Aristotle Eth. 1123b7, where the general principle is enunciated. Cf. also M. Treu Von Homer zur Lyrik (Munich 1955) pp. 35-47.

6. Cf. Stanford on Od. 18.195-196, where he calls attention to the epithet πριστοῦ "sawn." Ivory is white when first cut, but it yellows with age and exposure.

7. Deliberate, that is, in drawing a contrast between Penelope and Odysseus, although the passages are widely separated.

δέμας δ' ὤφελλε καὶ ἥβην.
ἂψ δὲ μελαγχροιὴς γένετο, γναθμοὶ δὲ τάνυσθεν,
κυάνεαι δ' ἐγένοντο γενειάδες ἀμφὶ γένειον.

"She made his form and youth thrive. He became dark-skinned
again, his jaws filled out, and the beard grew dark on his chin."[8]
Now the only other man in Homer who is dark-skinned is
Eurybates (Od. 19.246); he is "round-shouldered, dark-skinned
and woolly-haired": γυρὸς ἐν ὤμοισιν, μελανόχροος, οὐλοκάρηνος.
Wallace[9] assumes from this description that dark skin and
"woolly" hair are definitely not marks of beauty and wonders
whether they may be racial characteristics, comparing Herodotus'
description of the Colchians as "dark-skinned and woolly-haired"
(2.104): μελάγχροες καὶ οὐλότριχες. But Odysseus himself has
"woolly" hair as a mark of beauty (οὖλας κόμας) in Od.
23.157-158 where Athene restores him for Penelope and has his
hair curl "like a hyacinth blossom." (These lines are also found in
Od. 6.230-231 in the Nausicaa episode.) Woolly hair, then, need
not be foreign, and since Eurybates according to Il. 2.183-184 is
from Ithaca, it is likely that he, like Odysseus, was a Greek. The
unusually vivid personal description of Eurybates is part of the
fabrication Odysseus told Penelope when he posed as a Cretan
who had met Odysseus and his crew.[10] One would judge that
Eurybates' appearance was memorable, since Odysseus uses it to
establish his *bona fides*, but that does not mean that he was
unattractive. Indeed, since curly hair and dark skin were marks of
beauty in Odysseus, they ought to be taken here as distinguishing
features, not unhandsome ones.

It was suggested above that λευκός referred to texture as well
as fairness when it described women. Homer calls the flesh of
warriors χρὼς λευκός (Il. 11.573, 15.316).[11] Χρώς is the soft,
unprotected flesh at which an enemy directs his weapons.[12]
Consider the passage where Achilles brandishes his spear and scans

8. On κυάνεαι cf. chapter three, pp. 90-91.
9. Wallace p. 20.
10. Stanford on Od. 19.246.
11. In Il. 15.316 some mss. read καλὸν for λευκόν.
12. Cf. the Homeric epithet for χρώς, τέρην (Il. 4.237, 13.553, 14.406) and the
discussion of τέρην in chapter two.

Hector for the most vulnerable spot at which to direct his weapon
(*Il.* 22.321-325).

εἰσορόων χρόα καλὸν, ὅπηι εἴξειε μάλιστα.
τοῦ δὲ καὶ ἄλλο τόσον μὲν ἔχε χρόα χάλκεα τεύχεα, . . .
φαίνετο δ ἧι κληῖδες ἀπ᾽ ὤμων αὐχέν᾽ ἔχουσι
λαυκανίην, ἵνα τε ψυχῆς ὤκιστος ὄλεθρος.

"He [Achilles] scrutinized his fair flesh to see where it was
especially vulnerable. All the rest of his flesh was covered by his
bronze armour, but it was visible where the collar-bone divides the
neck from the shoulders at the throat, where the destruction of
the life is swiftest." It is clear from the passage that the χρώς
needs the protection of armour. Unlike the parts of the body
which are normally exposed, the face, arms, and legs, the χρώς is
not subject to weathering because it is protected by clothing or
armour.[13] Although men are "dark-skinned" generally, their χρώς
is λευκός. The epithet καλός seems to underline the tone of
vulnerability. We find λειριόεις used as an epithet of χρώς in
Hector's threat to Ajax (*Il.* 13.829-830; cf. Appendix I). Cole
thinks that the description of the χρώς as λευκός and λειριόεις
are taunts of cowardice, because of the later use of λευκός as
"cowardly."[14] But since λευκός is not so used by Homer, these
epithets rather reinforce the idea of vulnerability already present
in χρώς.

We shall see when we come to discuss bravery and cowardice
in connection with darkness and fairness, that there are several
steps involved in the development of this idea: first, that men who
lead outdoor lives are dark-skinned, in good physical condition,
and good fighters; then, that a certain species of eagle "dark-
tailed" was brave and another species "white-tailed" was a coward,
which epithets were by a vulgar comparison transferred to men
who were brave or cowardly; and also, that the response of the
inner man to grief, danger, anger and other emotions was dark, but
if for any reason he did not respond, his φρένες or whatever part

13. This difference in texture and colour of the skin may be observed in
sun-bathers in early summer when their faces and arms have been exposed to the summer
sun, but their bodies are still white and soft.
14. Cole vol. 1, p. 30. For a discussion of λευκός as "cowardly," see below on
λευκηπατίας and Hesychius' gloss λευκοί· οἱ δειλοί.

of him normally showed emotion was white. The roots of these ideas are found in Homer, but our chief evidence for the use of "white" to mean "cowardly" and "dark" to mean "brave" is found in the comic poets at the end of the fifth century (pp. 132,151). Therefore, I cannot accept the suggestion that λευκός is a taunt of cowardice in *Il.* 11.573, and 15.316. The contrast between men and women cannot have represented a great actual difference of skin tone, especially in an olive-skinned race such as the Greeks. It is suggested above, that this "artificial" contrast is evidence of the Greek tendency to polarize sexual characteristics; that it describes a difference not merely of skin colour, but of texture as well; and that it reflects an antithesis between fine-skinned, fragile women and tougher and hardier men.

III Whiteness of Women in Lyric and Tragic Poetry

Although Hera is the only goddess in Homer who is "white-armed" (λευκώλενος), later poetry extends the epithet to other goddesses:[15] Artemis (Bacch. 5.99); Persephone (Hes. *Theog.* 913); Selene (*h. Hom.* 32.17); Calliope (Bacch. 5.176); Cytherea (Adesp. fr. 975(c) *PMG*). Mortal women are also λευκώλενος: in Pindar, Harmonia (fr. 29.6), Thyone (*Pyth.* 3.98), Cyrene (*Pyth.* 9.17, v. 1.); and in Bacchylides, Europa, daughter of Phoenix (17.54) and Iole (16.27). This epithet is not found in tragedy, although the arms and other parts of the body are described as λευκός.

Bacchylides describes a girl's arm as λευκός when she lifts it in playing the game of cottabos (fr. 17). A reference in the fragment to the young men (νεανίαις) who were watching makes the adjective particularly relevant. Elsewhere, in the ode which relates the tale of Theseus and the seven youths and seven maidens on their way to Crete in the company of Minos, Bacchylides says that "the dread gifts of the goddess Cypris with the lovely diadem stung the heart of Minos and he no longer kept his hand from the maiden, but he touched her λευκᾶν cheeks," (17.8-13):

$$κνίσεν \ τε \ Μίνωϊ \ κέαρ$$
$$ἱμεράμπυκος \ θεᾶς$$

15. For Hera λευκώλενος in lyric, see Pind. *Paean* 6.87-88 and Bacch. 9.7-8.

Κύπριδος ἀγνὰ δῶρα.[16]
χεῖρα δ' οὐκέτι παρθενικᾶς
ἀτᾶρθ' ἐράτυεν, θίγεν
δὲ λευκᾶν παρηίδων.

Jebb debates briefly whether to translate λευκᾶν "pale" or "fair;"[17] he decides for "fair" because "the pallor of *fear* is expressed by χλωρός." Λευκᾶν emphasizes the beauty and desirability of the girl. As her distress is not mentioned until the following line (βόασέ τ 'Ερίβοια ...) it would be premature to take λευκᾶν as indicating this. In his comment on these lines, Jebb compares Sophocles *Antigone* 1238-1239, where Haemon, after stabbing himself, gathers the dead Antigone in his arms, "and, panting, sends forth a sharp stream of bloody drops on her fair cheek."

καὶ φυσιῶν ὀξεῖαν ἐκβάλλει ῥοὴν
λευκῆι παρειᾶι φοινίου σταλάγματος.

Jebb takes λευκῆι as "pale" here, since Antigone is dead, in spite of his preference for "fair" in Bacchylides 17.13.

Turning to Euripides, *Medea* 922-924, Jason asks Medea, "You, why do you wet your eyes with fresh tears, turning away your λευκήν cheek, and why do you not receive this word from me with joy?"

αὕτη, τί χλωροῖς δακρύοις τέγγεις κόρας,
στρέψασα λευκὴν ἔμπαλιν παρηίδα,
κοὐκ ἀσμένη τόνδ' ἐξ ἐμοῦ δέχηι λόγον;

It is possible to argue that here λευκήν represents the pallor accompanying emotion, since Medea is deeply moved. Later in the

16. 'Αγνά is Snell's restoration of the uncertain manuscript reading in Bacch. 17.10. F. G. Kenyon, *The Poems of Bacchylides* (London 1897) restored αἰνά here and most editors have followed him, e.g. Jebb, Smyth, and Blass (second edition). Jebb argued that ἀγνά was unsuitable in the context, since presumably the passion inspired by the goddess was far from "holy." He has been well answered on this point by D. Gerber (in *Phoenix* 19 [1965] 212-213) who points out that ἀγνός is closer in meaning to the English "awful," i.e. "inspiring awe or deep dread" than to "holy." 'Αγνός denotes both religious awe and the absence of any blemish. The gifts in the passage are the gifts of a goddess and therefore can be described as "awful." Gerber quotes other passages where ἀγνός is so used in support of his suggestion: Pind. *Pyth.* 1.21-22, fr. 34 (Snell), Lamproc. fr. 1(a).1 (735 *PMG*).

17. Jebb *Bacchylides* on 16.13.

same play, in the messenger's speech reporting Glauce's reaction to the gifts from Medea's children, we are told that she looked away, "turning aside her λευκήν cheek" (1148): λευκήν τ' ἀπέστρεψ' ἔμπαλιν παρηίδα. Since Glauce is the beautiful, young bride of Jason, it is reasonable to assume that λευκήν describes her "fair" youth and beauty, not her cheeks "pale" with emotion. If λευκήν means fair in line 1148 it ought to mean the same in 923.[18] Corssen argued, however, that line 923 is an interpolation, having been adapted from line 1148, since it is out of keeping with the situation to have Jason complimenting Medea: "laus a verbis Iasonis uxorem vehementer commotam alloquentis quam alienissima est."[19] Page countered that λευκός "is too conventional to be a compliment,"[20] and therefore Corssen's argument over the authenticity of the line finds no support there.

It is indeed true that Euripides uses λευκός frequently to denote beauty: in the Medea, besides the two examples already quoted, there is the description of Medea's neck as πάλλευκον δέρην (line 30); of Glauce's foot as παλλεύκωι ποδί (line 1164 below); and of Glauce's flesh λευκήν . . . σάρκα (line 1189).[21] (Note the intensive πάλλευκος in two of the above passages). But in spite of its frequent appearance, I am not sure that Page is right in considering λευκός simply as a conventional epithet; I suggest, rather, that Euripides intends to create a particular emotional tone when he uses this epithet for his heroines. In line 30, for example,

18. Cf. Page Euripides Medea on line 1148.
19. P. Corssen in Hermes 47 [1912] 476-480.
20. Page Euripides Medea on lines 923-924. For his view of repeated lines, see his note on lines 37-44.
21. The reading of most mss. is λεπτήν, but this is a peculiar epithet for flesh "thin, fine, delicate," as in clothing which clings to the body. One suspects that it has been introduced into the text by the proximity of λεπτοί (line 1188). A copyist could easily misread ΛΕΠΤΗΝ for ΛΕΥΚΗΝ. Page accepts λευκήν, the reading of mss. B and Haun., comparing Elec. 823: λευκὰς ἐγύμνου σάρκας (of the flesh of a freshly-skinned calf), although this does not seem to me to be an entirely satisfactory parallel. One cannot argue against λεπτήν solely on the grounds that the same adjective is used in the previous line, because Page has shown that Euripides, like other Greek writers, is unconcerned by repetition of words and phrases where English is careful to avoid it (Actors' Interpolations in Greek Tragedy pp. 122-129). But whereas one can explain the presence of λεπτήν as a misreading of λευκήν influenced by λεπτοί, it is much less easy to explain how λεπτήν could be corrupted into λευκήν. Considering Euripides' fondness for describing women as λευκός, we need not hesitate to accept λευκήν as the correct reading.

the reference to Medea's "all-white neck" serves to remind the audience that Medea, though rejected by her husband, is still attractive; moreover, as I shall attempt to demonstrate from Euripides' other uses, it suggests that she is vulnerable. Although Jason's reference to Medea's "fair cheek" (line 923) is not a deliberate compliment, by it he seems to acknowledge himself and to remind the audience that Medea is a woman — soft, vulnerable, and unable to fight back on his terms.

Professor D. Conacher of the University of Toronto has reminded me that Page allows two similar passages (like *Med.* 923 and 1148) to stand only on the basis of a "commonplace" epithet or description. If this view of repeated lines is right, and λευκός in Euripides is not merely conventional, then one of the two lines must be dropped. Of the two, line 923 would perhaps be less missed than 1148.

To return briefly to Sophocles. It is possible that Jebb is right to take λευκῆι as "pale" (in *Antigone* 1239), but in view of the Bacchylidean and Euripidean usages, is it not more likely that Sophocles was providing a poignant reminder of Antigone's beauty? It is not without significance that the reminder comes in a scene of violence, as it does so often in Euripides, and thus λευκῆι emphasizes Antigone's femininity and softness. (Although she died by her own hand, she was driven to it by Creon and was, therefore, his victim.) In Bacchylides 17.8-13 we saw the same tone. In the context, Eriboea was obviously distressed and unable to protect herself; she called out and Theseus came to her aid, his dark eye whirling (cf. pp. 155, 212-213). In mentioning her "fair cheeks," Bacchylides apparently intends to emphasize not only her beauty, but her helplessness in the situation (recall λευκός as a Homeric epithet of χρώς).

We shall turn now to other examples of the way Euripides uses λευκός to describe the women in his plays, with particular consideration to the tone produced by this epithet. In *Iphigeneia in Aulis* 875, an old man reports to Clytemnestra that Agamemnon intends to kill their daughter, bloodying the fair neck (λευκὴν δέρην) of the wretched girl with the sword. The chorus in *Hippolytus* 769-771 foresees that Phaedra will hang herself after her rejection by her step-son, fitting a noose to her fair neck (λευκᾶι δείραι). In *Electra* 1022-1023 we read how Agamemnon, held his daughter over the altar and slashed her fair cheek.[22] The nurse describes to the chorus how Alcestis prepared herself for death (*Alc.* 158-162). She bathed her fair flesh (λευκὸν χρόα) in the waters of the river, and choosing a dress from the cedar chambers, she adorned herself fittingly and stood before Hestia and prayed. Dale comments that here λευκὸν χρόα "is not proleptic but the conventional epithet for women's flesh, the white painted flesh on black-figure pots."[23] I quite agree, but would add that here again Euripides describes a victim as λευκός. Alcestis is not being slaughtered, as Iphigeneia was, nor is she committing suicide like Phaedra, but she is sacrificing herself to save her husband — a victim of her own selflessness, if you will. Creusa is another victim, although she suffers not death but shame (*Ion* 891-895). She reproaches Apollo who abducted her and grasping her fair wrists (λευκοῖς δ' ἐμφὺς καρποῖς χειρῶν), dragged her into the shelter of a cave. Here λευκοῖς καρποῖς χειρῶν emphasizes the helplessness of the girl.

Three times in Euripides the arm (πῆχυς) is λευκός, twice in the context of lament (*Phoen.* 1350-1351 λευκοπήχεις κτύπους χεροῖν, and *Orestes* 1467-1469 λευκὸν δ' ἐμβαλοῦσα πῆχυν στέρνοις). The third occasion is much more terrible. After the capture and rending of her son Pentheus, Agave speaks to her fellow-citizens (*Bacch.* 1203-1207):

> ἔλθεθ' ὡς ἴδητε τήνδ' ἄγραν
> Κάδμου θυγατέρες θηρὸς ἣν ἠγρεύσαμεν,
> οὐκ ἀγκυλητοῖς Θεσσαλῶν στοχάσμασιν,
> οὐ δικτύοισιν, ἀλλὰ λευκοπήχεσι
> χειρῶν ἀκμαῖσιν.

"Come see this catch of a wild beast which we daughters of Cadmus caught not with Thessalian javelins thrown with bent arm,

---

22. J. D. Denniston *Euripides Electra* (Oxford 1939) on line 1023 points out that one would expect "throat" here rather than "cheek." He suggests either πατὴρ δέρην or παιδὸς δέρην an emendation suggested by Kvičala, assuming a mutilation of the end of the line obliterating all but πα of παρηίδα. The copyist may have thought of *Medea* 923, 1148.

23. A. M. Dale *Euripides Alcestis* (Oxford 1954) on line 159.

nor with nets, but with our hands' white blades."[24] The horror of the deed is redoubled by the epithet λευκόπηχυς which should convey beauty, but here serves to heighten the contrast between the deed and the respectable matrons of Thebes who did it. It cannot be simply by chance that Euripides uses λευκός to emphasize the pathos of his heroines' predicaments, whether they are helpless victims, or whether, as in the case of Agave, their actions contrast with their feminity.

Our examples from Homer, the lyric poets, and the dramatists, then, suggest that λευκός indicated not merely beauty in women, but another quality that was thought to be characteristic of them – their helplessness and need of protection. This quality was naturally attributed to them because of their status and functions; women tended to the affairs of the house and remained at home, for the most part, in contrast to men who worked outside, became strong because of physical labour, and were able to protect themselves. This gulf between men and women seems to grow from the relatively equal relationship in the time of Homer to the unequal situation in fifth-century Athens, where the exploitation of women was recognized, and even portrayed by a dramatist such as Euripides.[25]

IV White Feet and Dark Feet

Just as the χρώς which is normally protected by clothing is described by Homer as λευκός, so the bare foot is in several places given this epithet. Four of these occurrences are found in

24. The rendering "with our hands' white blades" is owed to Dodds *Euripides Bacchae* on lines 1203-1207. He explains that "χειρῶν ἀκμαί are probably hands not fingers, as ποδοῖν ἀκμαί at Soph. O.T. 1034 are feet not toes. But the phrase suggests that the hands are sharp and deadly (cf. Aesch. *Pers.* 1060 πέπλον δ' ἔρεικε ἀκμῆι χερῶν). In λευκοπήχεσι the first part of the compound implies "feminine," the second repeats the meaning of the noun as in λευκοτρίχων πλοκάμων (line 112). Cf. *Phoen.* 1351."

25. The impression one gets from reading Homer is that men and women are social equals, although they have different functions. Most historians assume that this freedom between the sexes did not survive into the fifth century, but Gomme has argued convincingly that evidence to this effect has been misinterpreted (in *C.P.* 20 [1925] 1-25). Whether, in fact, they were confined to the house, as the popular view holds, or moved about in comparative freedom, is not really the question here. It is important to notice that Euripides shows an awareness of the vulnerable position of women, particularly in wartime, and the sufferings to which they are peculiarly susceptible. It is, perhaps, not the relative positions of men and women that have changed between Homeric times and the fifth century, but the understanding of these positions.

Euripides and in each of these cases the feet so described are women's; the fifth is found in Aristophanes and is clearly humorous.[26] In *Medea*, the unfortunate Glauce parades in her fatal finery, "stepping daintily with her all-white foot" (1164): ἀβρὸν βαίνουσα παλλεύκωι ποδί. We remarked earlier on the frequency with which Euripides uses λευκός in this play for both Medea and Glauce. The intensive form of the adjective (πᾶν+λευκός) concentrates attention on Glauce's beauty – a concentration which we have frequently marked in Euripides' plays at the fatal moment. The fact that she is barefoot is incidental in this passage – taken for granted, but not the reason for the epithet. Euripides' choice of adverb (ἀβρόν) is significant, since it, like λευκός, conveys a tone of feminity and softness. Judging from the frequency of its appearance in Sappho's poetry, it must have been one of her favourite adjectives to describe beauty, grace, and delicacy: the Graces (fr. 128), Andromache (fr. 44.7) and Adonis (fr. 140.1) were all ἄβρος and Aphrodite was besought to pour nectar ἄβρως for Sappho and her companions (fr. 2.13-16). Cf. also a gloss on ἀβρός in Anacreon (fr. 461 *PMG*): ὁ κούφως βαίνων, κατὰ στέρησιν τοῦ βάρους (Orion *Lex.* 3.11); "one who walks lightly because of loss of weight." The step is dainty and light, as if, I think the gloss means, the walker were not putting his weight down as he moved. This contrasts with a heavy, masculine tread; hence the suitability of ἀβρόν for Glauce's dainty gait.[27]

In the *Bacchae* (862-865), the chorus sings, "Shall I ever in the night-long dances set my bare foot in Bacchic revels, throwing back my neck to the dewy air?"

> ἆρ' ἐν παννυχίοις χοροῖς
> θήσω ποτὲ λευκὸν
> πόδ' ἀναβακχεύουσα δέραν
> εἰς αἰθέρα δροσερὸν ῥίπτουσ'.

26. In *Bacch.* 13.84-86, Jebb (*Bacchylides* on 12.84-86) suggested a possible restoration of λευκοῖς, agreeing with πόδεσσι, to a gap in the ms. Since this is merely a guess, with no ancient evidence to support it, it has not been considered here. In fact, is unlikely to be correct, since we find no other examples earlier than Euripides. Snell gives the following text for 13.84-86: καί τις ὑψαυχὴς κό[ρα/ ...]ρᾶν/ πόδεσσι ταρφέως; and for 85: στείχουσ' [λευκοῖς Jebb] ἀνὰ γᾶν ἱε]ρέν [Blass].

27. Cf. Treu pp. 176-177.

Earlier in the same play, Agave refers to the whiteness or bareness of the limbs of the Maenads (664-665):

Βάκχας ποτνιάδας εἰσιδὼν, αἳ τῆσδε γῆς
οἴστροισι λευκὸν κῶλον ἐξηκόντισαν.

"Beholding the revered Maenads whose white limbs flashed away from this land spear-swift in their madness."[28] Dodds comments that "λευκός is the traditional epithet for women's flesh in Greek poetry; but its use here suggests the bare feet of the Bacchants (called ἀπέδιλοι or ἀσάμβαλοι by Nonnus[29] and nearly always barefooted on vases)." A third reference to the bare feet of Maenads is made in Cyclops 72: Βάκχαις σὺν λευκόποσιν. There is a double suitability in this use of λευκός: first, as Dodds remarked, it is the traditional epithet for women's flesh, and so implies beauty and femininity; secondly, it implies bareness, because it suggests that the foot is visible, i.e. uncovered. Similarly the Homeric epithet λευκώλενος calls attention to the bare arms.

It was the custom in Greece to wear sandals when one walked out-of-doors; Socrates, to be sure, went barefoot, but this was regarded as one of his many eccentricities, evidence of his poverty and hardiness.[30] The Maenads went without sandals for different reasons: they attained greater freedom in running and dancing, and bare feet, along with wild attire and flowing hair, were an evidence of their possession by the god. They shook off all restraint, including confining shoes and clothes, and abandoned themselves to the revels. Whereas it was unusual for a woman to go barefoot out-of-doors and an evidence of her abandonment, it was apparently quite acceptable for her to go barefoot within the house, since Glauce modelled her robe in bare feet. It is sometimes argued that going outdoors without sandals was a sign of a hasty departure. (This is to some degree true of the Maenads insofar as

28. "Whose limbs . . . their madness" is Dodds' translation in Eur. Bacch. lines 664-667.

29. Nonnus Dionysiaca 32.256, 44.14 ἀσάμβαλος; 5.407 ἀπέδιλος.

30. For the general habits of the Greeks, see L. Whibley A Companion to Greek Studies (third ed., Cambridge 1916) p. 632, where Lady Evans writes "In houses Greeks seem to have gone barefoot, especially in summer . . . On entering a house it was customary for everyone to uncover the feet. Shoes were left at the door when paying calls, as nowadays in the East." For Socrates as barefoot, see Plato Symp. 220b where Alcibiades relates Socrates' behaviour in the campaign at Potidaea.

casual attire such as theirs goes hand in hand with haste.) The chorus of daughters of Ocean tells Prometheus, "I hastened without sandals in a winged car" (Aesch. *Prom.* 135): σύθην δ' ἀπέδιλος ὄχωι πτερωτῶι. In Theocritus (24.36), Alcmene, hearing the cries of the infant Iphicles, urges her husband, Amphitryon, "Up, nor stay to put your sandals on your feet": ἄνστα, μηδὲ πόδεσσιν ἑοῖς ὑπὸ σάνδαλα θείης. The second example is clearly a matter of haste, as Alcmene's tone of urgency indicates. (Here, however, Amphitryon does not propose to go outdoors, but simply to the children's sleeping quarters.) In the first example, ἀπέδιλος is usually taken with the verb σύθην,[31] "I left in such a hurry that I didn't put my shoes on." Page suggests an alternate explanation which deserves consideration. Alcman, in the *Partheneion* (fr. 1.15-16), warns his audience: "let not the unsandalled bravery of man soar to Heaven":

$$\text{ἀπέδιλος ἀλκὰ}$$
$$\text{μή τις]ἀνθρώπων ἐς ὡρανὸν ποτήσθω.}$$

The phrase ἀπέδιλος ἀλκά is puzzling. Page interprets thus: "ἀπέδιλος 'without walking shoes' signifies 'not walking on the ground (but being conveyed through the air)' here as in Aeschylus (*Prom.* 135, see above); the meaning is assisted by πτερωτῶι in Aeschylus, as by ποτήσθω in Alcman."[32] He translates, "let not the bravery of man leave the ground and soar to Heaven." This interpretation, though ingenious, is not altogether satisfactory. Hermes, after all, put on sandals "which bore him over sea and land" (*Il.* 24.339-342), unaware that sandals were for walking only. Though no other definite explanation is apparent, one cannot help thinking that the clue lies in the area of haste and disarray, rather than in a contrast between walking and flying.

The chorus of women in Euripides' *Ion* (219-221) ask permission of Ion to enter the temple:

$$\text{θέμις γυάλων ὑπερβῆ-}$$
$$\text{ναι λευκῶι ποδί γ' *33}$$

---

31. Haste is the interpretation of P. Groeneboom on Aeschylus *Prometheus* (Groningen, Den Haag 1928) line 135 and Gow *Theocritus* on 24.36.

32. D. L. Page *Alcman: The Partheneion* (Oxford 1951) pp. 34-35.

33. Hermann proposed βηλόν for the gap in line 221.

"Is it lawful to cross the sanctuary with white (bare) foot?" Now it would be unusual for the chorus, pilgrims to the temple of Apollo, to have arrived there barefoot; their question, then, indicates that they expected to remove their sandals before entering the shrine. Before we consider the matter of removing sandals, we ought to examine γυάλων. Γύαλον is a "hollow" (*LSJ* s.v.), but in the plural it is "especially applied to the sanctuary of Delphi." (cf., e.g., *Ion* 76, 245; Soph. fr. 460).[34] It is thought that the hollow referred first to the unique character of the ἄδυτον at Delphi which was a pit or cavern in the earth and was later extended to include the whole sanctuary. The chorus, then, intend to enter the temple, not merely the vales around it.

Commentators ignore the question whether the women are about to remove their sandals; λευκῶι being taken as a conventional epithet, an indication that the feet are women's.[35] This is, of course, true, but is only half the reason for the epithet, the other being the bareness of the foot. The Hebrews of the Old Testament removed their shoes when they entered the temple, because they were standing on holy ground; Moslems leave their shoes outside when they go into a mosque; there is not, however, much evidence that this was a Greek custom. In the famous passage in *Agamemnon* in which Clytemnestra entices Agamemnon to tread on the purple carpets (or vestments),[36] he first removes his shoes before stepping from the chariot (Aesch. *Ag.* 944-949). Fraenkel suggests that Agamemnon had two reasons for this action: he wished to avoid spoiling the carpets and he was showing respect for materials which were, in some way, connected with the gods.[37] Fraenkel gives one example of a prohibition of wearing shoes in a temple: μηδὲ ὑποδήματα ἐσφερέτω μηδὲ ὕειον μηθέν (a law of Ialysos for the sanctuary of Alektrona, about 300 B.C., C. F. W. Dittenberger *Sylloge Inscriptionum Graecarum* [3rd ed. Leipzig 1915-24] 338.25). Whether or not this rule was invariable, in some

---

34. A. C. Pearson *Fragments of Sophocles* (Cambridge 1917) on fr. 460; A. S. Owen *Euripides Ion* (Oxford 1939) on line 220 agrees.

35. Owen *Euripides Ion* on line 221.

36. Denniston and Page *Aeschylus Agamemnon* on line 909 argue that Agamemnon is treading on clothing, not carpets which are meant to be walked on.

37. Fraenkel *Aeschylus Agamemnon* on line 948.

places at least the Greeks removed their shoes before entering a temple or sacred place.[38]

The connection of λευκόπους with the Bacchic revels apparently prompted one of the poets of the *Anacreontea* to describe the mad Orestes as "whitefooted" (9.4-5):

> ἐμαίνετ' 'Αλκμαίων τε
> χὠ λευκόπους 'Ορέστης.

It was symptomatic of his frenzy that he, like the Maenads, went about without shoes. It should be noted that this late poem is one of two cases where men's feet are "white," the other being a pun in Aristophanes (see below). The double connotations of bareness and beauty are more suitably applied to women. Men went barefoot for different reasons and the effect was undoubtedly different: we have on the one hand the Maenads whose bare feet were evidence of their abandonment to the revels and the god and, along with their flowing hair and loose attire, suggested sensual attraction, and on the other Socrates whose habit of going about barefoot attested his ability to endure cold and discomfort as well as his voluntary poverty (see Plato *Symp.* 220b). It would seem likely, then, that the use of λευκός for women's feet is part of the general use of this epithet to describe women, carrying overtones of beauty, femininity, and vulnerability.

What, then, are we to say about the two examples of "white-footed" men? The description of Orestes as λευκόπους need not concern us except as evidence of a connection between madness and going barefoot, for the source originates long after the end of the fifth century, the limit of our study. The second instance of λευκόπους used of men occurs in Aristophanes, where part of the chorus of old men in the *Lysistrata* addresses the other part (665-670):

> ἀλλ' ἄγετε λευκόποδες, οἵπερ ἐπὶ Λειψύδριον ἤλθο-
>   μεν ὅτ' ἦμεν ἔτι,
> νῦν δεῖ νῦν ἀνηβῆσαι πάλιν κἀναπτερῶσαι

---

38. For other indications that shoes were removed before entering a shrine, see J. G. Frazer *The Fasti of Ovid* (London 1929) vol. ii 237f, on *Fasti* 1.629, and Varro *De lingua latina* 7.84 where the prohibition is related to a connection between leather, the hide of a dead animal, and death, which ought not to take place in a sacred enclosure.

πᾶν τὸ σῶμα κἀποσείσασθαι τὸ γῆρας τόδε.

"Come, then, white-feet, we who went to Leipsydrion when we were in our prime, now, now, we must become young again and set our whole body on the wing and shake off this old age." The reference to Leipsydrion is a reminder of the unsuccessful attempt of the Alcmaeonidae and their supporters to get rid of the tyranny of Hippias at Athens (Herod. 5.62) and actually took place about one hundred years before this play was first performed.[39] The manuscripts read λυκόποδες "wolf-footed" in place of λευκόποδες and the Scholiasts comment as if this was in their texts, but this reading is precluded by the metre. Some commentators regard this as evidence that λευκόποδες is a pun on λυκόποδες, the latter epithet implying that they were fierce fellows indeed, and perhaps concealing a reference to the Alcmaeonidae. Hesychius' gloss is thought to give support to this view, but I think that Wilamowitz was closer to the truth when he referred to it as a garbled (verstümmelte) gloss: λυκόποδες οἱ Ἀλκμαιονίδαι· οἳ μέν τινες διὰ τὴν ποδῶν λευκότητα· ἦσαν γὰρ ἀεὶ ὑποδεδεμένοι.[40] About all one can conclude from Hesychius is that both readings were known in antiquity. Wilamowitz goes on to suggest that the chorus speak of their white feet as if they were fine young fellows, whereas, in reality, they are old and their feet will be quite different in appearance. It seems doubtful that "fine young fellows" would refer to their feet as white, since, as we have seen, λευκός is elsewhere restricted to women. Van Leeuwen suggests that in poetic diction λευκόποδες indicates the whiteness of bare feet, but in popular speech seems to have meant "rascals," as the French va-nu-pieds and sansculottes.[41] The French terms developed presumably from those who went barefoot from poverty to the socially undesirable. To imagine a similar development in Greek is difficult, since the implications of going barefoot were quite different, especially among women of whom the adjective λευκός

39. Hippias was finally driven out of Athens in 510 B.C.; the attempt at Leipsydrion must have been earlier than this. *Lysistrata* was first produced in 411 B.C.

40. U. von Wilamowitz-Moellendorff *Aristophanes Lysistrate* (Berlin 1927) on line 665.

41. J. Van Leeuwen *Aristophanis Lysistrata cum prolegomenis et commentariis* (Leiden 1903) on line 665.

was chiefly used. More ingenious explanations are offered by Rogers who supposes that the old men are wearing white slippers[42] and Hopper who thinks that the whiteness is caused by dust and mud caked on the legs.[43] In both these cases, the humour of the epithet lies in the fact that λευκόποδες, a suitable description of a band of dancing Maenads, is applied to a group of old men, not in its usual meaning "with bare, beautiful feet," but in some literal way made clear on stage. We are in no position to decide how Aristophanes was using λευκόποδες except to conclude that it was a humorous, unexpected appellation; the error of the manuscripts seems to indicate that the ancients also found difficulty in interpreting the epithet.

Rogers remarked in his note that "the contention of Bothe and others that λευκόποδες here means 'barefoot' seems quite inadmissible . . . in truth, 'with bare, white feet' would be an epithet suitable to young girls rather than to old soldiers who would pride themselves on being μελάμποδες." But Rogers gives no examples of μελάμπους as an epithet of old men, or of anyone else, nor in all probability could he. Melampus "Blackfoot" occurs in Homer as the name of a seer (*Od.* 15.225); the plural Melampodes is said by various commentators to have been the name of the inhabitants of Egypt before they took their name from Aegyptus (Apollod. 2.1.4, Eustath. 37.23, Schol. Hom. *Il.* 1.42, Schol. Plato *Tim.* 25b). But I have found no instances of μελάμπους used as a descriptive epithet. That the Egyptians should be called "Blackfeet" is not surprising, since they were a dark-skinned race (Herod. 2.104), and this epithet may simply refer to that darkness. If, however, it is related specifically to the feet, the significance is apparently lost.[44] It is interesting that another race or tribe, perhaps fabulous, has a name which may mean "Blackfeet"; in Aristophanes' *Birds* (1553-1555) we find mention of the "Shadowfeet" (Σκιάποσιν) among whom the

42. B. B. Rogers *Aristophanes Lysistrata* (London 1910) on line 664.
43. R. J. Hopper in *CQ* N.S. 10 (1960) 242-247. Hopper refers to κονίποδες "dusty-footed" and the allusion to foot-washing in Aristophanes *Wasps* 608 to support his contention that λευκόποδες meant "with feet white from dust or mud."
44. Cf. the tribe of North American Indians known as Blackfoot, who were so named because they smeared ashes on their mocassins *Encyclopedia Canadiana* (Ottawa 1966) ed. John E. Robbins s.v. Blackfoot.

unwashed (ἄλουτος) Socrates calls up the spirits. The name "Shadowfeet" may be given to them because their feet are dirty (cf. *Il.* 16.234-235 on the Selloi with unwashed feet at Dodona, the fact that Socrates went barefoot, and the epithet ἄλουτος given to Socrates in this passage). The connection of dirty feet with philosophers may account for the name of the seer, Melampus, although the suggestion is not particularly attractive. Note in contrast the name Podaleiros "Whitefoot" or "Tender-footed" given to one of the sons of the physician Asclepius (*Il.* 2.732, 11.833, cf. n 23 Appendix I).

V Darkness and Fairness as a Reflection of Manliness and Effeminacy in Men

The Greeks thought that a dark complexion signified manliness, including virility and such manly virtues as courage and the ability to fight well. A fair complexion, on the other hand, signified effeminacy in men.

The Egyptians, Colchians and Ethiopians were dark to the Greeks. Hesiod says that in winter the sun "goes to and fro over the people and city of the dark men" (*W.D.* 527-528): ἀλλ' ἐπὶ κυανέων ἀνδρῶν δῆμόν τε πόλιν τε / στρωφᾶται. As the Greeks observed that the sun travelled in a lower, more southerly path through the sky in winter, it seems likely that the "dark men" were Egyptians or inhabitants of Africa where the sun was more nearly overhead than in Greece at this season.[45] Xenophanes, in expounding how men make gods in their own image, says that "the Ethiopians say their gods are snub-nosed and dark, but the Thracians that theirs are blue-eyed and red-haired" (fr. 14):

Αἰθίοπές τε [θεοὺς σφετέρους] σιμοὺς μέλανάς τε
Θρῆικες τε γλαυκοὺς καὶ πυρροὺς [φασι πέλεσθαι].

It is to be presumed that the Ethiopians themselves are snub-nosed

---

45. The height of the sun in the sky as seen from the earth changes with the season and the latitude of the observer. For example, the sun at the winter solstice appears to an observer on earth to reach a height of 90° *minus* the latitude of the observer *minus* 23 1/2° (the tilt of the earth's axis). In Athens (latitude 38°) the sun at mid-winter would reach a height of 28 1/2°; at Memphis in Egypt (latitude 30°) a height of 36 1/2°, noticeably higher in the sky. See *Exploration of the Universe* G. Abell, (2nd ed. New York 1969) pp. 127-129.

and dark. Pindar describes the Colchians as dark (κελαινώπεσσι *Pyth.* 4.212). Herodotus compares the Colchians to the Egyptians in appearance (2.104) describing them as "dark-skinned and woolly-haired": μελάγχροες καὶ οὐλότριχες (cf. section two above).[46]

There are several references in the *Supplices* of Aeschylus to racial darkness. The reader will recall that Io, a Greek, driven to Egypt by a gad-fly, bore there a son Epaphus to Zeus. Two of his descendants, the brothers Aegyptus and Danaus, had fifty children apiece. The fifty sons of Aegyptus sought to marry the fifty daughters of Danaus, but the Danaids rejected them and fled for protection to Argos, the home of their ancestor Io. Both the Danaids and the Aegyptioi are dark-skinned in spite of their Greek ancestry. Stress is laid on their non-Greek appearance (lines 277-290) by the fact that the king can hardly believe the tale of the Danaids because they are not like Argive maidens, but like Libyans, Egyptians, Amazons, or Nomads – all, presumably, of dark complexion. The maidens speak of their "soft cheek summered by Nile's sun" (70-71): τὰν ἀπαλὰν / Νειλοθερῆ παρειάν.[47] It is interesting that, although their cheek is "warmed by the Nile," it remains "soft"; there may well be an internal tension (even an oxymoron), between ἀπαλὰν "soft and feminine" and Νειλοθερῆ "darkened by the southern sun," since the Greeks grouped softness and fairness together in their standard of feminine beauty. Later in the same play, the Danaids describe themselves as a "dark, sunburned family" (154-155): μελανθὲς / ἡλιόκτυπον γένος.

Later Danaus reports to his daughters the approach of the sons of Aegyptus; "the men on board ship are conspicuous to behold with dark limbs showing from white garments" (719-720):

πρέπουσι δ᾽ ἄνδρες νάϊοι μελαγχίμοις
γυίοισι λευκῶν ἐκ πεπλωμάτων ἰδεῖν.[48]

---

46. For a discussion of κυάνεοι ἄνδρες, cf. pp. 98-99.

47. "Summered by Nile's sun" is from the translation of H. W. Smyth (London 1922) "Sun" is implied by -θερη which includes the ideas of warmth and harvesting. Cf. the Scholiast: τὴν ἐν τῶι Νείλωι θερισθεῖσαν ὅ ἐστι βλαστήσασαν ἐν Αἰγύπτωι ἀπὸ τῶν σταχύων δὲ ἡ μεταφορά.

48. On the form of μελάγχιμος which is a variant for μέλας, cf. δύσχιμος.

Here is a striking picture of contrast, suggesting that the sons of Aegyptus, like the Egyptians, wore linen clothing, the whiteness of which made their skin seem all the darker. The epithet is repeated later (745): πολεῖ μελαγχίμωι ξὺν στρατῶι. "with a large, dark-skinned army."[49] But if the Aegyptioi are "many and dark," the Argives are like them in both respects (746-747):

πολλοὺς δέ γ᾽ εὑρήσουσιν ἐν μεσημβρίας
θάλπει βραχίον᾽ εὖ κατερρινημένους.

"Yes, but they will find (the Argives) many and with arms made sinewy in the heat of mid-day." The primary reference is to their good condition because of exercise, but the mention of the "heat of mid-day" suggests that they are tanned. It seems to me that Aeschylus mentioned this deliberately to correspond to the darkness of the enemy.[50] There is a definite correlation between fighting ability and darkness of complexion here and elsewhere in Greek thought.[51] Surely the concept of manliness is at the heart of this association; a man ought to be hardy, accustomed to hard work outside the protection of the house, and able to protect himself and his family. If a man looked "manly," i.e. dark, it followed that he would quit himself like a man. If, however, he was fair, it was assumed that his behaviour, like his complexion, would be effeminate.

In Aristophanes' play *Ecclesiazousae*, in which women dis-

49. Further examples of racial darkness are found in tragedy: Eur. fr. 228.3: μελαμβρότοιο Αἰθιοπίδος γῆς; Eur. fr. 771.4: γείτονες μελάμβροτοι (neighbours of Egypt); Aesch. fr. 370 (Schol. Apol. Rhod. 4.1348 στέρφεσι· τοῖς δέρμασιν) μελα[ν]στέρφων γένος "dark-hided race"; Aesch. *Prom.* 807-809: ... τηλουρὸν δὲ γῆν/ ἥξεις κελαινὸν φῦλον οἳ πρὸς ἡλίου/ ναίουσι πηγαῖς, ἔνθα ποταμὸς Αἰθίοψ, 851: κελαινὸν Ἔπαφον.

50. For a further comment on racial darkness resulting from the heat of the sun cf. Ptolemy *Tetrabibl.* 2.2, p. 122 (ed. F. E. Robbins London 1940). On the effect of sun on the complexion, cf. *Trag. Adesp.* fr. 161: χρόαν δὲ τὴν σὴν ἥλιος λάμπων φλογί/ αἰγυπτιώσει "the sun shining with his light will make your skin Egyptian."

51. For further references to the contrast between men who are exposed to the sun and so in good condition for fighting and athletics, in contrast to men who live effeminate lives, see Plato *Rep.* 556d: πολλάκις ἰσχνὸς ἀνὴρ πένης ἡλιωμένος παραταχθεὶς ἐν μάχηι πλουσίωι ἐσκιατροφηκότι πολλὰς ἔχοντι σάρκας ἀλλοτρίας. See also Lucian *Anacharsis* 25: ἐννοεῖς γάρ, οἶμαι, τὸ μετὰ τοῦτο, οἵους εἰκὸς σὺν ὅπλοις ἔσεσθαι τοὺς καὶ γυμνοὺς ἂν φόβον τοῖς δυσμενέσιν ἐμποιήσαντας, οὐ πολυσαρκίαν ἀργὸν καὶ λευκὴν ἢ ἀσαρκίαν μετὰ ὠχρότητος ἐπιδεικνυμένους οἷα γυναικῶν σώματα ὑπὸ σκιᾶι μεμαρασμένα.... and οὗτοι δὲ ἡμῖν ὑπέρυθροι ἐς τὸ μελάντερον ὑπὸ τοῦ ἡλίου κεχρωσμένοι.

guised as men take over city affairs, there are several jokes about the contrast in complexion of the sexes. One of Praxagora's companions anointed her body and stood facing the sun all day, in an effort to acquire a manly appearance (63-64). If we had any doubt as to the meaning, the Scholiasts' comment sets it down in black and white: ὥστε μέλαινα γένεσθαι ὡς ἀνήρ. Chremes tells his friend about the assembly of women in disguise at 385-387:

> καὶ δῆτα πάντας σκυτοτόμοις ἠικάζομεν
> ὁρῶντες αὐτούς, οὐ γὰρ ἀλλ᾽ ὑπερφυῶς
> ὡς λευκοπληθὴς ἦν ἰδεῖν ἡ ἐκκλησία.

"Indeed, when we saw them all, we likened them to shoemakers, for it was marvellous how full of white people the assembly was to behold." The reference to shoemakers is explained by the Scholiast "because shoemakers sit and work in the shade." The Scholiast on *Peace* 1310 reports a proverb "there is no work for fair-skinned men except shoemaking": οὐδὲν λευκῶν ἀνδρῶν ἔργον εἰ μὴ σκυτοτομεῖ.

White-skinned men might resemble women in physical condition if, like Plato's rich oligarch, they lived within the shelter of their homes (*Rep.* 556d, cf. n. 51), or if they were regarded as effeminate. In the *Ecclesiazousae*, Chremes reports on various speakers in the assembly. One of them was "a fair, good-looking youth, like Nicias" (427-428): εὐπρεπὴς νεανίας/ λευκός τις ὅμοιος Νικίαι. The comparison of Nicias to the young speaker who is, in fact, a woman, is a clear hint of his effeminate ways and appearance. Pentheus taunts Dionysus with his effeminate appearance (Eur. *Bacch.* 457-458):

> λευκὴν δὲ χροιὰν ἐκ παρασκευῆς ἔχεις
> οὐχ ἡλίου βολαῖσιν, ἀλλ᾽ ὑπὸ σκιᾶς.

"You have a fair skin purposely, not from the shafts of the sun but from the shade." Here there is a suggestion of effeminacy and a connection of λευκός with the deliberate attempt to avoid the sun, as μέλας was with exposure to the sun. Agathon, the tragic poet, is ridiculed by Aristophanes (*Thesm.* 190-192):

> ἔπειτα πολιός εἰμι καὶ πώγων᾽ ἔχω
> σὺ δ᾽ εὐπρόσωπος, λευκός, ἐξυρημένος,

γυναικόφωνος, ἀπαλός, εὐπρεπὴς ἰδεῖν.

Euripides is the speaker: "I then am grey and have a beard, but you [Agathon] are handsome, fair, smooth-shaven, with a woman's voice, soft and attractive." If we were in any doubt about the tenor of his remarks, γυναικόφωνος should settle the question. It is worth noting that here again ἀπαλός "soft" also indicates feminine characteristics. Poor Agathon is the object of Aristophanes' barbs in the same connection earlier in this play (29-32):

Εὐριπίδης:	ἐνταῦθ᾽ Ἀγάθων ὁ κλεωὸς οἰκῶν τυγχάνει ὁ τραγωιδοποιός.
Μνησίλοχος:	ποῖος οὗτος Ἀγάθων;
Εὐ:	ἔστιν τις Ἀγάθων
Μν:	μῶν ὁ μέλας, ὁ καρτερός;
Εὐ:	οὔκ, ἀλλ᾽ ἕτερός τις.

Euripides:	This is the house of the famous Agathon, the tragic poet.
Mnesilochus:	What kind of man is this Agathon?
Eur:	He's an Agathon. . . .
Mnes:	Is he dark and strong?
Eur:	Oh, no, he's quite different.

And on it goes mercilessly. (Notice the association here of μέλας and καρτερός "strong, powerful.")

In the *Frogs* (1089-1093), Dionysus gives a word picture of one of the contestants in the Panathenaea:

ἀφαυάνθην
Παναθηναίοισι γελῶν, ὅτε δὴ
βραδὺς ἄνθρωπός τις ἔθει κύψας
λευκός, πίων, ὑπολειπόμενος,
καὶ δεινὰ ποιῶν.

"I laughed myself dry at the Panathenaea when a slow, white, fat fellow with his head down was running on far behind the rest and doing very badly." The unfortunate runner's poor physical condition is indicated by his pallor and overweight. In a different context, Aristophanes uses χροιὰν λευκήν to mean "clear skin" (*Clouds* 1011-1013). The Just Cause lists the rewards of right living:

ἔξεις ἀεί
στῆθος λιπαρὸν, χροιὰν λευκήν,
ὤμους μεγάλους, γλῶτταν βαιάν,
πυγὴν μεγάλην, πόσθην μικράν.⁵²

If one followed the Unjust Cause, the results would be far different (1017-1018):

χροιὰν ὠχράν, ὤμους μικρούς,
στῆθος λεπτὸν, γλῶτταν μεγάλην.

The contrast in this passage between λευκήν and ὠχράν makes it plain that λευκήν is not simply "pale" and may even be opposed to it. We are reminded of our earlier discussion of λευκός describing cheeks, where we debated whether "whiteness" was an indication of fairness or pallor. We called attention there to Jebb's comment on Bacchylides 16 (17).13; he chose to translate λευκᾶν παρηίδων "fair cheeks" because "the pallor of *fear* is expressed by χλωρός." The contrast in Aristophanes between λευκήν and ὠχράν supports our contention that λευκός describes a healthy "whiteness" on women's cheeks, not a sickly or fearful pallor. It seems, then, that λευκός can be a mean between μέλας and ὠχρός. (Cf. my discussion of μελίχλωρος which, I have suggested, is a shade of complexion lying somewhere between μέλας and λευκός, chapter two pp. 57-60). As Aristotle says,⁵³ all means are likely to be more significant in relation to one extreme than the other; λευκός is usually opposed to μέλας, but certain passages indicate either directly (as Aristophanes *Clouds* 1012, 1017) or by implication (as Bacch. 17.13, Soph. *Ant.* 1239, Eur. *Med.* 923, 1148) the opposition of λευκός to ὠχρός. The latter contrast is

52. The two oldest mss. R and V read χροιὰν λευκήν, others χροιὰν λαμπράν. In our opinion λευκήν is likely the right reading here and λαμπράν a gloss, because λευκός is the more unusual word, λαμπρός being found as the description of a healthy appearance in prose and poetry, e.g. Aristoph. *Peace* 859, Plato *Phaedr.* 250b, Hippocr. *Aer.* 24. Moreover, λευκήν corresponds better to ὠχράν.

53. Aristotle says (*Eth.* 1107a28 — 1108b10) that a mean implies the existence of an excess and a defect, but that it is not simply the middle point between them, as a mathematical mean is. He adds (1108b10 — 1109a19) that the extremes are opposed to the mean and to one another and the mean is opposed to the extremes. However, one of the extremes may be more like the mean than the other. For example, courage is the mean between rashness (the excess) and cowardice (the defect); rashness and cowardice (the two extremes) are opposed, and so are courage and cowardice (the mean to one extreme), whereas courage (the mean) is somewhat like rashness (the extreme).

probably related to the presence or absence of good health.

Plato, in discussing the pet names lovers give to their beloved to excuse faults in appearance, says (*Rep.* 474d, e) that the "dark" (μέλανας) are called manly (ἀνδρικούς) and the "fair" (λευκούς) children of gods (θεῶν παῖδας). Instead of taking "fair" in the pejorative sense "effeminate," the lover turns the fairness by hypocorism into a compliment. The significance of "children of gods" I take as a reflexion of the fact that many Olympians, notably Apollo, were ξανθός "blond" and presumably fair-skinned. In a generally olive-skinned, dark-haired race, the rare blond may have been attributed in jest to "some divine blood in the family a few generations back." What was acceptable, or at least excusable, in a boy was much less desirable in a grown man, hence the usual suggestion of effeminacy in λευκός. It would probably be fair to assume that it carried much the tone of "pretty" in English; girls and women may be pretty, even small boys may be called pretty, but to call a man pretty is no compliment!

VI Dark and Light in Connection with the Emotions

A. φρένες μέλαιναι

Four times in the *Iliad* and once in the *Odyssey* Homer speaks of φρένες μέλαιναι. This formula always occurs at the end of the line in the nominative φρένες ἀμφὶ μέλαιναι (*Il.* 1.103, *Od.* 4.661) or the accusative φρένας ἀμφὶ μέλαινας (*Il.* 17.83, 449, 573). Its invariable position suggests that it is a traditional formula and may be very ancient. Agamemnon's anger is roused against Achilles; "his dark φρένες were mightily filled round with fury and his eyes blazed like fire" (*Il.* 1.103-104):

> μένεος δὲ μέγα φρένες ἀμφὶ μέλαιναι
> πίμπλαντ', ὄσσε δέ οἱ πυρὶ λαμπετόωντι ἐίκτην.

These two lines recur in the *Odyssey* (4.661-662) where Antinous, one of the suitors, is the subject. The other three occurrences in the *Iliad* are all from the seventeenth book. Automedon's φρένες are "filled round with valour and might" (17.499): ἀλκῆς καὶ σθένεος πλῆτο φρένας ἀμφὶ μέλαινας. The courage of the gnat (μυίη) "filled Menelaus around his dark φρένες" (17.573): τοίου μιν θάρσευς πλῆσε φρένας ἀμφὶ μέλαινας. When Hector heard of the death of Euphorbus, "dreadful grief shadowed him around his dark φρένες" (17.83): Ἔκτορα δ᾽ αἰνὸν ἄχος πύκασε φρένας ἀμφὶ μέλαινας. There are two problems which demand our attention here, the identification of the φρένες and the reason for their darkness. The context in which the formula appears suggests that the emotion (anger, grief, courage) comes from outside the φρένες, filling (a form of πίμπλημι) or covering (a form of πυκάζω) them round (ἀμφί).[54] The fact that in each case the φρένες are affected by emotion is an indication that the emotion is the cause of the darkness.

Onians argues at considerable length and with convincing detail that the Homeric φρένες were the lungs.[55] This identification suits better than the traditional translation "midriff, diaphragm" the frequent use of the plural, the place of the φρένες in relation to the rest of the body and its organs, and the interconnection between φρένες and θυμός, which Onians interprets as "breath." The diaphragm is a "pink muscular sheet dividing the organs of the thorax from those of the abdomen"; it cannot claim "to be considered as a plurality, φρένες, or, as the latter are, to be described as μέλαιναι." The lungs, on the other hand, are in two parts and have a dark exterior. The φρένες are said to "enclose the liver" (Od. 9.301), to "shut in the dense heart" (Il. 16.481); the lungs surround both heart and liver. They come out when Patroclus pulls his spear from Sarpedon's chest, a feat which the diaphragm, "taut muscle firmly attached all around," could scarcely accomplish (Il. 16.504). Onians suggests that the most decisive evidence is the word μετάφρενον "the part behind the φρένες." This is clearly and unmistakably defined in Homer as the upper part of the back between the shoulders. This position only makes sense if the φρένες are the lungs not the diaphragm.[56] The θυμός, something "vaporous" (cf. θυμιάω) is in

54. Some editors write ἀμφιμέλαιναι (cf. Homeri opera ed. D. B. Munro and T. W. Allen (3rd ed. Oxford 1920) at Od. 4.661-662), but the Alexandrian critics preferred to write ἀμφὶ μέλαιναι, construing ἀμφί adverbially (according to LSJ s.v. ἀμφιμέλας).

55. Onians pp. 23-40.

56. Onians pp. 23-27; on p. 25 he quotes Piersol's Human Anatomy (Philadelphia 1907) p. 1846: "The adult lung is bluish grey, more or less mottled with black."

the φρένες, i.e. contained by them (Il. 8.202, 9.462). Onians suggests that this vapour is breath contained by the lungs and that it arises from the hot blood concentrated around the heart and lungs.[57] The identification of the φρένες as the midriff or diaphragm is made by the Hippocratic school (V.M. 1.54 ed. C. G. Kühn, Leipzig, 1825-27) and by Plato (Tim. 70a); the transfer assumed by Onians from an earlier meaning "lungs" can be explained by the lack of a proper term for diaphragm, the existence of another term for lungs (πλεύμων), and the closeness in position in the body and in its function in the act of breathing of the diaphragm to the lungs.[58] If the reader finds difficulty in associating the lungs and breathing with emotion, let him consider the list of reactions in terms of breathing given by Onians. "To *pant* with eagerness, to *gasp* or *whistle* with astonishment, to *snort* with indignation, to *sob* with grief, to *yawn* with weariness, to *laugh* with mirth, to *sigh* with sadness or relief are some of the more marked variations of breathing that have found distinct expression in everyday speech. The '*breast heaving with emotion*' is a commonplace. We '*catch our breath*' at a sudden sound, '*hold our breath*' in suspense, '*breathe more freely,*' and so the list might be continued."[59] He is not, of course, relying on modern English idioms to support his argument, but simply giving them as parallel so that we can more easily comprehend the Greek position. He gives many examples from Homer on to illustrate the association of breathing with the emotions; I shall repeat only one of his examples here. Achilles, at the point of reconciliation with Agamemnon, says that "anger waxes like smoke in the breasts of men; so now Agamemnon, king of men, angered me. But we shall let go what has passed, although we are grieved, subduing our own (dear) θυμός in our breasts by necessity" (Il. 18.108, 110-113):

καὶ χόλος
ἀνδρῶν ἐν στήθεσσιν ἀέξεται ἠύτε καπνός·
ὡς ἐμὲ νῦν ἐχόλωσεν ἄναξ ἀνδρῶν Ἀγαμέμνων.
ἀλλὰ τὰ μὲν προτετύχθαι ἐάσομεν ἀχνύμενοί περ,
θυμὸν ἐνὶ στήθεσσι φίλον δαμάσαντες ἀνάγκηι.

57. Onians pp. 44-48.
58. Onians p. 39.
59. Onians p. 50.

The comparison of anger to smoke reminds us of θυμός "vapour" and its cognates: Latin *fumus* "smoke," Sanskrit *dhumah* "vapour, smoke," and Old Slavonic *dymu* "smoke," *duchu* "breath, spirit."[60] Moreover, Achilles' intention to "let bygones be bygones" involved "subduing his θυμός," on Onians' interpretation, "restoring his breathing to normal." We are in a position to appreciate the comparison of anger to smoke, when we understand that the Homeric hero felt anger in his lungs (φρένες) and that this feeling was accompanied by a change of breathing.

Onians takes the formula φρένες μέλαιναι as descriptive of the normal condition and appearance of the lungs, i.e. the lungs are regularly dark. I cannot agree with him on this point, for it seems to me that the darkness is caused by the emotion experienced by their possessor. Professor Woodbury has suggested that the darkness of the φρένες may have been thought to be caused by a sort of smoke. We saw that Achilles compared anger to smoke filling men's breasts. We considered some of the evidence offered by Onians for the identification of the θυμός with "breath," particularly the etymological evidence relating it to cognates meaning "smoke, vapour." Such a smoke or vapour may have been pictured as darkening the φρένες. We called attention to the fact that on each of the occasions when φρένες μέλαιναι is used, the verb is either πίμπλημι "fill" or πυκάζω "cover," with an adverbial ἀμφί. This idea of filling, covering round, or engulfing is quite compatible with the action of smoke. If, as Onians surmised, the vapour arises from the blood, the darkness of the blood may account for the darkening of the φρένες.[61] (For emotion, particularly anger, as dark in Homer, see the following passages where an angry person is compared to night: *Il.* 1.47; *Il.* 12.462-463, and *Od.* 11.606. The last example contains a specific indication of darkness as the point of similarity.) This explanation seems to me to take into account the meaning of φρένες, the Homeric view of emotion, and the particular evidence of the passages in which φρένες μέλαιναι occurs.

Grošelj, in a discussion of this formula, suggested a connection

60. Boisacq s.v. θυμός.
61. Homer describes blood as μέλας frequently: e.g. in *Il.* 4.149, 7.262, 10.298, 469, 11.813. 13.655, 16.529, 18.583, 20.470, 21.119, 23.806, *Od.* 3.455.

between this darkness and bravery.[62] He referred in his argument to Lobeck who related φρένες μέλαιναι to μελάμπυγος, an epithet given to a species of eagle and also to brave, strong men. In support of a connection between the two, he quoted two glosses of Hesychius: s.v. μελάμπυγος · ἀνδρεῖος "brave" and s.v. μέλαιναι φρένες · αἱ δειναὶ καὶ ἰσχυραί "clever and strong." The latter gloss appears to be a guess, with no particular relevance to the Homeric contexts. I do not think that the darkness of the φρένες can be a reference only to bravery, although two of the five occurrences mention bravery or valour (p. 135, Il. 17.499, 573). I take the epithet rather as descriptive of the effect of any emotion on the inner part where a man feels emotion.

B. μελάμπυγος and πύγαργος

The question of the meaning of μελάμπυγος and its opposite, πύγαργος, is somewhat complicated. The Greeks had a proverb "Watch out that you don't meet the Blackrump" — Blackrump standing for "someone brave and strong" as the lexicographers and paroemiographers tell us.[63] The earliest occurrence of this saying is found in Archilochus (fr. 93D), apparently in the story of Heracles and the Cercopes: μή τευ μελαμπύγου τύχῃς.[64] (The fact that it occurs in Archilochus shows that it is a very old saying, since Archilochus is one of the earliest lyric poets; moreover, his use of the expression suggests that it was proverbial in his time, and therefore even earlier than he.) This was the warning a mother gave her two mischievous sons, but they continued heedlessly in rascality until they annoyed Heracles who picked them up and slung them head-down over his shoulder. Then, remembering their mother's warning about the Blackrump, they laughed aloud to

---

62. M. Grošelj in *Ziva Antika* 2 (1952) 77. The reference to C. A. Lobeck is *Aglaophamus* (Regimontii Prussorum 1829) p. 1299. Cf. also F. Buffière *Les mythes d'Homère et la pensée grecque* (Paris 1956) p. 264.

63. Lexicographers: Hesychius s.v. μελάμπυγος · ἀνδρεῖος, τοὺς γὰρ δασεῖς τὰς πυγὰς ἀνδρείους ἐνόμιζον; also s.v. λευκόπυγος · ὁ ἄνανδρος; Photius s.v. μελαμπύγους · ἀνδρείους; Suda s.v. μελαμπύγου τύχοις relates the story of Heracles, giving δασύπρωκτος as a synonym for μελάμπυγος; he adds ὅτι τοὺς λευκοπύγους ὡς γυναικώδεις ἐκωμῴδουν. Paroemiographers: Zenobius 5.10; Anonymous in *Paroemiographi graeci* ed. T. Gaisford (Oxford 1836) p. 74 [629 e cod. Bodleiano]. Cf. also Herod. 7.216, a reference to the "so-called Rock of Melampygus and the seats of the Cercopes."

64. The Cercopes were a race of dwarfs or monkey-men.

find its literal fulfilment in Heracles, whose "black rump" they were in a position to appreciate! (Several ancient commentators explain the darkness as hairiness, see n. 63). As a result of this encounter, the epithet μελάμπυγος came to mean "someone brave and strong," because Heracles was the personification of these virtues. Compare the semantic relationship between ἀνήρ "man" and ἀνδρεῖος, the adjective which describes manly behaviour, with the special meaning "brave, courageous"; the particular virtue of men is bravery.

Scholiast B (Porphyry ?) on Il. 24.315 says that Archilochus called the black eagle μελάμπυγος. Apparently then, as Fraenkel argues from this and other ancient evidence,[65] the proverb referred originally to the eagle, perhaps the same species whose prowess was mentioned in the Iliad (21.252 where Achilles is likened to this, the mightiest and swiftest of birds):

αἰετοῦ οἴματ᾽ ἔχων μέλανος τοῦ θηρητῆρος[66]
ὅς θ᾽ ἅμα κάρτιστός τε καὶ ὤκιστος πετεηνῶν.

Fraenkel points out that in many fables and prophecies an animal is mentioned, but the fulfilment turns out to be a man. Here, he suggests, the warning intends "Watch out for the eagle," but is fulfilled by Heracles.

After the first transfer of the epithet from the eagle to Heracles, μελάμπυγος was used generally of anyone who, like him, was brave and strong. In Aristophanes' Lysistrata, the chorus of old men tell the women that "Myronides was rough (i.e. hairy) and black-rumped to all his foes" (801-803):

καὶ Μυρωνίδης γὰρ ἦν
τραχὺς ἐντεῦθεν μελάμπυ-
γός τε τοῖς ἐχθροῖς ἅπασιν.

The epithet is undoubtedly meant to recall the tale of Heracles; the phrase μελάμπυγος τοῖς ἐχθροῖς could be rendered "a Heracles

65. Fraenkel Aeschylus Agamemnon on line 115.
66. The use of the article (in τοῦ θηρητῆρος) is late; several conjectures have been proposed to remove it. According to Fraenkel, Ahrens suggested μελανόρσου "black-rumped" for μέλανος τοῦ; if he were right, the Homeric eagle could be identified with the μελάμπυγος. Fraenkel clearly likes this emendation, but is cautious about accepting it. Leaf (The Iliad vol. 2 on Il. 21.252) describes it as "still more plausible" than other conjectures such as μελανόσσου "black-eyed" or μελανόστου "black-boned."

to his foes." Eubulus, the 4th century comic poet, writes (fr. 61), "You thought I had no gall and spoke to me as to a fish (*hepatos*, a kind of fish) but I am still one of the Blackrumps":

οὐ ᾤου [σύ] με
χολὴν ἔχειν, ὡς δ᾽ ἡπάτωι μοι διελέγου
ἐγὼ δὲ γ᾽ εἰμὶ τῶν μελαμπύγων ἔτι.

Eubulus apparently connects the epithet μελάμπυγος with the possession of χολή "gall" or "bile." The Greek medical writers thought that there were four humours (χυμοί) in man: phlegm, blood, yellow bile, and black bile.[67] If the humours remained in balance, a man enjoyed good health, but if any one element became too strong or too weak, the man became sick. This applied to mental and emotional as well as physical well-being. Eubulus, then, assigns a lack of spirit or courage to the man who lacks χολή; presumably the man with χολή is also μελάμπυγος. Since one of the forms of bile in the body was black (μέλαινα χολή), it seems likely that Eubulus was explaining the blackness in μελάμπυγος by the blackness of the bile. It does not seem likely that this was the traditional explanation of the epithet; rather Eubulus is offering a new explanation in terms of a modern theory. (Further discussions of the influence of the theory of humours with respect to λευκαὶ φρένες, λευκηπατίας, and μελαγχολία occur later in this section.)

In contrast to μελάμπυγος with its associations of bravery and strength, another species of eagle, πύγαργος is characterized as cowardly and despicable.[68] The earliest mention of it is found in Archilochus (fr. 93D *testimonia*). To preserve the contrast which is obviously intended between μελάμπυγος, "blackrumped" and πύγαργος, it seems best to translate the latter "whiterumped" although ἀργός has a wider meaning than simply "white." Sophocles used πύγαργος for "coward" (fr. 1085 Pearson), as we learn from an entry in the *Etymologicum Magnum* (p. 695, 50 s.v. πύγαργος). Lycophron, a tragic poet of the third century B.C.,

67. The theory of humours is first clearly stated in the Hippocratean *Nature of Man* (see *Hippocrates*, Loeb vol. 4, pp. 10-13, ed. W. H. S. Jones London 1931).

68. For descriptions of the eagles, see D'Arcy Thompson, p. 255 πύγαργος (a) and p. 197 μελάμπυγος and μελανάετος. It is interesting that the Peripatetic writer of the *History of Animals* (618 b 18) ignores the tradition that makes πύγαργος a coward and says that he flies to mountains and woods διὰ τὸ θάρσος.

called Paris a "whiterumped sailor" (90-91): ναύτην πύγαργον.[69] Tzetzes, in a comment on these lines, gives as synonyms for πύγαργον, δειλὸν, αἰσχρὸν ἢ ἅρπαγα, "cowardly, shameful, or rapacious"; he gives Archilochus as his authority for ἅρπαξ. Over the span of several centuries, then, these two eagles, with dispositions as unlike as their tail feathers, gave their species names to men who behaved as they were supposed to behave. The Peripatetic who compiled a history of animals mentions several species of eagle, among them πύγαργος, also called νεβροφόνος, and μελανάετος, also called λαγωφόνος (Arist. H.A. 618b19ff), but he does not draw any distinction in disposition between them (see also n. 68). It seems likely that the Greeks were influenced in their characterization of the eagles by the implications of dark and light in regard to people and to disposition, rather than by actual observation of the birds. Animals in popular lore have very definite characteristics which are not always upheld by natural historians.[70] Once these characteristics are fixed in the popular mind by fables, they are almost impossible to erase. And so with blackrumped and whiterumped eagles. Whether or not the two species behaved as heroes or cowards is irrelevant in the face of Greek belief that they did.

These two eagles appear again, Fraenkel suggests, in Aeschylus' *Agamemnon* where the chorus recounts the omen which appeared at the outset of the Trojan expedition (110-115):

> ὅπως Ἀχαιῶν δίθρονον κράτος
> πέμπει . . .
> θούριος ὄρνις Τευκρίδ᾽ ἐπ᾽ αἶαν
> οἰωνῶν βασιλεὺς βασιλεῦσι νεῶν ὁ κελαινὸς ὅ τ᾽ ἐξόπιν
> ἀργᾶς[71]
> φανέντες ἴκταρ μελάθρων. . . .

(I can tell) "how the rushing bird [or omen] sent the two-throned

69. Cf. E. Scheer's edition of Lycophron (Berlin 1881-1908) with scholia. It is interesting that both Helen's husbands, Menelaus and Paris, were considered second-rate by antiquity. On Menelaus, see below.

70. In fable, the fox is cunning, the lion king of the beasts, but naturalists dispute both these characterizations.

71. Ἀργᾶς is taken by J. D. Denniston and D. L. Page *Aeschylus Agamemnon* (Oxford 1957) on lines 114f as a contraction of ἀργάεις just as τιμῆς is of τιμήεις (*Il.* 9.605).

might of the Achaeans against the land of Teucer, the king of birds, the black-tailed and also the white-tailed, appearing hard by the palace to the kings of the ships." The two eagles were identified by Calchas as the two sons of Atreus (line 122). We have two problems to consider here: first, are the eagles in *Agamemnon* the μελάμπυγος and πύγαργος; secondly, do they have the characteristics of the blackrumped and whiterumped eagles? On first reading, the Greek text might seem to mean that one eagle was dark (κελαινός) and the other white-tailed (ἐξόπιν ἀργᾶς). This does not necessarily exclude a reference to the black-tailed eagle. Wilamowitz, however, has seen that in the construction of this sentence (the *schema Pindaricum*) the two singular subjects are closely bound together; he takes ἐξόπιν with both ἀργᾶς and κελαινός, translating "Das Schwanzgefieder des einen weiss, des anderen schwarz."[72] This seems to me to be the correct understanding of the lines. But even if the two eagles can be identified as the blackrumped and the whiterumped, some commentators argue that they do not represent the brave man and the coward.[73] There is, to be sure, nothing specific said about their characters, but certain indications in the text allow us, even encourage us, to draw conclusions about Agamemnon and Menelaus from the symbol of the eagles. As one hears or reads lines 110-115 one might assume that there was only one bird (θούριος ὄρνις, οἰωνῶν βασιλεύς); the white-tailed eagle appears almost as an afterthought, his assistance acknowledged in the participle (φανέντες). This word order encourages us to think of the black-tailed eagle as the leader and the white-tail as very much a follower. Then, the two sons of Atreus are described as "differing in character (or courage)" (lines 122-123): δύο λήμασι δισσούς/ Ἀτρείδας. This seems to me to imply a reference to the well-known difference between the eagles. Although the quarrel was Menelaus' since Helen was his wife, the expedition was organized and led by

72. U. von Wilamowitz-Moellendorff *Euripides Herakles* (Berlin, Leipzig 1889) on line 237.
73. Denniston and Page on line 122 argue that the reference is not to courage, but to character, i.e. Menelaus is a "less dominating character" than Agamemnon. They call attention to the epithet μαχίμους which, they say, applies "equally to both kings." The word, however, could refer simply to the fact that both are "at war" not necessarily "warlike."

Agamemnon. Menelaus was described by Homer as a "faint-hearted warrior" μαλθακὸς αἰχμητής (*Il.* 17.588). He receives much harsher treatment in the hands of later writers (cf. Plato *Symp.* 174c, Eur. *Orest.* 754, 1201-1202). Considering what the Greeks felt about the two brothers' characters and believed about the eagles, it is simply perverse to refuse to see the black-tailed eagle here as the brave fighter and leader, typifying Agamemnon "king of men," and the white-tailed eagle as the coward typifying Menelaus, "the faint-hearted warrior." The fact that they are not called μελάμπυγος and πύγαργος Fraenkel attributes to Aeschylus' delicacy, πυγή being more suited to comedy, satire or satyr plays, than to tragic diction.[74]

It was mentioned earlier that to translate πύγαργος as "white rumped" in order to contrast with μελάμπυγος, does not give the most accurate rendering of the Greek. Ἀργός combines brightness and movement in a way which we sometimes find difficult to comprehend. Objects, often animals, which move quickly or have a sheen or gloss are so described; brightness combined with swiftness or play of light seems to be the characteristic indicated (cf. Appendix II). So the epithet πύγαργος is well chosen; for when a bird is at rest, any white tail feathers are folded in, but when he rises in flight, they flash out brightly and suddenly. Compare the English expression (which similarly implies cowardice) "to show the white feather," which is derived from the fact that a game-cock with a white feather in his tail shows by it that he is not bred true (*ONED* s.v. white, feather). Although the origins of the expressions are apparently unrelated, it is interesting that the Greek -αργος (flash of white) and the English "show" both suggest that the coward is suddenly manifest, perhaps as he turns tail in the midst of the action.

C. The Dark Heart and Its Opposite

Several times in poetry after Homer the φρήν and the heart (καρδία) are given the epithet μέλας "dark." Theognis, deprived of his property, reports that he heard the voice of the bird which

---

74. Note the later coinage λευκόπυγος for πύγαργος in Alex. 321; and λευκοπρωκτός in Call. *Com.* 11.2; in both contexts the epithet signifies cowardice.

comes as herald of the ploughing season, "and it smote my dark heart because other men hold my flowery fields" (1199-1200)

καί μοι κραδίην ἐπάταξε μέλαιναν,
ὅττι μοι εὐανθεῖς ἄλλοι ἔχουσιν ἀγρούς.

The poet's reaction is one of grief and indignation; here, I suggest, as in the case of the Homeric formula φρένες μέλαιναι, darkness of heart is associated with emotion. It looks as if Theognis were simply adapting a traditional formula in his poetry.[75]

Pindar twice describes the heart as dark. He comments on change in human fortunes in a fragment preserved by the Scholiast in connection with *Olympian* 2.23-24, which reads "Grievous sorrow falls in the presence of greater good": πένθος δὲ πίτνει βαρὺ/ κρεσσόνων πρὸς ἀγαθῶν, i.e. good fortune has the power to make one forget past sorrow. The Scholiast comments: ἐὰν δὲ χωρὶς τοῦ σ γράφηται (i.e. πρὸ instead of πρὸς), ἔσται τὸ νόημα τοιοῦτον. πρὸ τῶν ἀγαθῶν τοῖς ἀνθρώποις τὰ κακά. ὅπερ καὶ ἐν ἑτέρωι φησίν (fr. 225):

ὁπόταν θεὸς ἀνδρὶ χάρμα πέμψηι,
πάρος μέλαιναν κραδίαν ἐστυφέλιξεν.[76]

The Scholiast understands Pindar to mean "before good things, evils come to men" in this fragment. I therefore translate "Whenever a god sends joy to a man, hitherto he struck hard at his dark heart." Bowra interprets differently "When God sends delight to a man, He knocks hard on the heart which was black before."[77] He takes the blackness of heart to be melancholy.[78] The first difficulty I find in Bowra's translation concerns the meaning of the verb στυφελίζω which elsewhere implies an unpleasant use of

75. Kober pp. 34-35 argues μέλας is associated with undesirable qualities, especially in mental attitudes. She interprets Theognis' reaction as "jealousy," Pindar in fr. 225 and fr. 123.5 as "hard-heartedness" and *Scol. Anon.* 32.4 D. as "general wickedness"; but it is hardly reasonable to attribute "undesirable qualities" to a man who grieves because his lands have been expropriated.

76. *Scholia Vetera in Pindari Carmina* vol. 1 ed. A. B. Drachmann (Leipzig, 1903) on *Olymp.* 2.42e.

77. C. M. Bowra *Pindar* (Oxford 1964) p. 246.

78. H. W. Smyth *Greek Melic Poets* p. 373 interprets the darkness of heart in this fragment as sadness, but he comments on a general level, "The epithet 'black' is often applied to the heart and mind when filled with passion;" hence one supposes that he translates μέλαινα "sad" because of a connection with passion, rather than with gloom. For a discussion of μέλας and sadness, see chapter five, section three.

power "strike hard, treat roughly, maltreat" (*LSJ* s.v.). Although Bowra's translation "He knocks hard" may sound rough, the sense requires that the action be, in fact, pleasant, a change from former sadness. It seems to me that the verb is far more suitable to the earlier action of the god in sending unhappiness and I have indicated this in my translation. The second difficulty in Bowra's interpretation relates to the comment of the Scholiast who tells us that, in the fragment, Pindar is saying "before good things, evils befall men." This suggests that the Scholiast understood one line to be describing present good fortune, and the second, past misfortune. On Bowra's interpretation, the misfortune has to be supplied from the phrase πάρος μέλαιναν κραδίαν "his formerly dark heart." But from our examination of μέλας in connection with emotion, it seems unlikely that a Greek would supply the meaning "sad, melancholy" for μέλαιναν and the sense "the heart of a man who has suffered misfortune" for the phrase. The darkness of heart is related here, not to sadness, but, more appropriately, to the poetic convention derived from Homer of describing the φρήν or the heart as dark with emotion. Would Bowra argue that the man with the "heart which was black before" has now a "white" heart; and if so, what light does this shed on *Pythian* 4.109-110? It seems likelier that Pindar and other Greeks pictured the normal condition of the heart as μέλας, in contrast to which λευκαὶ φρένες represented a deviation from the norm (see the discussion of Pelias' λευκαὶ φρένες below).

The phrase μέλαιναν καρδίαν is apparently also an *epitheton ornans* in the poem addressed to Theoxenus (fr. 123):

χρῆν μὲν κατὰ καιρὸν ἐρώτων δρέπεσθαι, θυμέ, σὺν ἁλικίαι,
τὰς δὲ Θεοξένου ἀκτῖνας πρὸς ὄσσων
μαρμαρυζοίσας δρακείς
ὃς μὴ πόθωι κυμαίνεται, ἐξ ἀδάμαντος
ἢ σιδάρου κεχάλκευται μέλαιναν καρδίαν

ψυχρᾶι φλογί, πρὸς δ' Ἀφροδίτας ἀτιμασθεὶς ἑλικογλεφάρου
ἢ περὶ χρήμασι μοχθίζει βιαίως
ἢ γυναικείωι θράσει
ψυχὰν φορεῖται πᾶσαν ὁδὸν θεραπεύων.

ἀλλ᾽ ἐγὼ τᾶς ἕκατι κηρὸς ὡς δαχθεὶς ἕλαι

ἱρᾶν μελισσᾶν τάκομαι, εὖτ᾽ ἂν ἴδω
παίδων νεόγυιον ἐς ἥβαν.

"It is right to pluck the blooms of love in season, in one's youth, my heart. Whoever beholds the dazzling rays from the eyes of Theoxenus and does not swell with passion, has had his dark heart forged from adamant or iron with a cold flame. He is dishonoured by dark-eyed Aphrodite[79] and either is compelled to labour for money or is borne along all the road nurturing his life with womanly courage. But I melt because of her, like the wax of the sacred bees when pricked by heat, whenever I look at young-limbed boys in their prime." There are many difficulties of reading and interpretation in these few lines, some of which we shall consider. Pindar's basic meaning is, I think, clear; anyone who is not moved by Theoxenus' beauty is unnatural. This is shown in three ways: he has been dishonoured by the goddess of love and is either money-mad or (and this is debatable) a coward. Pindar, himself, is not like this. Since we are interested in the meaning of μέλαιναν καρδίαν, we shall concentrate our attention on the immediate context of this phrase (lines 4-6) and also on Pindar's definition of the type of man who is not affected by passion (lines 6-9).

Farnell relates the darkness of the heart to the metaphor of forged metal; "the *dark* metal of his heart has never been heated to a *red* glow."[80] If we had no other occurrences of the phrase "dark heart," the simplicity of this view in the context would recommend itself very strongly. The heart is dark because the metal out of which it is made is dark; if it were heated in the *fire*, instead of an ineffective cold flame, it would glow red with emotion. We do, however, have other examples of "dark heart" where there is no question of a similar connection; on the contrary, "darkness" is a normal state for the heart. Our suggestion is that μέλαινα καρδία is a rephrasing of the traditional

---

79. On ἑλίκωψ see Page *History and the Homeric Iliad* pp. 244-245 and p. 283, nn. 70-71, where he argues convincingly for the meaning "black-eyed."
80. G. Farnell *Greek Lyric Poetry* (London 1891) p. 421 on Pind. fr. 123.

formula φρένες μέλαιναι. Van Groningen argues that blackness is applied by Pindar "à tout ce qui est laid et vil, triste et sombre, inhumain."[81] Of the four examples he gives to illustrate this quality in Pindar, two are traditional; the darkness of death (*Pyth.* 11.56) and of the house of Hades where the dead make their abode (*Olymp.* 14.20) occur in poetry as early as Homer (see chapter five, section three). His third example is "le silence qui plonge dans l'obscurité celui qui ne possède rien" (fr. 94a.9-10): ὁ δὲ μηδὲν ἔχων ὑπὸ σιγᾶι μελαίναι κάρα κέκρυπται. Here there is an opposition implied between the brightness of fame and the darkness of obscurity; I suggest that this is an example of synaesthesia and that, for Pindar, fame was a kind of light which illumined its possessor, whereas the man who was not talked about seemed to be covered in darkness (see chapter five, section six). The qualities of ugliness and sadness which van Groningen sees in these examples are, I suggest, incidental or derived. The fourth example is Pindar's fragment 225 which we examined earlier. Van Groningen interprets μέλαιναν κραδίαν as "le coeur privé de lumière"[82]; he offers no justification for this, but presumably he is thinking of the grouping of joy and light in Greek thought. In our opinion van Groningen has not been able to show that darkness connotes sadness, ugliness or wickedness in Pindar. We submit, then, that in view of the examples of dark φρένες or dark heart, the phrase μέλαιναν καρδίαν in fr. 123 should be treated as a traditional formula, with little if any difference from the bare καρδίαν. (For a further discussion of fr. 123, see Appendix V.)

Pindar shows the unnatural quality of a man in fr. 123 by his figure of forging without heat; the heart, the organ of affection, is forged with a cold flame, i.e. ineffectively or falsely.[83] In *Pythian* 4.109-110, Pelias is described by Jason as "trusting in his white φρένες":

πεύθομαι γάρ νιν Πελίαν ἄθεμιν λευκαῖς πιθήσαντα φρασίν
ἀμετέρων ἀποσυλᾶσαι βιαίως ἀρχεδικᾶν τοκέων.

---

81. B. A. van Groningen *Pindare au banquet* (Leiden 1960) p. 57.
82. *Ibid.* p. 57.
83. Another metaphor of forging is found in *Pyth.* 1.86 where the tongue is the member on the anvil. See L. Woodbury in *TAPA* 86 (1955) 31-39.

"For I hear that unrighteous Pelias, trusting in his white heart, took power by force from my parents, the legitimate possessors." There are points of similarity between the insensitive man of fr. 123 and Pelias. We might say that Pelias was "cold-hearted" (as in fr. 123), but Pindar chooses instead to call him "white-hearted" in contrast with the Homeric φρένες μέλαιναι. What I am suggesting in this discussion is that both images have the same purport. The insensitive man was compelled to labour for money (βιαίως); Pelias took from Jason's parents what was theirs by force (βιαίως). It is true that force *acted upon* the first man, whereas it was *used* by Pelias, but I suspect that the Greeks would think that a man who used force to gain his ends was being forced by the desire for gain, i.e. that Pelias was compelled to behave as he did. (The reverse is, of course, not necessarily true, that a man who is compelled to labour for profit will use force to gain what he wants.) Secondly, both the insensitive man and Pelias were dishonoured by the gods: the former was "dishonoured by Aphrodite," the latter disregarded what the gods laid down (ἄθεμιν) and was rejected by the Moirae because of this behaviour (line 145). The insensitive man might be "carried along all the way with womanly courage caring for his life." Pelias did not undertake the search for the Fleece himself, so he was apparently careful of himself. (Cf. below the connection between whiteness of the liver [λευκηπατίας] and cowardice, and our earlier observation of bile as an indication of bravery). He contrasts his age with Jason's youth, using the same verb to describe the burgeoning of youth as was used in fr. 123.4 for the swelling of passion (157-158):

ἀλλ᾽ ἤδη με γηραιὸν μέρος ἁλικίας
ἀμφιπολεῖ σὸν δ᾽ ἄνθος ἥβας ἄρτι κυμαίνει.

"Already old age is my companion, but the flower of your youth is just now swelling." If youth and passion both swell (κυμαίνω), we can assume an affinity between them. Old age, by implication, being incapable of "swelling" is also incapable of passion. I suggest that this lack of passion is a third resemblance between the insensitive man and Pelias. Since they are alike in behaviour, it seems to me that Pelias' "trusting in white φρένες" is similar in meaning to "a black heart forged with a cold flame." There is a negative quality in each man, expressed in the one case by the abnormal whiteness of the φρένες and in the other by the coldness of the flame (which would not be effective in forging). There are other influences at work in the phrase λευκαῖς πιθήσαντα φρασίν. Obviously λευκαῖς φρασίν are in contrast to the Homeric φρένες μέλαιναι. If we were right in interpreting the Homeric formula as the normal and healthy response to emotion then Pelias' φρένες are unresponsive. Perhaps Pindar and his hearers would think of the comment of Agamemnon when he confessed that his actions against Achilles had been wrong (Il. 9.119): ἀλλ᾽ ἐπεὶ ἀασάμην φρεσὶ λευγαλέῃσι πιθήσας. "But since I was deluded trusting in my shameful heart . . ." The expressions are so similar that it is hard to believe that Pindar was not thinking of the Homeric passage.[84] The coincidence of participle and noun suggest that the adjectives are also related.

Stanford connects the "pallor" of Pelias' φρένες with a thread running through the poem by which Pelias (πολιός) is characterized as the "Grey Man" and Jason the golden youth.[85] Pelias is preoccupied with age and greyness: he stresses his advanced years (lines 157-158, above); he asks Jason's parentage in an odd manner (line 98): καὶ τίς ἀνθρώπων σε χαμαιγενέων πολιᾶς ἐξάνηκεν γαστρός; "Who bore you from a grey womb?" Because he is the Grey Man, his φρένες, the seat of emotion, are pale, colourless. Stanford offers good reason for Pindar's substitution of "white" for "dark" as an epithet of the φρένες. This is the artistic or poetic reason, with λευκαί φρένες as part of the imagery; but there is also an historic reason, an opposition to φρένες μέλαιναι and an echo of φρεσὶ λευγαλέῃσι πιθήσας. Each of these reasons complements the other.

I suggest that, since φρένες μέλαιναι are those which react to emotion the best English rendering for λευκαῖς πιθήσαντα φρασίν is "trusting in his insensitive heart." (Although we saw that φρένες

84. Farnell Pindar vol. 2 on Pyth. 4.109; Farnell suggests that Pindar may have written λευγαῖς, a variant of λευγαλέῃσι "wretched, sad, sorry"; if this were shown to be the case, this passage would have no connection with light and dark contrasts. But Hesychius' glosses (cf. n. 86) bear witness to λευκαῖς as the reading in antiquity, as well as the mss. tradition itself. It is possible that Pindar read λευκαλέῃσι in Homer.

85. W. B. Stanford "Pelias and his Pallid Wits" in Phoenix Supplementary Volume I ed. M. E. White Studies in Honour of Gilbert Norwood (Toronto 1952) pp. 42-45.

can be read as the lungs in early poetry, it seems better in translating to substitute the English seat of emotion, the heart, when the emotions are clearly involved.)[86]

Whiteness was connected with the liver in the word λευκηπατίας "white-livered," a by-word, according to the Peripatetic Clearchus, for the coward (fr. 40):[87] Κλέαρχος [ἐν] τῶι περὶ βίων φησὶ/ συμβαίνειν τι περὶ τὸ ἧπαρ ἐπί τινων, ὃ δειλοὺς ποιεῖ. εἰρῆσθαι οὖν ἐπὶ τῶν τοιούτων τὴν παροιμίαν. This rather vague account suggests that whiteness was an abnormal state for the liver and caused cowardice. Λευκηπατίας reminds us of the English "lily-livered," also a synonym for "coward." An account similar to Clearchus' is preserved in the Suda s.v. λευχηπατίας (sic). An unknown comic poet, however, used λευκηπατίας as a synonym for ὁ εὐήθης "simple-minded" (Com. Adesp. 1072 K). This suggests that the reference in λευκηπατίας was not limited to cowardice. Εὐήθης is often used in a bad sense "simple, silly, foolish" (LSJ s.v. εὐήθης). The connection of whiteness and the liver is likely related to the theory of humours and in particular to black bile, since bile is produced by the liver. A lack of black bile in the system would result in a white liver. Compare Eubulus (fr. 61 above) who contrasts someone who has no "gall" or "bile" with a brave man (μελάμπυγος). He credits bile (presumably black, since it makes a man μελάμπυγος) with giving courage. On the other hand, an excess of black bile causes depression, as in μελαγχολία (see below).

In the writing of the dramatists we find blackness (or darkness) associated with organs of the body, and in their uses there is some indication of a movement toward the English concept of "black-hearted" in the sense of "wicked," and away from the associations of the Homeric formula. The chorus in the Persae consider with foreboding the expedition which had gone out against Greece. They depict their feeling in a vivid phrase: "for this reason, my dark-clad heart is gashed with fear" (115-116):

---

86. Hesychius' gloss on λευκαὶ φρένες: μαινόμεναι, ἀγαθαί, λαμπραί, ἥμεροι, is apparently a string of guesses, none of which fits Pindar's context. His gloss on λευκῶν πραπίδων· κακῶν φρενῶν is closer to the correct meaning, although it is too general to be helpful.

87. In Die Schule des Aristotles ed. F. Wehrli (Basel 1948) Heft 3, as reported by Zenobius 4.87.

ταῦτά μοι μελαγχίτων
φρὴν ἀμύσσεται φόβωι.

Broadhead thinks that the latter part of the compound
μελαγχίτων is meant to suggest the garments of mourning.[88] In
their minds, the chorus has already put on mourning. This gives a
highly poetic interpretation to the passage and fits well with the
verb ἀμύσσω "gash, tear," since the laceration of the cheeks was
also a sign of mourning. Onians, on the other hand, takes the
epithet as an anatomical description; the lungs are covered with a
dark protective casing, the *chiton* (cf. n. 56). Both these
explanations contribute to our understanding of μελαγχίτων.
Whatever the φρὴν is for Aeschylus, it is normally dark; hence the
epithet fits in the poetic tradition with an added significance. In
this example, darkness is caused by emotion (fear) and no
suggestion of wickedness is involved. Fear is also the cause of
darkness in two other cases in Aeschylus. The chorus in the
Supplices declares, "My dark heart is shaken" (line 785):
κελαινόχρως δὲ πάλλεταί μοι καρδία. The chorus in the *Choe-
phoroe* expresses the same reaction in similar words. "My dear
heart again is shaken and my inward parts are darkened" (line 410,
413-414):

πέπαλται δ᾽ αὐτέ μοι φίλον κέαρ. . .
σπλάγχνα δέ μοι κελαινοῦται.

The σπλάγχνα include heart, lungs, liver, and kidneys (*LSJ* s.v.) so
this seems to belong in the same poetic tradition, although
κελαινός has replaced μέλας. But in the *Eumenides* we find, for
the first time, a possible suggestion of dark *qua* wicked rather than
dark *qua* emotionally responsive. Orestes relates the murder of his
father, Agamamnon, by his mother, Clytemnestra (459-461):

ἀλλά νιν κελαινόφρων ἐμή
μήτηρ κατέκτα, ποικίλοις ἀγρεύμασι
κρύψασ᾽ ἃ λουτρῶν ἐξεμαρτύρει φόνον.

"But my dark-hearted mother killed him, covering him with an
intricate net which bore witness to the slaughter in the bath."

---

88. H. D. Broadhead *The Persae of Aeschylus* (Cambridge 1960) on lines 115-116.

Since Orestes is clearly censuring his mother's action, one is inclined to translate κελαινόφρων as "black-hearted" i.e. "wicked." Perhaps the change to κελαινό- was made here to avoid recalling the Homeric φρένες μέλαιναι, although κελαινός sometimes appears to be a synonym for μέλας (see *Choeph.* 413-414, and *Supp.* 785).

In Sophocles' one reference to "dark soul," there is a suggestion of wickedness and it is noteworthy that he uses κελαινό-. The chorus in *Ajax* refers to Odysseus: "the much-enduring man exults arrogantly in his dark heart" (line 955-956):

η ρα κελαινώπαν θυμὸν ἐφυβρίζει
πολύτλας ἀνήρ.

Stanford interprets κελαινώπαν as "deeply stirred," thus preserving the traditional connection with emotion;[89] Jebb, on the other hand, prefers to take the darkness as wickedness and also gives full value to the suffix -ωπ-: "the dark soul which watches from its place of concealment with malevolent joy"(cf. *Philoct.* 1013-1014 ἀλλ᾽ ἡ κακὴ σὴ διὰ μυχῶνδ βλέπουσ᾽ ἀεὶ ψυχή).[90] Since Sophocles uses other compounds in -ωπ- without stress on the suffix, as Stanford points out, this interpretation of Jebb's seems rather far-fetched. But his interpretation of dark as "malevolent" is preferable to Stanford's since it suits the censuring tone of the chorus better (cf. ἐφυβρίζει, *hybris*). Like κελαινόφρων in *Eumenides* 459, κελαινώπαν seems to indicate wickedness.

In a scolion attributed to Solon (but undoubtedly later in date), we read "A double-speaking tongue sounds forth from a dark heart" (*Scol. Anon.* 32.4): γλῶσσα δέ οἱ διχόμυθος ἐκ μελαίνας φρενὸς γεγωνῆι. Since the tongue is criticized, we may assume that the darkness of the φρήν betokens wickedness. Since the composer of a "popular song" is not so likely to show sensitivity in his diction as a dramatic poet like Aeschylus or Sophocles, we can account for the appearance of μέλας in the scolion, rather than κελαινός which the dramatists were careful to use when they meant "wicked." If the scolion is later than the fifth century, this may be another reason for the use of μέλας. For

89. W. B. Stanford *Sophocles Ajax* (London 1963) on line 954.
90. R. C. Jebb *The Ajax of Sophocles* (London 1898) on line 955.

the tongue drawing on the φρήν cf. Pindar *Nemean* 4.6-8. Since the tongue draws on, or sounds forth from the φρήν, the double-dealing of the tongue is the result of the darkness of the φρήν in the scolion. (For μέλας suggesting wickedness elsewhere, see Plut. 2.12d μέλανες ἄνθρωποι and Marcus Antoninus 4.28 μέλαν ἦθος).

In the *Frogs* of Aristophanes there is a reference to the "dark-hearted rock of Styx" (line 470): Στυγός μελανοκάρδιος πέτρα, on which the Scholiast comments: ἐκ μεταφορᾶς τῶν ἀγρίων ἀνθρώπων, οὓς διὰ τὴν ἐνοῦσαν αὐτοῖς ἀγριότητα μελαγκαρδίους φασί. We know that the Scholiast, at any rate, thought that "black-heartedness" was evidence of savagery, perhaps even cruelty, of character. In the context in Aristophanes, the compound is a (ἅπαξ λεγόμενον) parody of tragic style and seems to have been chosen for effect, although the meaning "savage, cruel" is not inappropriate to the rock of Styx.

We find several occurrences in comedy of the verb μελαγχολάω "to be melancholy-mad" (Aristoph. *Birds* 14, *Eccles.* 251, *Plutus* 12, 366, 903; *Com. Adesp.* fr. 553). This verb and its noun μελαγχολία are derived from the humour of black bile, μέλαινα χολή. An excess of black bile was as bad, in its way, as a lack. A man in whom black bile became too powerful (in relation to the other humours) suffered from "melancholia." Jones has an interesting discussion of melancholia, which, he says, in popular speech, could mean anything from biliousness to a nervous breakdown, but, in medical writers, meant the period of prostration physical and mental which followed malaria and which was supposed to be caused by black bile.[91] Symptoms which resembled this prostration were popularly supposed to be caused by melancholia, hence the comic poets' use which is as vague as our "nervous breakdown."

---

91. W. H. S. Jones *Malaria and Greek History to which is added The History of Greek Therapeutics and the Malaria Theory* by E. T. Withington (Manchester 1909) pp. 98-101. The author's brother, Dr. G. E. Gray, who has practised for a number of years in Thailand and is familiar with malaria, explained the physical basis for thinking that prostration following malaria was caused by black bile. Malaria destroys the red blood cells and liberates the haemoglobin (haemolysis); these protein molecules escape in the urine in the most severe cases, giving it a black appearance; in less severe cases, they are gradually cleared in the bile, which is also black.

Finally, there is a passage which, though a little farther afield, might further demonstrate the connection between μέλας and emotion. Bacchylides describes the scene on board ship as the fourteen Athenians and Theseus return with Minos to Crete. Minos is attracted by one of the maidens, reaches his hand to touch her cheeks, when Theseus intervenes (17.16-19):

ἴδεν δὲ Θησεύς,
μέλαν δ᾽ ὑπ᾽ ὀφρύων
δίνασεν ὄμμα, καρδίαν τε οἱ
σχέτλιον ἄμυξεν ἄλγος. . . .

"But Theseus saw and his dark eye whirled beneath his brow and cruel pain pricked his heart." As far as we know, Bacchylides had no poetic precedent for describing the eye as μέλας. Dark eyes in Homer and the lyric poets are represented as κυανῶπις and perhaps ἑλίκωψ (n. 79.) (In prose, however, μέλας is used; see chapter three pp. 27, 101). From the context we see evidence of Theseus' anger: δίνασεν ὄμμα illustrates his agitation; ὑπ᾽ ὀφρύων outlines his disapproving frown; and μέλαν can be taken as a detail of his spirited resistance to Minos. (Recall the use of κυάνεος to describe the eyebrows of Zeus and Hera [Il. 1.528, 15.102, 17.209] in chapter three). This interpretation of μέλαν becomes even more convincing after an examination of the meaning of λειρίων ὀμμάτων in the same poem (17.94-96, see Appendix I).

VII Conclusion

With respect to outward appearance, the early Greek poets reinforced their observations of the differences between the sexes by describing women as "white" and men, less frequently, as "black." This is the literary expression of a convention which is as old as Egyptian art and persisted for many years in the Greek world, that of painting women's flesh white and men's dark. By marking the contrast in this way, the ideal of manly or womanly beauty is emphasized. It is similar in spirit to "Vive la difference." It was a compliment to describe a woman as λευκός, but an insult to a man who ought to be μέλας. A real man was characterized above all by bravery, the manly virtue, and so darkness of complexion was thought to be indicative of courage.

When the poets were writing of the inner man, they regarded darkness as the normal state. It is difficult for us to equate good (or normal) with blackness, because of the Judaeo-Christian influence in our background where, in matters of the heart, white is good and black evil. This association is supported by the figure of cleansing resulting in purity or whiteness and connections between blackness and dirt or sin. This view is foreign to the early Greeks; they thought of darkness as the normal state of the internal organs, probably because they were familiar with their physical appearance. (Homer's understanding of the reasons for internal darkness certainly differs from the understanding of later writers.) Whiteness of the internal organs was indicative of abnormality as we found in Pelias in Pindar (*Pyth.* 4.109).

It is interesting to see in these cases the Greek tendency to polarize by describing one extreme as white and the other as black.

Five
Dark and Light Contrasts, Part Two

I Introduction

In this, the second part of the study of contrasts, we shall be looking at the physical and religious world of the Greeks and at the way they tended to describe opposites in their world as "dark" or "light." We shall look first at the division between day and night, as this was one of the basic distinctions for the early Greeks and on it they based many other contrasts. On the side of night and darkness, they placed storm, death, and sadness; on the side of day and brightness, fair weather, life, and joy. In the study of life and death, we shall see that death was like dark night, whereas life was "seeing the light of the sun"; because death was dark, the Greeks wore dark clothing for mourning and in contrast considered white clothing most suitable for a festive occasion. In section four we shall consider the division of the gods of the Greeks into Olympian and chthonian, and shall see that the chthonian gods are dark and for the most part receive dark animals in sacrifice. The Olympians, however, appeared in human form and therefore fell into the general division between the sexes (dark men and light women) rather than being characterized as "white" in opposition to the nether gods. There was a tendency to offer white animals to those who, like the Sun and the Dioscuri, were connected with light and brightness. Certain gods were described as "white": Leucothea, the sea nymph who helped Odysseus, and the Dioscuri who brought calm to sailors in a storm.

In section five we investigate the opposition of earth and sky, which seems to have been the basis for describing earth as "dark."

157

We shall also examine the various "tables of opposites" based on what is known of Parmenidean and Pythagorean opposites and shall see a definite relationship between the opposites on one side of the scale as against those on the other side.

Finally, we turn briefly in section six to three dark and light contrasts: hair, water, and fame and oblivion. The second and third are related to other sections of this chapter, the first seems to be a contrast unto itself.

II Night and Day

Cleobulus, one of the seven wise men of ancient Greece, is supposed to have composed this riddle (fr. 1D.):

εἷς ὁ πατήρ, παῖδες δὲ δυώδεκα τῶν δὲ ἑκάστωι
κοῦραι ἑξήκοντα διάνδιχα εἶδος ἔχουσαι·
αἳ μὲν λευκαὶ ἔασιν ἰδεῖν, αἳ δ' αὖτε μέλαιναι·
ἀθάνατοι δέ τ' ἐοῦσαι, ἀποφθινύθουσιν ἅπασαι.

"There is one father and twelve sons; each of the sons has sixty daughters who are of two different forms; some are white in appearance and others in contrast are black. All are immortal, yet they perish." The answer to the riddle is, of course, that the father is the year, his sons the twelve months, and their daughters the thirty days and thirty nights of each month. Instead of treating day and night as a unit, as we usually do, the author of the riddle regarded them as separate entities.[1] The opposition of day and night, reinforced by the description of night as "black" or "dark" and day as "white" or "light," is very common in Greek poetry from Homer to the end of the fifth century. It is not surprising to find day and night opposed, because ordinarily this is the first change in his world which a child perceives. The Greeks must have been keenly aware of this cycle since it limited their actions far more than it does ours, who with the aid of electricity can turn night into day. Moreover, although we often describe night as

1. On separate dwelling places for day and night, see Job 38.19: "Where is the way to the dwelling of light/ and where is the place of darkness"; 26.10: "He has described a circle upon the face of the waters/ at the boundary between light and darkness" (R.S.V.). On the house of Night, see Hes. *Theog.* 744-745, Parmenides B1. On day in Greek thought, see H. Fraenkel, "Man's 'Ephemeros' Nature according to Pindar and Others" *TAPA* 77 (1946) 131-145.

"black" or "dark," we do not usually describe day as "white."[2]
The original opposition of day and night seems to be made
without reference to the sun as the cause of light. Day, then, is
light and night dark. In Genesis 1.3-5 we read that God separated
the light from the darkness, calling the light day and the darkness
night. The realization that the sun brought light came later. Since
the sun rose after daylight came, its function as the cause of
daylight was not obvious. The sun belonged in the day, as the
moon and stars in the night, but daylight as such had an existence
independent of the sun. In this section, we shall consider the
occurrences of "dark night" and "white day" in Greek poetry and
shall then proceed to an examination of related contrasts: fair
weather and storm, night and day as typical of danger and
deliverance, and to particular phrases, a "white" day as being an
especially happy one and a "white" wind.

The epic poets had at their disposal several formular expres-
sions for "dark night." Most frequently they described night as
μέλας, in various cases and positions in the hexameter.[3] Evening is
also μέλας twice in the *Odyssey* (1.423, 18.306). In addition to
being μέλας, night is δνοφερός (*Od.* 13.269, cf. δνόφος "dark-
ness"), κελαινός (*Il.* 5.310, 11.356), ἐρεμνός (*Od.* 11.606), and
ἐρεβεννός (*Il.* 8.488, 9.474, 5.659, 22.466-467, Hes. *W.D.* 17).
Both descriptions of night as κελαινός refer to the night of death
(see section three), but later poets use this epithet for literal night
(cf. Aesch. *Pers.* 428, Eur. *H.F.* 834, Aristoph. *Frogs* 1331-1332).
The epithets ἐρεμνός and ἐρεβεννός (which occurs in the *Iliad* but
not in the *Odyssey*) are related to Ἔρεβος, the dark underworld
(see Appendix III). The epic poets, then, had a variety of ways to
say "dark night" and this suggests that it was a common idea.

Later poets repeated and varied the epic description. Alcman
called Mount Rhipa "the breast of dark night" (fr. 90 *PMG*):

2. There is a strange French expression *nuit blanche*, a night in which one does
not sleep, and an English counterpart "a white night." Ordinarily night is dark and used
for sleep, whereas this night, not being used for sleep, is therefore not dark, but white. In
this use of *blanche* and white there is a blankness, a lack of accomplishment, quite unlike
the tone of λευκός which often connotes joy.

3. Final position in the hexameter, in the dative *Il.* 8.502, 9.65; *Od.* 7.253,
12.291, 14.314; in the accusative *Il.* 10.297, 394, 468, 24.366, 653; Hes. *Theog.* 20, 481,
788; other occurrences, *Il.* 15.324, *h. Herm.* 67, 290, 358; Hes. *Theog.* 123, *Il.* 14.439,
8.486.

νυκτὸς μελαίνας στέρνον. Stesichorus tells the story of the sun sailing in his cup "to the depths of dark, holy night" (fr. 185.3 PMG): ἰαρᾶς ποτὶ βένθεα νυκτὸς ἐρεμνᾶς. Simonides pictures the babe Perseus "stretched out in the dark gloom" (fr. 543.12 PMG, cf. chapter three, section four): κυανέωι δνόφωι ταθείς. Pindar varies the Homeric formula in Nemean 7.2-4 (addressed to Eleithuia, goddess of childbirth):

ἄνευ σέθεν
οὐ φάος,οὐ μέλαιναν δρακέντες εὐφρόναν
τεὰν ἀδελφεὰν ἐλάχομεν ἀγλαόγυιον Ἥβαν.

"Without you we would not see the light nor the dark night [lit. kindly time] and we would not attain your sister, Hebe of the glorious limbs." This is a good Pindaric example of chiaroscuro, the juxtaposition of light and dark.[4] The Greeks often used "see the light" as a synonym for "live," but here Pindar has expanded the phrase by adding "and the dark night" and provided further contrast in the epithet of Hebe ἀγλαόγυιον. Pindar also describes night as dark in his comment on an eclipse (fr. 108b, μελαίνας ἐκ νυκτός, κελαινεφέι δὲ σκότει).

We read in Bacchylides an apostrophe to "torch-bearing Hecate, daughter of great-bosomed Night" (fr. 1B3 Snell):

Ἑκάτα δαιδοφόρε, Νυκτὸς
μεγαλοκόλπου θύγατερ.

Some editors follow the conjecture of Ursinus and read μελανοκόλπου "dark-bosomed," giving us another reference to the darkness of night. Snell keeps the ms. reading, but gives in his apparatus a parallel for μελανόκολπος, κυανόκολπος, which is found in Hibeh Papyri 2.172.11, a poetical onomasticon of compound adjectives. One point in favour of the emendation is that it provides a contrast between the bright moon (torch-bearing Hecate) and the dark night sky in which she appears. (Cf. Pindar's liking for contrast above, and the contrast between dark night and its "golden stars," Eur. Electr. 54, below). However, since it is hard to imagine why such an obvious epithet of night should be miscopied, we must be cautious about this conjecture.

4. G. Norwood Pindar (Berkeley and Los Angeles 1956) pp. 92-93.

Similar descriptions of night are found in the dramatists. In Aesch. *Eumenides* 745, the chorus of Furies appeals to their mother, dark Night: ὦ Νὺξ μέλαινα, μῆτερ. Aeschylus also speaks of night "with its dark horses" (fr. 69.5, μελανίππου). There are several references in the *Persae* to the darkness of night, particularly that night before the Persian defeat at Salamis. The Greek who pretended to betray Greek plans to Xerxes says that the Greeks will flee with the gloom of dark (μέλας) night (line 357). Xerxes commanded the fleet to form in battle order when the sun ceased to illumine earth with its beams and darkness (κνέφας) held the precinct of the sky (364-365). The sailors boarded when the light of the sun faded and night came on (377-378). The dawn of the next day is described in these words (386-387):

> ἐπεί γε μέντοι λευκόπωλος ἡμέρα
> πᾶσαν κατέσχε γαῖαν εὐφεγγὴς ἰδεῖν. . .

"when, however, radiant, white-horsed day shone over all the land." With the day comes a song of triumph from the Greeks, a presage of the victory they would win that day (388-391). The day closes with a view of the Persian disaster; groans and shrieks together filled the open sea, till the eye of dark (κελαινῆς) night hid them (426-428). In the messenger's account, then, bright day represents the good fortune of the Greeks and dark night the misfortune of the Persians. Although the speech ostensibly is told from the Persian viewpoint, it is in fact a glorification of the Athenians and the symbolism of bright day and dark night emphasizes this orientation. Aeschylus gives a clear indication of the symbolism of day and night in the words with which the messenger tells Queen Atossa that Xerxes is still alive (line 299): Ξέρξης μὲν αὐτὸς ζῆι τε καὶ φάος βλέπει "Xerxes himself is alive and sees the light": and in the words of Atossa's reply (lines 300-301):

> ἐμοῖς μὲν εἶπας δώμασιν φάος μέγα
> καὶ λευκὸν ἦμαρ νυκτὸς ἐκ μελαγχίμου.

"To my house your words bring great light [i.e. joy] and a white day after dark night." Since this interchange precedes the messenger's speech, we can be certain that in it Aeschylus intended to symbolize victory and happiness by day or light and defeat and sorrow by night. (Night may, in other circumstances, be welcome, as for instance in Aesch. *Ag.* 355 where night is φιλία, because darkness helped the Greeks in the final destruction of Troy).

A similar association of night with sorrow and day with joy is found in Sophocles' *Electra*. The Paedagogus comments to Orestes at the beginning of the play that the bright torch of the sun is stirring the clear morning songs of the birds and the dark (μέλαινα) night of stars has failed (lines 17-19). Jebb comments that "the sights and sounds of early morning are in unison with the spirit of this play in which the παννυχίδες (1.92) of Electra's sorrow are turned to joy and the god of light prevails."[5] Dark night is mentioned again (1.91): δνοφερὰ νύξ.

Euripides describes night as "dark" several times. Sleep is the child of dark (μέλας) Night (*Cyc.* 601); and Madness the unwed maiden (daughter) of dark (κελαινός) Night (*H.F.* 834). Night is μέλαινα (fr. 101) and "dark-robed" μελάμπεπλος (*Ion* 1150), where Night is depicted on a tapestry driving a chariot and the epithet is a description of the personification. (But it might also be used for actual night, cf. Hipponax fr. 37.1 D., below). Electra addresses night, "O dark night, nurse of golden stars" (*Electra* 54): ὦ νὺξ μέλαινα, χρυσέων ἄστρων τροφέ. Denniston quotes Camper: *siderum nutrix, ea nempe quae siderum augeat per tenebras suas splendorem*, on which Denniston remarks, "I think that this is right, though the conceit is a trifle precious."[6]

Aristophanes also calls night "dark." In the birds' account of the creation of the world, first of all dark-winged (μελανόπτερος) Night laid a wind-egg (*Birds* 695).[7] "Dark-winged night" may very well have occurred elsewhere in Greek poetry in a more serious vein (cf. "white-winged day," Eur. *T. W.* 848-851, and "white-winged morning star" Ion of Chios fr. 9D). But in Aristophanes

---

5. R. C. Jebb *Sophocles Electra* (Cambridge 1908) on line 17 f.
6. J. D. Denniston *Euripides Electra* (Oxford 1939) on line 54.
7. "Wind-egg" *LSJ* s.v. ὑπηνέμιος "full of wind," of eggs which produce no chickens: Aristoph. fr. 186, Pl. Com. 19; but in Aristoph. *Birds* (the passage under discussion here) "produced by Night alone without impregnation." Cf. Luc. *Sacr.* 6 where Hephaestus is called the ὑπηνέμιος·παῖς of Hera, and is said to have been conceived without intercourse. Cf. the Spirit moving on the waters, Genesis 1.2.

the epithet is made comic by the transformation of Night into an egg-laying bird. In a passage of the *Frogs* which parodies Euripides and is full of what Stanford calls "romantic" references to gloom and darkness,[8] a dream is seen as the child of dark (μέλας) night (1334-1335), and night is addressed thus (1331) "O dark-gleaming gloom of night" (ὦ Νυκτὸς κελαινοφαὴς ὄρφνα).[9]

Day is not described directly as "white" in Homer, but we have a few pieces of evidence connecting the brightness of day with whiteness. In *Iliad* 14.184-185, Hera puts on a head-dress which is white (λευκόν) like the sun. In *Odyssey* 6.44-45 the poet describes the beautiful weather on Olympus, home of the gods, where the atmosphere is cloudless and a white brightness (λευκὴ αἴγλη) is spread over it. We may assume from this that Homer found λευκός a suitable epithet for a clear, sunny day. In *Odyssey* 23.246 we read that the names of the horses which bring Dawn are Lampus "Bright" and Phaethon "Shiner;" names suggestive of white coats. It is probably to this passage that later poets owe their description of day or dawn as "white-horsed" (λεύκιππος or λευκόπωλος). Bacchylides is the earliest poet to use this combination (fr. 20C.22 Snell): λε[ύκι]ππος Ἀώς. (Cf. also Aesch. *Pers.* 386, λευκόπωλος; Soph. *Ajax* 673 λευκοπώλωι ἡμέραι,[10] and in contrast, Aesch. fr. 69.5, μελανίππου. The epithet is elaborated by Euripides *I.A.* 156-158 with a reference to the fire of the team of Helios' horses "whitening" λευκαίνει).

The image is changed from that of a team of horses drawing day or dawn to that of day as a great bird with white wings (Eur. *T. W.* 848-849 λευκοπτέρου ἀμέρας). In contrast to this epithet we saw that Aristophanes described night as "dark-winged (*Birds* 695). Ion of Chios called the morning star "the white-winged forerunner" of the sun (fr. 9 D.): λευκοπτέρυγα πρόδρομον. He is probably depicting the brightness of the star in the first part of the

---

8. W. B. Stanford *Aristophanes Frogs* (London 1958) on lines 1331 ff.

9. The epithet κελαινοφαὴς is a parody of Euripides' style, which leaned to compounds in φάος and also to oxymorons. Cf. O. Hense in *Phil.* 60 (1901) 389 on compounds in φάος and T. Mitchell *The Frogs* (London 1839) on oxymorons, where 36 examples are given from Euripides. Cf. *Helen* 518, μελαμφαές.

10. There may be a contrast in Soph. *Ajax* 672-673 between "white-horsed day" and the "dark circle of night"; cf. W. B. Stanford *Sophocles Ajax* (London 1963) on lines 672-673.

compound (λευκο-) and its speed in the second part (-πτερυγα), as the morning star seems to speed away before the rising sun.

In a different image which was probably influenced by the epic "saffron-robed Dawn" (κροκόπεπλος Ἠώς, Il. 8.1, 19.1, etc.), Hipponax calls day "white-robed" (λευκόπεπλον fr. 37.1 D.; cf. Eur. Ion 1150, above). The eye of Dawn is white (λευκόν) in Euripides Electra 102 and her face white (λευκὸν πρόσωπον) in line 730 of the same play.[11] Λευκός, then, is readily applied to daylight by the Greek poets, most frequently in an indirect manner, i.e. "white-horsed," "white-robed," "white-winged." When day is described directly as white, it has a special meaning (see below). In connection with daylight, we can interpret the epithet λευκός to mean not white but bright. Euripides says that Thetis comes "passing through the white air" (Androm. 1228-1229), meaning the bright, clear atmosphere: λευκὴν αἰθέρα πορθμευόμενος. Similarly in Medea 829-830 the Athenians are said to tread "delicately through the brilliant air": διὰ λαμπροτάτου βαίνοντες ἀβρῶς αἰθέρος. (Cf. also Homer's description of the clear atmosphere on Olympus, cited above.) This combination of bright and white is clearly seen in the comments of the Peripatetic writer of the treatise on colours (De Color. 794a13-15), as he explains why the air which surrounds us is colourless, while the sky appears blue. "Air when examined from nearby appears to have no colour (οὐδὲν ἔχειν φαίνεται χρῶμα) but when examined in depth, it seems very nearly dark blue (κυανοειδής) in colour because of the rarity. For where light fails, there interspersed with darkness it appears dark blue. But when it is dense, as is also the case with water, it is the whitest of all things (πάντων λευκότατόν ἐστιν)." It is interesting to observe that the author feels no strangeness in equating colourless and white with regard to air.

The Greeks called day white when it was a time of good weather, happiness, or delivery from danger. In Sophocles' Ajax the chorus hears Ajax' apparent change of plan and hopes that the "white light of fair weather" will come to the ships (708-709):

11. The eye of dawn is here dawn itself, although in Soph. Ant. 103 the eye of day is the sun. Cf. Job 3.9 "neither let it behold the eyelids of the morning." For the eye of night as a periphrasis for night, cf. Aesch. Pers. 428, Eur. Phoen. 543; but in Aesch. Sept. 390 the eye of night is the moon.

λευκὸν εὐάμερον φάος. In this context, λευκός conveys the double significance of "bright" and "happy." Just as clear weather after a storm is both bright and welcome, so the change in Ajax' intention marks the beginning of good times and happiness. Twice Aeschylus uses the phrase λευκὸν ἦμαρ. When Queen Atossa learns that Xerxes is safe, she tells the messenger that his words bring a great light (φάος) to her house, and "white day after dark night" (λευκὸν ἦμαρ νυκτὸς ἐκ μελαγχίμου, Pers. 300-301; for φάος as "joy, safety," see below and n. 44). "White day after dark night" contrasts the brightness of safety and Atossa's joy with the dark night of danger and sorrow. (Recall the comments on day and night in the messenger's speech in Persae). The second example of λευκὸν ἦμαρ occurs in Agamemnon in the messenger's speech to the chorus relating the storm which fell on the Greek ships as they left Troy and swept Menelaus' vessel out of sight (Ag. 667-669):

ἔπειτα δ᾽ Ἅιδην πόντιον πεφευγότες
λευκὸν κατ᾽ ἦμαρ, οὐ πεποιθότες τύχηι,
ἐβουκολοῦμεν φροντίσιν νέον πάθος.

"Then having escaped death on the deep, in the white day, not trusting fortune, we brooded over the recent experience in our hearts." Here the whiteness of day, coming after a storm, suggests not only the brightness of the weather, but also their deliverance. (Cf. for the sentiment "dawn most fair to look upon after storm": κάλλιστον ἦμαρ εἰσιδεῖν ἐκ χείματος 900.) It is hardly surprising, that a storm is described as dark: cf. the examples from Il. 11.747 12.375, 20.51 below.

The phrase λευκὴ ἡμέρα becomes proverbial for "a good day." There are reports of a number of authors using it with this meaning: Sophocles fr. 6 P.[12] Eupolis fr. 174, Menander fr. 315 III 90 K., and Herodian (Philet. ed. J. Pierson Leiden 1759 p. 477). There is no dispute at all over its meaning; its origin, however, is explained in various ways. In our discussion of day and night we have seen that day was described by the Greeks as "white-horsed," "white-robed," or "white-winged," so that white is suitable indirectly for ordinary daylight. We have also seen that a specially

12. For a discussion of λευκὴ ἡμέρα, see A. C. Pearson The Fragments of Sophocles (Cambridge 1917) on fr. 6.

brilliant atmosphere, like that around Olympus (*Od.* 6.44-45), or
that through which Thetis was passing (Eur. *Androm.* 1228-1229)
was described as "white." We noted also the particular suitability
of "white" to fine weather after a storm, whether actual or
symbolic (Cf. Aesch. *Pers.* 300-301, *Ag.* 667-669, Soph. *Ajax*
708-710). It would seem a fairly obvious explanation of the phrase
to connect it with the earlier poetic tradition and to interpret the
"whiteness" as descriptive of the contrast implied between this
day and others which were, one might say, like night in
comparison. There are, however, other explanations. Plutarch
relates that in the siege of Samos Pericles had more soldiers than
he could use, so he had them draw lots for service each day, and
those who chose a white bean had the day off; this, says Plutarch,
is the origin of the phrase λευκὴ ἡμέρα (*Pericles* 27).[13] It is
interesting to note that this tale is roughly contemporary with the
first appearance of the phrase in literature and that Eupolis in the
Flatterers (where we find his reference to λευκὴ ἡμέρα) men-
tioned the same siege (fr. 154 I 299 K, 154.3 Edmonds). Others,
however, give credit for the phrase to the custom of various tribes
by which each member put into his quiver at the day's end a stone
to represent his experiences, a white stone for a happy day or a
black one for a sad day (Suda s.vv. λευκὴ ἡμέρα, τῶν ἐν φαρέτρων
of the Scythians, Plin. *N.H.* 7.40 of the Thracians). The
connection between white stones and good days is found not
infrequently in Latin poetry,[14] but I have not seen any explicit
references to marking a day with a white stone in Greek poetry. It
seems most reasonable to associate the phrase λευκὴ ἡμέρα with

13. Callimachus twice mentions a "white day." In fr. 191.37, the plural appears in
the proverbial sense "happy"; in fr. 178. 1-2 a white day was apparently a day off from
work, as it was in Plutarch's account.

14. For Latin references see C. J. Fordyce *Catullus A Commentary* (Oxford 1961)
on Catullus 107.6 *candidiore nota* (cf. also 68.148: *lapide illa diem candidiore notat*).
"The white mark for a lucky day appears in various forms: so Pliny *Ep.* 6.11.3 *o diem
laetum notandumque mihi candidissimo calculo*; Mart. 9.53.5 *diesque nobis/ signandi
melioribus lapillis*, 8.45.2 *hanc lucem lactea gemma notet*; Hor. *Od.* 1.36.10 *cressa* (i.e.
chalk) *ne careat pulchra dies nota.* The cliché was popularly connected with the habit
imputed to some primitive tribes (Thracians in Pliny's version, *N.H.* 7.132) of putting a
white or a black pebble every day in a jar to represent the happiness or unhappiness of
each individual and by a final count assessing the happiness of his life, but it probably
goes back to the practice of marking lucky days on a primitive calendar, and so has a
similar origin to our "red-letter day."

earlier poetic passages in which "white days" are times of fair weather after storm or rescue from danger.

Apparently akin to the description of fair weather and good days as white is the Alexandrian use of the epithet for spring and summer. Theocritus speaks of "white spring" λευκὸν ἔαρ (18.27), and Callimachus depicts part of the festival of Demeter (Cer. [VI] 120-123): as four white horses bring the ceremonial basket, "so the great wide-ruling goddess will come bringing for us *white spring, white summer*, autumn and winter and will guard us into another year": λευκὸν ἔαρ, λευκὸν δὲ θέρος. In Kober's view the phrases "may refer to the increasing brightness of the light as the sun approaches its greatest effectiveness at the summer solstice, or to the fairness and clearness of the weather at that time."[15] There is no need to separate these ideas; undoubtedly both play a part in the intention of the poets. We ought to consider whether a similar phrase in Hesiod has any connection with these occurrences. In *Works and Days*, Hesiod twice describes spring as "grey": the phrase occurs in line 477 πολιὸν ἔαρ and is elaborated in lines 491-492:

μηδέ σε λήθοι
μήτ' ἔαρ γιγνόμενον πολιὸν μήθ' ὥριος ὄμβρος.

"Do not let the coming of grey spring escape you nor the seasonable rain." "Grey" for us in a weather description suits an overcast sky, so the author's first impression was that Hesiod's "grey spring" was quite unlike the Hellenistic "white spring." This impression tended to be confirmed by the grouping in line 492 of "seasonable rain" with "grey spring."[16] It was with considerable surprise, then, that references were discovered in Mugler suggesting that, at times, πολιός was almost identical in meaning to λευκός.[17] Air, for example, is πολιός in Euripides *Orestes* 1376:

15. Kober p. 12.
16. H. G. Evelyn-White *Hesiod and the Homeric Hymns* (London 1936) on *W.D.* 477 suggests that spring is grey because of "iron-grey husks on buds," but this seems quite unconvincing. T. A. Sinclair *Hesiod Works and Days* (London 1932) on *W.D.* 477 interprets πολιός as "misty," comparing our use of "grey" for skies (never a safe course, unless one can show from elsewhere that the Greeks had a similar use). He argues that Eur. *Orest.* 1376 and Ap. Rh. 3.275 display a similar use of πολιός, i.e. the "air" is "misty" (see text, p. 168), referring for support to Wilamowitz on *W.D.* 492.
17. Cf. C. Mugler *Dictionnaire historique de la terminologie optique des grecs* (Paris 1964) s.v. πολιός.

πολιόν αἰθέρα; and in Apollonius Rhodius 3.275: πολιοῖο δι᾽ ἠέρος. It is possible for air to be misty, but we have seen that the Greeks called clear air white. Particularly in Euripides where the *aether* (clear atmosphere) is πολιός, it is hard to believe that the poet intended a misty connotation. Even more illuminating is the description of hair as "whiter than a swan" in Aristophanes *Wasps* 1064: κύκνου τε πολιώτεραι τρίχες. The bird is proverbial for whiteness,[18] and if this hair is more "swan-coloured" than a swan, we must assume logically that πολιός here is white. Let us consider in the light of these πολιός passages whether Hesiod's πολιὸν ἔαρ may not refer to a clear rather than a misty spring, as it is usually taken. If this is so, the Hellenistic λευκὸν ἔαρ is a variation on the older formular expression. (Cf. the discussion of hair colour in section six). In contrast to the brightness of spring and summer, we find in Pindar that winter is dark (*Isthm.* 4.18-19):

> νῦν δ᾽ αὖ μετὰ χειμέριον ποικίλα μηνῶν ζόφον
> χθὼν ὥτε φοινικέοισιν ἄνθησεν ῥόδοις
> δαιμόνων βουλαῖς.

"Now in turn after the wintry darkness of the months [the family fortune of Melissus] blossoms like the many-hued earth with red roses at the will of the gods."[19] Winter contrasts with spring as the past experiences of Melissus contrast with his present victory. Winter is dark because no bright flowers bloom,[20] but perhaps the factors of poorer weather and less intense light also enter into this description.[21]

The Greeks described certain winds as white; some commentators interpret the whiteness as "bringing fair weather,"[22] while

---

18. Cf. Juvenal 6.165 "rara avis in terris/ nigroque simillima cycno."

19. For the mss. reading μετὰ χειμέριον ποικίλων μηνῶν ζόφον/ χθὼν "after the wintry darkness of the many-hued (or changeful) months, the earth," Hartung proposed χειμερίων ποικίλα "after the darkness of the wintry months, the many-hued earth." For a defence of ποικίλα see L. Woodbury in *TAPA* 78 (1947) 368-375. He rejects the emendation χειμερίων as does Snell.

20. For the connection of spring and red (purple) flowers, see Pind. *Pyth.* 4.64, fr. 63. 15-16 (Bowra); and Verg. *Ecl.* 9.40; *ver purpureum Georg.* 2.319 *vere rubenti*.

21. Norwood argues (*Pindar* pp. 172-175) that *Isthm.* 3 and 4 were not written by Pindar. He calls attention to a number of strange phrases which he regards as un-Pindaric. But for our purposes, some poet, whether Pindar or another, contrasted dark winter with the flowers of spring.

22. Kober p. 17; R. C. Seaton in *CR* 8 (1889) 220.

others, noting that this is not always the result, translate "with bright, white clouds."[23] Homer twice describes the south wind as white: at *Iliad* 11.305-306:

ὡς ὁπότε νέφεα Ζέφυρος στυφελίξῃ
ἀργεστᾶο Νότοιο, βαθείῃ λαίλαπι τύπτων,

"as when Zephyrus scatters the clouds brought by white Notus, smiting with a deep hurricane . . ."; and at *Iliad* 21.334-335:

αὐτὰρ ἐγὼ Ζεφύροιο καὶ ἀργεστᾶο Νότοιο
εἴσομαι ἐξ ἁλόθεν χαλεπὴν ὄρσουσα θύελλαν,

"and I (Hera) shall go and rouse a harsh gust of Zephyrus and white Notus from the sea . . ." In the first example, the south wind brought clouds which were driven before the west wind in a violent storm; in the second, both south and west winds were to be involved in bad weather. It seems perverse, in the Homeric occurrences, to try to establish a connection between whiteness and fair weather.

In Hesiod it is the west wind which receives this epithet. In the account of the births of the gods, he tells us that Dawn bore to Astraeos the winds "white Zephyrus, swift-speeding Boreas and Notus" (*Theog.* 379-380): ἀργεστὴν Ζέφυρον Βορέην τ᾽ αἰψηροκέλευθον/ καὶ Νότον. Later in the same poem, he explains that "the wet strength of winds that blow is from Typho, except Notus, Boreas and white Zephyrus; their lineage is from the gods" (*Theog.* 869-871):

ἐκ Τυφωέος ἔστ᾽ ἀνέμων μένος ὑγρὸν ἀέντων
νόσφι Νότου Βορέω τε καὶ ἀργεστέω Ζεφύροιο
οἵ γε μὲν ἐκ θεόφιν γενεήν

Paley felt unhappy about the fact that only three winds were mentioned by Hesiod, whereas four cardinal winds are named in Homer (*Od.* 5.295-296):

σὺν δ᾽ Εὖρός τε Νότος τ᾽ ἔπεσον Ζέφυρός τε δυσαὴς
καὶ Βορέης αἰθρηγενέτης.

He, therefore, suggested reading Argestes as a proper name for the

23. Leaf *Homer The Iliad* on 21.334.

east wind (commonly Euros).[24] It is true that Argestes is later used as the proper name of a wind, but as that of the north-west, and the connection with Zephyrus accords well with its later role (see below). In spite of the difficulty posed by the mention of only three (cardinal) winds in Hesiod, Paley's conjecture is not generally adopted.

A folk song provides a rule of thumb for predicting weather (*Carm. Pop.* 40 Bgk):

Λίψ ἄνεμος ταχὺ μὲν νεφέλας, ταχὺ δ' αἴθρια ποιεῖ·
ἀργέστηι δ' ἀνέμωι πᾶσ' ἔπεται νεφέλη.

"The south-west wind quickly brings clouds, quickly fair weather, but all cloud accompanies the north-west wind." (Since the south-west wind is mentioned in the first line, it seems likely that ἀργέστης is the north-west wind, rather than simply a descriptive epithet white). In the popular view, the south-west wind might bring cloud (perhaps rain?) or fair weather, but the north-west wind always brought clouds. (Cf. πᾶς with the force "nothing but," *LSJ* s.v.).

These five occurrences in the poetry of our period are supplemented by several references in prose.[25] We find, in the Peripatetic treatise on weather, a careful account of the names of

---

24. F. A. Paley *The Epics of Hesiod with an English Commentary* (London 1861) on *Theog.* 870 and 379. See also M. L. West *Hesiod Theogony* (Oxford 1966) on lines 379 and 871. West translates ἀργεστήν "the cleanser," an epithet of Zephyrus in both passages, and makes the point that the three winds form a triad, a common pattern in Hesiod, usually three proper names, the last qualified by an epithet. (See further West on line 140). West prefers to accent ἀργεστήν as an oxytone, attested as the correct accent for the epithet by the Scholiast on *Iliad* 11.306, although all the mss. of Hesiod accent ἀργέστην, correct for the proper name. He also prefers to read γενεήν in line 871, where there is a disagreement among the mss. I have followed him on both these points.

25. We find two references in later poetry as well: *Ap. Rh.* 2.960 Ἀργέσταο ... ἐπιπνείοντος, where Argestes is a proper name, glossed by the Scholiast Ζεφύρου; and 4.1627-1628, where ἀργέστης is an epithet of Notus as it was in Homer. In Bacch. 5.65-67 we find a description of the souls by Cocytus "As many as the leaves which the wind stirs on the bright, sheep-rearing slopes of Ida":

οἷά τε φύλλ' ἄνεμος
Ἴδας ἀνὰ μηλοβότους
πρῶνας ἀργηστὰς δονεῖ.

Snell distinguishes between ἀργεστής and ἀργηστής commenting in his *apparatus criticus* on line 67: *ventus* ἀργεστής *montes claros* (ἀργηστάς) *reddit*, cf. Schol. A. *ad* Λ 306; *ne putes hic* ἀργεστάς *scribendum esse.*

winds with the direction from which they blow. We are told that Argestes blows from the sun's summer setting (i.e. north-west) and that it blows towards the south-east (*Meteorol.* 363b24); its source is between Boreas, the north wind and Zephyrus, the west wind. (Cf. also Diodorus Siculus 1.39). Plutarch groups Argestes and Zephyrus as winds that sometimes bring soft showers to certain Atlantic islands but mostly cool them with moist breezes and gently nourish the soil (*Sert.* 8). By the fourth century the epithet of wind in epic poetry has become a proper name, presumably because the characteristic expressed by ἀργεστής was found commonly in the north-west wind. Whatever this characteristic was, it does not seem to have been a habit of bringing fair weather (cf. *Carm. Pop.* 40, Plut. *Sert.* 8).

The name of another wind must be mentioned at this point, since it is often wrongly considered analogous. The usual south wind brought rain (see Herod. 2.25), but there was a wind from the south which cleared the weather, the Leuconotus "white-south-wind" ([Arist] *Meteorol.* 362a14. *Vent.* 973b10-12). White-ness in this connection is clearly related to the earlier description of good weather as white. Since Homer described the south wind as ἀργεστής, some commentators assume that he meant the Leuconotus. But as we pointed out, there is no suggestion in Homer that the white south wind brought good weather – quite the reverse. Horace translates the Leuconotus as *albus Notus* (*Odes* 1.7.15-17):

> albus ut obscuro deterget nubila caelo
> saepe Notus neque parturit imbres
> perpetuo. . . .

"As often white Notus clears clouds from an overcast sky and does not always bring rain." In acknowledging the fact that the south wind commonly brought rain but sometimes brought good weather, Horace indicates his dependence on the Greek meteorological sources.[26]

---

26. Cf. also Verg. *Georg.* 1.460: *et claro silvas cernes Aquilone moveri. Clarus* seems strongly reminiscent of λαμπρός and, like it, indicates a *strong* wind, since in Vergil it moves the trees. Commentators like to translate *claro* as "sky-clearing," or some similar term. See H. H. Huxley *Virgil: Georgics I and IV* (London 1961), on this passage: "the late H. J. Rose has shown that the phrase [the sky-clearing North wind] depends

We conclude that ἀργεστής as an epithet of wind differs in its meaning from the λευκός, as in Leuconotus, "the fair-weather wind." What then did the epic poets mean when they described a wind as white? We find a clue in the description of a wind as λαμπρός. Herodotus says that when boats travel upstream they need a λαμπρὸς ἄνεμος (2.96), presumably meaning a strong rather than a bright wind. In *Agamemnon*, Aeschylus makes Cassandra say that no longer will her prophecy peep forth like a bride behind a veil, "but it will rush as a clear wind blowing against the sun's risings" (1180-1181): λαμπρὸς δ' ἔοικεν ἡλίου πρὸς ἀντολὰς/ πνέων ἐσαίξειν. Fraenkel points out that λαμπρός is doubly suitable: as an epithet of wind (implied by πνέων) and as a description of her prophecy which will be clarified.[27] (We note in passing that this is a west wind, since it blows towards the east, the sun's risings). In Aristophanes, the Paphlagonian compares himself to a strong wind (*Knights* 430):[28] ἔξειμι γάρ σοι λαμπρὸς ἤδη καὶ μέγας καθιείς "For I shall come out, swooping like a bright, strong breeze." Since λαμπρός is used with μέγας, it perhaps also suggests the strength of the blast (cf. Eur. *Heracl.* 280).

Our suggestion, then, is that the solution to the problem of the "white" wind may be found in a comparison with λαμπρός as an epithet for wind. It is a mistake to understand ἀργεστής as descriptive of the effect of wind "clearing the sky," "bringing fair weather." We have in λαμπρός authority for taking it as a direct description of wind. Kober wrestles with the problem and decides that "there is nothing in the other uses of the words from the same stem [i.e. ἀργ-] that warrants the translation 'rapid.' The expression ἀργὸς κύων can be translated 'swift dog' only on the

not merely on Aratus, but also on Homer (*Od.* 5.296 Βορέης αἰθρηγενέτης, 'Boreas, begetter of clear sky')." Vergil may well have had the Homeric passage in mind, but *clarus* is more likely to be Vergil's rendering of λαμπρός. (Huxley refers to W. F. Jackson Knight's suggestion that Vergil may be here giving the noun *Aquilo* (from *aquilus* "dark") an adjective which contradicts its etymology, *clarus* "bright"). But the ancient commentators did not connect *aquilus* with *aquilo* but *aquila* "eagle." See further A. Ernout and A. Meillet *Dictionnaire étymologique de la langue latine* (Paris 4th ed. 1967) s.v. *aquilo, aquilus*.

27. Fraenkel *Aeschylus Agamemnon* on line 1180.

28. Cf. J. van Leeuwen's comment (*Aristophonis Equites* [Leiden 1900] on lines 430-431) *Claro aquiloni se assimulat*. It is clear that van Leeuwen is reminded of Vergil, above n. 26.

supposition that rapid motion causes a flickering or glancing that may be expressed by ἀργός. Since, however, a wind is invisible, it is hard to see how it can be accompanied by flickering."[29] On the contrary, while we limit brightness to things we see, the Greeks did not. A bright or white wind did not have to be seen; the Greeks felt it, probably heard it. We speak of "blinding light," and "blinding speed"; the Greek description of a rapid wind as white similarly associates brightness and speed.

In short, the epithet ἀργεστής seems not to be connected with the presence or absence of clouds, and not descriptive of the action of bringing fair weather, but rather a characteristic of wind itself. It seems to be most closely parallelled by λαμπρός, also an epithet of wind. Why the Greeks called a strong wind white, we can perhaps guess. It may be comparable to our feeling that a good breeze "blows away the cobwebs," that a windy day is in some way invigorating. On the other hand, perhaps the smooth rush of air past them felt like the smoothness of a bright, white surface. For whatever reason, brightness and whiteness were characteristic of a strong wind.

III Life and Death

Death is described as dark (μέλας) five times in Homer: *Il.* 2.834, 11.332, 16.687; *Od.* 12.91-92, 17.326).[30] The darkness of death is contrasted with the light of this world in Hesiod (*W.D.* 154-155):

θάνατος δὲ καὶ ἐκπάγλους περ ἐόντας
εἷλε μέλας, λαμπρὸν δ' ἔλιπον φάος ἠελίοιο.

"Dark death seized them, although they were terrible, and they left the bright light of the sun." (Cf. Pind. *Pyth.* 11.56-57, "the verge of dark death" μέλανος ἐσχατιὰν θανάτου, and Eur. *Alc.* 843-844, "dark-robed Death," μελάμπεπλον . . . Θάνατον). Death is sometimes spoken of as a dark cloud which covers its victim; it is μέλας in *Iliad* 16.350, *Odyssey* 4.180; Theognis 707, and it is

29. Kober p. 17.
30. Fate and death are closely connected in Homer; fate, then, is often dark (μέλαινα): in *Iliad* (2.859, 3.360, 454, 5.22, 652, 7.254, 11.360, 443, 14.462, 21.66) and *Odyssey* (2.283, 3.242, 15.275, 17.500, 22.14, 330, 363, 382). Cf. B. C. Dietrich *Death, Fate and the Gods* (London 1965) pp. 243-245. Cf. also Eur. *Phoen.* 950, Hes. *Theog.* 211.

κυάνεος in *Iliad* 20.417-418, and Simonides fr. 121.2 D.[31] At other times death is like dark night which overwhelms the eyes: κελαινός in *Iliad* 5.310, 11.356; ἐρεβεννός in *Iliad* 5.659, 13.580, 22.466; and μέλας in *Iliad* 14.438-439. In a slightly different application of the phrase, Idomeneus is said to long "to cover one of the Trojans with dark night" (*Il.* 13.425): τινα Τρώων ἐρεβεννῆι νυκτὶ καλύψαι (i.e. to put one to death). In *Iliad* 22.466 the formula "dark night covered [her] eyes" is applied to Andromache who has fainted. Fainting, and in particular the loss of vision involved, seemed to the Greeks like death. The dark night of death is related to the fact that the dead no longer see things in this world. (Cf. the "dark eyes" of Eurydice, Soph. *Ant.* 1302 κελαινὰ βλέφαρα which Kober interprets rightly as the darkness of death).[32] With the similarity between death and faintness, we may compare the representation of Sleep and Death as twin brothers (*Il.* 14. 231, 16.672, 682).[33] Pindar describes sleep in terms of a dark cloud on the eagle asleep on Zeus' sceptre (*Pyth.* 1.7-8). This darkness over the eyes is to be contrasted with the Greek synonym for "to live" – "to see the light of the sun."

The underworld, the abode of the dead, was a gloomy place where, according to Homer, the sun did not shine (*Od.* 12.383; cf. also Aesch. *Sept.* 859, and *Prom.* 1028, reference to sunlessness). But Pindar says that the good dwell in equinox (*Olymp.* 2.61-62) and that the sun shines below during our night (fr. 129, 1-2).[34] Hades, god of the underworld, is dark (Soph. *O.T.* 29, μέλας; Eur. *Alc.* 439, μελαγχαίτας; and *h. Dem.* 347, κυανοχαῖτα). Objects and locations in the underworld are described as dark by many authors and with a variety of adjectives. The house of Hades is called both μέλαν (Theogn. 1014) and μελαντειχέα (Pind. *Olymp.* 14.20-21). The recesses are κελαινός (Aesch. *Prom.* 433) and

31. There are other ways of saying "he died" which relate specifically to darkness covering the eyes: *Il.* 16.316 "darkness covered his eyes" τὸν δὲ σκότος ὄσσε κάλυψε; *Il.* 16.344 "a mist was shed on his eyes" κατὰ δ' ὀφθαλμῶν κέχυτ' ἀχλύς; *Il.* 16.333-334 "on his eyes came turbulent (?) death and mighty fate" τὸν δὲ κατ' ὄσσε/ ἔλλαβε πορφύρεος θάνατος καὶ μοῖρα κραταιή.

32. Kober p. 37.

33. Cf. Heraclitus B21; also the Christian synonym for the dead, "those who have fallen asleep," as in I Corinth. 15.18. οἱ κοιμηθέντες.

34. On the significance of "equal days and equal night," see L. Woodbury *TAPA* 97 (1966) 597-616.

ἐρεμνῶν (Eur. *Heracl.* 218). μελαμβαθεῖς is applied to river-banks (Soph. fr. 480). The Styx appears as μελάγχρωτα (Eur. *Hec.* 1105), and the rock of the Styx is μελανοκάρδιος (Aristoph. *Frogs* 470). The gates loom κυανέας (Theogn. 708-709). Erebus, whose very name means "dark place" (Appendix III) is dark in Euripides *Helen* 518 (μελαμφαές; cf. n. 9), and in Aristophanes *Birds* 693 (μέλαν). Tartarus, the place of punishment, is described as dark three times in Aeschylus' *Prometheus*: 219-220 (μελαμβαθής), 1028-1029 (κνεφαῖα), and 1050-1051 (κελαινόν).[35]

We saw that death was a dark night which covered the eyes, life a luminous existence where brightness is reinforced by the common synonym for living, "seeing the light of the sun." This idea is expressed in a variety of forms; hence our conclusion that this view of life as brightness was basic. In some contexts both verbs (live and see) appear, e.g. in *Iliad* 18.61: ὄφρα δέ μοι ζώει καὶ ὁρᾶι φάος ἠελίοιο "so long as he lives and sees the light of the sun."[36] In other contexts seeing is used by itself as a synonym for living: (Eur. *I.A.* 1218-1219): ἡδὺ γὰρ τὸ φῶς/ βλέπειν "for it is sweet to see the light."[37] Birth is a coming to the light or seeing the light (Pind. *Olymp.* 6.43-44):

ἦλθεν δ' ὑπὸ σπλάγχνων ὑπ' ὠδῖνός τ' ἐρατᾶς Ἴαμος
ἐς φάος αὐτίκα

"immediately Iamus came forth from her womb with the lovely birth-pang to the light."[38] Death is "not being in the light" or "not seeing the light" and dying is "leaving the light," as in Praxilla (Min. *PMG* fr. 747): κάλλιστον μὲν ἐγὼ λείπω φάος ἠελίοιο "I am leaving the fairest light of the sun."[39] A spirit, called up from the

35. Cf. also *Adesp. PMG* fr. 963: δέσποτα Πλούτων μελανοπτερύγων "Pluto, lord of dark-winged...." Bergk supplies ὀνείρων, but Page prefers (ψυχῶν). Cf. Aristoph. *Clouds* 192.

36. For living and seeing the light of the sun, see also *Od.* 4.540, *Adesp. PMG* fr. 934.21-22; Eur. *Ion* 853. For living and seeing, see *Il.* 1.88; Aesch. *Pers.* 299, *Ag.* 677 s.v.1. (cf. chapter two, p. 74). For the combination of seeing and breathing, see Soph. *Philoct.* 883.

37. For "seeing the light" as a synonym for living, see also Aesch. *Eum.* 746; *Ag.* 1646, [Eur.] *Rhesus* 971; Soph. *O.T.* 375, *Trach.* 269; Eur. *Phoen.* 1084, *Trojan Women* 269; *Adesp. PMG* fr. 994. Seeing opposed to death, Soph. *Philoct.* 1349, *Ajax* 962.

38. For birth as "coming to the light" or "seeing the light," see also Hes. *Theog.* 451, Pind. *Nem.* 7.1-4 (above, p. 160).

39. For dying as "leaving the light," see Hes. *W.D.* 155; as "not seeing," Soph.

lower world of darkness, comes "to the light," as in Aeschylus
Persae 630: πέμψατ' ἔνερθεν ψυχὴν ἐς φῶς, "send from below the
spirit [of Darius] to the light."[40]

I should like to call attention to several matters which show a
connection between light and seeing. First, one of the verbs of
seeing in Greek, λεύσσω, is related to λευκός "white, bright" (see
further, Appendix III). Snell suggests that λεύσσω means "see
something bright" and often connotes joy.[41] (Cf. αὐγάζω a rare
verb for "see," related to αὐγή "light of the sun.") Secondly, the
Greek word for light φάος is occasionally used by the poets for
"eye" (*Od.* 16.15, 19.417; Pind. *Nem.* 10.40; Eur. *Cyc.* 633).[42]
Thirdly, the Sun is characterized as "the god that sees everything,"
and this may very well be because he brings light to everything.[43]

Since the Greeks thought of life as light, it is natural to find in
Greek poetry a particular enjoyment of light and brightness. We
saw earlier in this chapter that a white day was a specially happy
one. Light (φάος) was used frequently in poetry to mean "joy,
deliverance, help, safety"; we conclude, then, that for the Greeks,
these states were bright. In the couplet attributed to Simonides
which honours the exploit of Aristogeiton and Harmodius the
"tyrantslayers," one can picture a brilliance (glory?) settling on
Athens (fr. 76D.):

ἦ μέγ' Ἀθηναίοισι φόως γένεθ' ἡνίκ' Ἀριστο-
γείτων Ἵππαρχον κτεῖνε καὶ Ἁρμόδιος.

"Surely a great light came to Athens when Aristogeiton and
Harmodius slew Hipparchus."[44] A discussion of Greek joy in light

---

Trach. 828, [Eur.] *Rhesus* 967; as "no longer being in the light," Soph. *Philoct.* 415,
Eur. *Hec.* 704-707 (specifically "light of Zeus").

40. For the return from the underworld to the world above as a change from
darkness to light, see also Soph. *Philoct.* 624-625, Hes. *Theog.* 157, 652 (sending the
offspring of Earth and Heaven to the upper world).

41. B. Snell *The Discovery of the Mind* (Oxford 1953) p. 3.

42. Cf. Matt. 6.22, "the light of the body is the eye."

43. For the sun as the god "that sees everything," see Soph. *O.C.* 868 and Mugler
s.v. λεύσσω.

44. For φάος as "joy, help, deliverance," see also *Il.* 15.741, 16.95-96, 17.615,
21.538, 6.5-6; of persons, *Il.* 16.39, 8.282 and *Od.* 16.23; Pind. *Olymp.* 4.11, *Isthm.*
2.17; Anacr. fr. 380 *PMG*; Aesch. *Pers.* 300; Soph. *Ant.* 599-600, *Ajax* 709, *Electra*
1224, 1354; Eur. *Hec.* 841. Also Mimnermus fr. 13.9-11 D. on the brave warrior who
went "like the beams of the sun."

would not be complete without reference to Sappho's lines (fr. 58. 25-26 *PLF*):

ἔγω δὲ φίλημμ' ἀβροσύναν   τοῦτο καί μοι
τὸ λά [μπρον ἔρος τὠελίω καὶ τὸ κά] λον λέ [λ] ογχε-

"But I love luxury; this also has been allotted to me — brightness, love of the sun, and beauty."[45]

The brightness of life and happiness were in sharp contrast to the darkness not only of death but of sadness and gloom. It is interesting to note that the use of μέλας to mean sad is found almost exclusively in Homer and Aeschylus. In Homer we find pain described as "dark" (*Il.* 4.117, 191, 15. 394); grief as "a dark cloud" (*Il.* 17. 591, 18.22, *Od.* 24.315). Pain was probably linked with death in the poet's mind and may well have been dark because death was; grief is not always associated with death, although it may be, so the fact that it is dark probably reflects a general connection between darkness and sorrow. (Cf. the discussion of φρένες μέλαιναι chapter four.) The specific association between darkness and mourning for the dead is found in the convention of wearing dark clothes for mourning and in the description of grief or mourning as dark, as, for example, in the following (Pind. *Pyth.* 4.112-113): κᾶδος ὡσείτε φθιμένου δνοφερὸν/ εν δώμασι θηκάμενοι, "making dark mourning in the house as for someone who had died," and (Aesch. *Pers.* 535-536): ἄστυ/ πένθει δνοφερῶι κατέκρυψας. "You [Zeus] covered the city with dark grief."

There are a number of examples in Aeschylus' plays in which dark apparently means "sad, gloomy." The blows struck in mourning in *Persae* 1052 are dark: μέλαινα . . . πλαγά. (Sidgwick takes μέλαινα as "gloomy,"[46] but Broadhead prefers "blackening," a realistic epithet for the result of the blows.)[47] In *Suppliants* 89, chance (τύχα) is μέλαινα;[48] in line 888 a dream (probably a

45. D. L. Page *Sappho and Alcaeus* (Oxford 1955) p. 130, n. 1., remarks (on fr. 58. 25-26); "I have no conception of the meaning of these last two lines." It is hard to believe that the association of brightness, the sun, and beauty strike no familiar note in Page's mind; presumably his difficulty lies in fitting the lines into the larger context of the fragment.
46. Sidgwick *Aeschylus Persae* on line 1052.
47. Broadhead *The Persae of Aeschylus* on line 1052.
48. H. W. Smyth *Aeschylus* vol. 1 (London 1922) p. 11 translates μελαίναι ξὺν

nightmare) is ὄναρ μέλαν; in line 530 the ship in which the sons of Aegyptus are pursuing the Danaids is a "dark-benched cursed thing" (τὰν μελανόζυγ᾽ ἄταν), recalling Homer's dark ships and also suggesting unhappiness. Oedipus' curse is dark (μέλαινα ... ἀρά), perhaps "fatal," as it resulted in the death of his sons (*Septem* 833). (Cf. *Ag.* 770 μέλαινα ἄτα, 1511 μέλας Ἄρης; Eur. *Hec.* 70-71, 705 "dark-winged dreams"; and the description of the Erinyes as dark).

The Greek convention of wearing black or dark clothing for mourning, a familiar practice for us, may seem quite unremarkable; but it is interesting to find it as far back as Homer, when Thetis chose a dark (κυάνεος) veil as a symbol of mourning (*Il.* 24.93-94, see chapter three). Similarly, Demeter wore κυάνεος clothing to mourn the loss of her daughter (*h. Dem.* 42, 182-183, 319, 360, 374, 442; see chapter three). From Dionysius of Halicarnassus we learn that such festivals as the rape of Persephone and the sufferings of Dionysus are "festivals of dark clothing" (ἑορτὴ μελανείμων 2.19).

The earliest connection of μέλας clothing with mourning and death is found in the dramatists. Charon's ship is "dark-sailed" (μελάγκροκον Aesch. *Sept.* 857) both because it is a ship of the dead and also as if it were draped in mourning.[49] A chorus of women "in dark cloaks" come carrying libations to Agamemnon's tomb (μελαγχίμοις Aesch. *Choeph.* 11).

In Euripides' *Alcestis*, a play in which death and mourning are frequently in the minds of the characters, there are several mentions of dark clothing for mourning: lines 215-217, 427, 819. Death himself wears dark robes (843 μελάμπεπλον). Admetus contrasts the white (λευκῶν πέπλων) clothing he wore at his wedding with the black (μέλανες στολμοί) raiment he put on for his wife's funeral (922-923). This move from one extreme to the other is repeated in *Helen* 1088, 1186-1187, where white clothing is her everyday dress and black her proposed apparel in mourning

---

τύχαι "by events obscure"; cf. section six C: for the darkness of obscurity in Greek poetry.

49. Smyth *Aeschylus* vol. 1 p. 395, n. 1, comments that this ship of the dead is meant to contrast with the ship that goes to the festival of Apollo at Delos, the "clear-seen" land.

for Menelaus. (Cf. also *Phoen.* 322-324 ἄπεπλος φαρέων λευκῶν, δυσόρφναια . . . τρύχη and 372 πέπλους μελαγχίμους).⁵⁰

The cropping of hair as a sign of mourning is frequently mentioned along with the wearing of black. In *Orestes* Tyndareus appears on stage "in dark clothing, his hair shorn in mourning for his daughter (i.e. Clytemnestra)" (457-458):

μελάμπεπλος
κουρᾶι τε θυγατρὸς πενθίμωι κεκαρμένος.

(Cf. also *Phoen.* 371-373, *Alcest.* 427, 819). We find a clear indication that dark clothing was put on in mourning in *Iphigeneia in Aulis* 1438, 1448, where Iphigeneia, now reconciled to her fate and playing the part of a willing victim, tells her mother Clytemnestra not to wear dark clothing after her death and not to allow her sisters to wear it, either.⁵¹

In Aristophanes *Acharnians* (1024) Dicaeopolis, hearing from a farmer all his bad luck, exclaims, "O miserable wretch, and you're wearing *white?*": ὦ τρισκακόδαιμον, εἶτα λευκὸν ἀμπέχει; The implication is certainly that he should, with all his misfortune, be in black. Van Leeuwen sees a further implication that since dirty clothes are characteristic of a farmer, his clothes were probably not very white, but this is perhaps unnecessarily subtle.⁵² Certain divinities and personifications wear dark clothing, for various reasons: Death (Eur. *Alcest.* 843); Night (Eur. *Ion* 1150); the Furies (Aesch. *Eum.* 370, cf. line 352: παλλεύκων δὲ πέπλων ἀπόμοιρος ἄκληρος ἐτύχθην), and darkness (Bacch. 3.13).

White clothing can, of course, be ordinary wearing apparel, made presumably of undyed cloth, as opposed to cloth dyed purple, for example, which was very costly. Among Priam's household linens are "white cloaks" (*Il.* 24.231); Patroclus' body is prepared for burial and covered "with fine linen from head to foot and over the linen a white cloak" (*Il.* 18.352-353); the

---

50. We translate λευκός as "white" rather than "light" in this discussion of clothing, because "light" is ambiguous; it might refer to weight as well as colour.
51. Prose references to the wearing of dark clothing: Plut. *Mor.* 2.838f (Isocrates wore black for Socrates' death); Dion. Hal. 2.19 see above); Plut. *Per.* 38 (Pericles on his death-bed declares that no one of Athenians alive ever on his account put on a black cloak).
52. J. van Leeuwen *Aristophanis Acharnenses* (Leiden 1901) on line 1024, where he compares line 120.

common colour for sails in Homer is white (*Il.* 1.480, e.g.);[53] Hera's head-band was "white like the sun" (*Il.* 14.185), and Penelope's web shone like the sun or moon, (*Od.* 24.148). Sometimes we find the connotation "clean, freshly-washed" associated with white. At Apollo's birth, the goddesses who were present "wrapped him in a fine, white, freshly-washed cloak" (*h. Ap.* 121-122): σπάρξαν δ' ἐν φάρεϊ λευκῶι/ λεπτῶι νηγατέωι·[54] (Cf. below Aristoph. *Birds* 1115-1117). Aeschylus contrasts the dark skins of the sons of Aegyptus with their white, probably linen,[55] clothing (*Supp.* 719-720, cf. chapter four, p. 130).

White clothing may symbolize the goodness and purity of the wearer, e.g. of Aidos and Nemesis in this passage from Hesiod when they returned from earth to Olympus "covering their fair flesh with white cloaks" (Hes. *W.D.* 198): λευκοῖσιν φάρεσσι καλυψαμένα χρόα καλόν. Similarly, it was apparently their purity and their priestly office that prompted the prophets of Zeus in Crete to wear white (Eur. fr. 472. 16-19):

> πάλλευκα δ' ἔχων εἵματα φεύγω
> γένεσίν τε βροτῶν καὶ νεκροθήκης
> οὐ χριμπτόμενος τὴν τ' ἐμψύχων
> βρῶσιν ἐδεστῶν πεφύλαγμαι.

"Wearing all-white robes, I shun the generation of mortals, and not touching a coffin, I have kept myself from eating the flesh of animals [lit. meat with life in it]." There is particular stress in this fragment on ritual purity, and it seems reasonable to assume that the wearing of white was part of this purity. Boughs crowned with white wool were suitable for a suppliant; Aeschylus *Suppliants* 191 (λευκοστεφεῖς ἱκτηρίας) and 334 (λευκοστεφεῖς κλάδους); and Aeschylus *Eumenides* 45 (ἀργῆτι ... μαλλῶι). The chorus in Euripides' *Bacchae* sings, "Gird for a consecration your cloaks of

53. Other references to white sails: *Od.* 2.426, 4.783, 8.54, 9.77, 10.506, 12.402, 15.29; Theogn. 671; Eur. *Helen* 1535. Cf. Eur. *Hipp.* 752-753.
54. We are used to white clothing for a new-born infant but we should note that it was not invariably used by the Greeks; the new-born Jason was wrapped in purple swaddling clothes (Pind. *Pyth.* 4.114,) and the infant Heracles in saffron (*Nem.* 1.38). The dyed materials probably were evidence of the wealth of their families. For white or bright clothing connoting cleanliness, see *Il.* 22.153-154: εἵματα σιγαλόεντα. But in *Od.* 6.26 σιγαλόεντα is conventional.
55. Cf. *Supp.* 121, 132.

dappled fawnskin with white curls of braided wool" (111-113):[56]

στικτῶν τ' ἐνδυτὰ νεβρίδων
στέφετε λευκοτρίχων πλοκάμων
μαλλοῖς.

It seems possible that here too the white wool may have a ritual significance.

Three examples in Aristophanes suggest that white clothing was particularly appropriate for festivals. This representation of happiness by white clothing contrasts strongly with the wearing of dark clothing for mourning and reminds us of the association of white and joy as shown by the Greek expression noted earlier λευκὴ ἡμέρα "a good/ happy day." In a fragment, the chorus in *Tagenistae* says (fr. 491):

τί οὖν ποιῶμεν; χλανίδ' ἐχρῆν λευκὴν λαβεῖν
εἶτ' Ἰσθμιακὰ λαβόντες, ὥσπερ οἱ χοροὶ
ᾁδωμεν ἐς τὸν δεσπότην ἐγκώμιον.

"What, then, are we to do? We ought to get white cloaks and then putting on Isthmians (a kind of wreath) as the choruses do, let us sing a hymn of praise to our master." White cloaks and wreaths were suitable attire for a celebration. In the parabasis of the *Thesmophoriazousae* the chorus mentions the mother of Hyperbolus sitting in the audience "dressed in white and with flowing hair" (840–841): ἠμφιεσμένην/ λευκὰ καὶ κόμας καθεῖσαν. Van Leeuwen comments: "candida veste crinibusque demissis festo die liberaliter contam atque ornatam."[57] Probably whiteness indicated not only the colour but the cleanliness of apparel worn at festivals. One might surmise that ancient standards of cleanliness were not so high as ours and that a special occasion called for the washing and bleaching of one's outfit. It seems to be a reference to cleanliness as much as to colour in the *Birds* where the chorus warns, "Whoever of you doesn't have a moon, when you are wearing a white cloak (χλανίδα λευκήν), then especially you will give us satisfaction, soiled by all the birds" (1115-1117). "Moons" were protectors placed over the heads of statues to keep them

---

56. For the translation of these lines, see Dodds *Euripides Bacchae* on line 112.
57. Van Leeuwen *Aristophanis Thesmophoriazousae* (Leiden 1904) on line 840.

from being soiled by birds.[58] The emphasis on a "white cloak" in this context suggests that it was just cleaned and therefore the annoyance of the wearer would be all the greater.[59]

IV The Gods: Olympian and Chthonian

We saw that the Greeks pictured Olympus, the seat of the gods above, as a bright abode in clear, brilliant air (*Od.* 6.44-45). The gods of the lower world, in contrast, were dark themselves and lived in darkness, either in the underworld or in the earth (cf. γαῖα μέλαινα, below, section five, and χθών chthonian). Not only did they live in very different places, but their whole character and the manner in which they were worshipped form a study in contrasts.[60] Can we find evidence of a division into "light" Olympian and "dark" chthonian deities? One factor which complicates the picture is that the Olympians appeared in human form, showing the same sex-based contrast of light and dark as is found in their human counterparts. Goddesses, it will be recalled, are "white-armed" (λευκώλενος) in Homer and later poets, but this epithet portrays their femininity, not their connection with Olympus (see chapter four). Dionysus is taunted for his fair skin by Pentheus (Eur. *Bacch.* 457, see chapter four), but this whiteness is an evidence of his effeminacy. The light/dark antithesis between the sexes seems to take precedence over a light/dark antithesis between the gods above and the gods below.

Fates and Furies are frequently described as dark. Fate in Homer (in the singular) is always connected with death; the poet says "he avoided dark fate," meaning "he avoided death." The darkness of fate in Homer is a result of its connection with death,

---

58. On "moons" see W. W. Merry *Aristophanes The Birds* (Oxford 1889) on line 1114 and van Leeuwen *Aristophanis Aves* (Leiden 1902) on line 1114. Merry describes the moons as crescent-shaped; van Leeuwen points out that the purpose demands a full moon shape.

59. Van Leeuwen *Aristophanis Aves* on line 1116 sees a reference to cleanliness: "χλανίδα λευκήν   pulchram puramque vestem, φανήν, a fullone recentem (*vid. ad Eq.* 1256)."

60. W. Headlam "Ghost-raising, Magic and the Underworld" in *CR* 16 (1902) 52-55 gives contrasts in the method of worshipping Olympian (Heavenly) and chthonian (Nether) deities: he extends this contrast to time of day, time of month and posture of worshipper. See also W. K. C. Guthrie *The Greeks and their gods* (London 1950) pp. 221-222.

which is dark (see above, section three, and n. 30 for references to
"dark fate" in Homer). The plural "Fates," however, seems closer
to personification; e.g. in *Iliad* 2.834 "the Fates of dark death led
them": κῆρες γὰρ ἄγον μέλανος θανάτοιο. In the lyric poets
Mimnermus (fr. 2.5 D) and Tyrtaeus (fr. 8.5-6 D.), reference is
made to "dark Fates." Again, specifically in Tyrtaeus, the Fates
are connected with death and in their darkness are like death.

In the case of the Furies or Erinyes, however, we are dealing
with chthonian deities and it seems reasonable to suppose that
their darkness is a result of their earthly origin. Most of these
references are found in Aeschylus: in *Septem* the Fury (Erinys) is
dark (977, 988 μέλαιν᾽ Ἐρινύς) and "dark-aegised" (699-700
μελάναιγις); in *Eumenides* where the Furies form the chorus, they
are dark (52, cf. *Ag.* 462-463 κελαιναί Ἐρινύες), wear dark
clothing (370, cf. 352), and are the daughters of Night (745).[61]
Other authors report that the Erinyes are the daughters of Earth
(Ge, Hes. *Theog.* 185, Soph. *O.C.* 40) but whether of dark Night
or of dark Earth, both accounts of their parentage stress their
darkness. Euripides calls them the "dark-complexioned Eumeni-
des" (*Orest.* 321: μελάγχρωτες εὐμενίδες), the only reference I
have found which describes them in their "reformed" state as
"dark." Compare Euripides' *Electra* 1345 where the Furies are
"dark in complexion": χρῶτα κελαιναί and *Orestes* 408 where
they are "like night": νυκτὶ προσφερεῖς. It is interesting that most
references to dark Erinyes occur in plays dealing with the Orestes
cycle which concerned a particular cult of the Eumenides at
Athens. Aeschylus' references in *Septem* are, unlike the other
dramatic occurrences, in the singular, though there too the Erinys
is "dark." We may speculate that contrasts of dark and light were
more widely used in cult worship than we might suspect from
literary remains (cf., e.g., below Aphrodite Melainis and Demeter
Melaina). Dietrich argues that the Eumenides had a dark and light
side, adducing as evidence Pausanias (8.34.3):[62] "they say that
these goddesses, when they were about to make Orestes mad,

61. Cf. also *Eum.* 321, 416, 791-792, 821-822, 844, 876, 1034.
62. Dietrich p. 120 n. 2. Cf. also Servius on Verg. *Ecl.* 5.56: "[candidus] significat
benignos et bonos; sicut e contra malos nigros dicimus"; and Suda s.v. λευκόν· ὅτι τὸ
λευκὸν ὁμώνυμον ὥσπερ τὸ ἀγαθόν.

appeared dark to him . . . and again they seemed to him to be white . . . and he sacrificed to the white goddesses." But it is probably a later refinement that made the Eumenides dark when they were hostile and white when they were kindly disposed.

There are two cults which interest us because the goddess who is worshipped is described as "dark": the cults of Demeter Melaina and Aphrodite Melainis. Demeter Melaina was worshipped at Phigalia in Arcadia (Paus. 8.5.8); Dietrich compares this title to Demeter Erinys and concludes that both titles reflect the aboriginal character of Demeter as an earth-goddess. (See the discussion of γαῖα μέλαινα below.) Pausanias says that Aphrodite is dark because men indulge in sexual intercourse at night (8.6.5), but Dietrich rejects this interpretation in favour of a connection with death. Flacelière, too, sees a reference to death in Melainis and compares the cult title Epitumbia "protectress of tombs," found at Argos and Delphi. He also refers to ceremonies of a funereal type held at Corinth in Aphrodite's honour.[63]

It is harder to establish a connection between the gods above and whiteness, although Radke argues that white indicates "protecting" or "helping" deities and gives many examples to support his view. Much of his evidence is later than the fifth century, for example, the "white maidens" who were supposed to have helped the inhabitants of Delphi against the Celts (279 B.C.). Some of his interpretations are disputed; for instance, he suggests that the title Leucos under which Hermes was worshipped at Tanagra signified "helper," and that Hermes Leucos helped "those who do wrong and are not able to escape," although *LSJ* say the proverb applied when a rogue was detected.[64] For the period of this study, we are chiefly interested in Leucothea, the "white" sea-goddess who helped Odysseus when his raft broke up (*Od.* 5.333ff) and the epithet "white-horsed" given to the Dioscuri who come to the aid of sailors.

The "White Goddess" Leucothea is, in her mortal origins, Ino

63. For Demeter, see Dietrich pp. 104-105, 121 n. 3, where he quotes in support L. R. Farnell *The Cults of the Greek States* (Oxford 1906) vol. 3, p. 51. For Aphrodite, see R. Flacelière *Love in Ancient Athens* (tr. James Clough, London 1962) p. 33.

64. G. Radke in *Philol.* 92 (1937) 387-402. References to this oracle: Aristid. *Or.* 26.75 (*Paroem. Gr.* 1.403), Suda s.v. ἐμοὶ μελήσει; Schol. Aristoph. *Clouds* 144, Tzetz. Chil. 11. 394f; in prose Diod. Sic. 22.20, Cic. *De Divin.* 1.81.

daughter of Cadmus and Harmonia and therefore sister of Semele who bore Dionysus to Zeus (Hes. *Theog.* 976). She is said to have leaped into the sea a mortal, Ino, and emerged an immortal, Leucothea. Farnell argues that she is primarily a chthonian goddess, because of her association with Semele and Dionysus, and because of certain cult practices peculiar to chthonian deities (Arist. *Rhet.* 1400 b quoting Xenophanes). He suggests that her association with the sea is chiefly literary (Hom. *Od.* 5.333-335, Alc. fr. 50 *PMG*, Hes. fr. 70.1-7 MW) and that Leucothea was given as a name of brightness and good omen. She bears the title "Saviour" once in an Athenian inscription: C.I.A. 3.368 [Λευκο] θέας Σωτῆρας (sic). She certainly appears as a maritime helper in Homer, whatever her role elsewhere, and the inscription is evidence that she appeared later in this role. Her name is suitable for a sea-deity, especially for one who helps those in distress on the water.[65]

With reference to the Dioscuri let us consider briefly the epithet λευκόπωλος or λεύκιππος. White horses were admired in antiquity (see *Il.* 10.427, the horses of Rhesus), and the ownership of such horses seems to have been a mark of wealth and ancestry (Pind. *Pyth.* 4.117, 9.83, fr. 202; Soph. *Elect.* 706). Day or dawn we saw is "white-horsed" because of the brightness of daylight. Certain gods were described as "white-horsed"; but, with one exception,[66] these were twins of the pre-Trojan War period: Castor and Polydeuces (Pind. *Pyth.* 1.66, Eur. *Helen* 639); Amphion and Zethus (Eur. *H.F.* 29, and probably also *Phoen.* 606)[67] – and the Molionids (Ibyc. fr. 285.1 *PMG*). These twins all belong to the time when battle was conducted from chariots in which two rode, one to drive and one to fight, and the epithet seems to be a reflection of this custom.[68] After their earthly life, however, the

---

65. L. R. Farnell *Greek Hero Cults and ideas of Immortality* (Oxford 1921) pp. 35-47, especially pp. 36, 39.

66. The exception is found in Pind. *Olymp.* 6.95 where Persephone is "white-horsed," possibly a cult title, since a festival is mentioned.

67. The reference is simply to "white-horsed gods"; because of the Theban connection, the reference is usually taken to be of Amphion and Zethus, sons of Zeus and Antiope (*Od.* 11.260-265), co-founders of Thebes (*Od.* 11.263).

68. Castor is connected with horses by tradition: Κάστορά θ' ἱππόδαμον *Il.* 3.237. The Molionids were, according to some reports, Siamese twins (Leaf *Homer The Iliad* on *Il.* 23.638). In Homer they are always charioteers (*Il.* 11.709, 750, 23.638).

Dioscuri became deities who brought help to sailors during a storm. Their presence was indicated by electricity playing on the ship's rigging (known as St. Elmo's fire, cf. Alc. fr. B(2)a.9-12 PLF). "White-horsed" may have acquired a new significance in connection with this light.

In connection with Leucothea and the Dioscuri who bring help in storms we are also reminded of the description of a calm as "white" in Homer (Od. 10.94): λευκὴ δ' ἦν ἀμφὶ γαλήνη. Moreover the action of the Dioscuri in ending a storm is thus given (h. Hom. 33.15): κύματα δ' ἐστόρεσαν λευκῆς ἁλὸς ἐν πελάγεσσι, "they laid to rest the waves on the surface of the white sea." In this context λευκῆς may very well be considered proleptic. I suggest that the association of white with deities who bring calm is related to the whiteness of calm itself (see further section six).[69]

There is a general division in sacrifices offered to the gods above and those below.[70] The earliest evidence of differentiation by colour is found in Homer, where Priam gives orders for a truce between the Greeks and the Trojans and commands, "Bring sheep, a white ram for the Sun and a black ewe for the Earth" (Il. 3.103-104):

> οἴσετε ἄρν' ἕτερον λευκὸν, ἑτέρην δὲ μέλαιναν
> Γῆι τε καὶ Ἡελίωι·

In the example both colour and sex of the victim are appropriate to the god to whom it is sacrificed (dark and female for Earth, white and male for Sun). In Homeric Hymn 33.10 white lambs are offered to the Dioscuri, Castor and Polydeuces. Black victims were customarily offered to the Erinyes (see Schol. Soph. O.C. 39 and above),[71] and were also sacrificed to the dead. Odysseus is told by Circe to sacrifice a black ram to Teiresias when he arrived in Ithaca (Od. 10.524-525, 11.32-33) and a black ewe when he reached

---

69. The Dioscuri are closely connected with light and brightness. They are "white-horsed," they appear as electricity on the ship's rigging, and they are a heavenly constellation (Gemini). Cf. Hesychius s.v. Διόσκουροι· ... καὶ ἀστέρες οἱ τοῖς ναυτιλλομένοις φαινόμενοι.

70. Radke pp. 400-402 quotes Porphyry in Euseb. Praep. Ev. 4.9.145c: φαιδρὰ μὲν οὐρανίοις, χθονίοις δ' ἐναλίγκια χροῆι and Verg. Aen. 3.120. Cf. also Headlam pp. 52-55.

71. In contrast white victims are sometimes offered to chthonic deities: to Despoina in Lycosura Syll.³ 999.18f and to Mystery gods in Andania Syll.³ 736,67. Radke pp. 400-402 argues that white is chosen to propitiate.

Erebus to provide blood for the ghosts to drink (*Od*. 10.527-528). In Euripides *Electra* 513 a black sheep is offered in sacrifice to the dead. On the other hand, the cattle killed for the funeral banquet of Patroclus are white (*Il*. 23.30): πολλοὶ μὲν βόες ἀργοὶ ... σφαζόμενοι. Kober remarks, "Since the Greeks did not usually kill white animals in honour of the dead, it has been suggested that the adjective here means 'sleek, fat' ... or that it is from a root which means 'idle' (ἀ-εργός)."[72] More probably, the poet merely thought of the banquet rather than a sacrifice when he specified the colour of the cattle.

Sometimes the colour of the victim seems to have been chosen for a particular aspect of the deity rather than an Olympian/chthonian distinction. Odysseus and his men sacrificed pure black bulls to Poseidon under his title "Earth-shaker with dark hair" (*Od*. 3.6): ταύρους παμμέλανας ἐνοσίχθονι κυανοχαίτηι.[73] But in Pindar (*Olymp*. 13.69), Bellerophon is instructed to offer a white bull to Poseidon the Horse-tamer: Δαμαίωι ... θύων ταῦρον ἀργᾶντα. In the first example, Poseidon appeared as the god of earthquakes and storms, in the second as the more peaceful god of horses. We find reference to a black victim for a storm-god in Aristophanes *Frogs* 847, where Dionysus in response to Aeschylus' stormy violence (825), calls "Boys, bring a black ram, for Typho is getting ready to blow":

ἄρν' ἄρνα μέλανα, παῖδες, ἐξενέγκατε
τυφὼς γὰρ ἐκβαίνειν παρασκευάζεται.[74]

V Earth and Sky

We saw in section one that the Greeks built much of their understanding of the world and their reactions to it on the contrasts of day and night. Thus, unlike states such as joy and sadness, are made even more unlike by descriptions as dark and white. But the opposition of night and day is not the only one which influenced the Greek view of the world. Indeed, a division of qualities and objects may be reconstructed from the remains of

72. Kober p. 14.
73. For κυανοχαίτης, see chapter three, section two.
74. W. B. Stanford *Aristophanes Frogs* (London 1958) on lines 847-848.

Parmenides and the Pythagoreans and represented in two columns of opposites. Guthrie has drawn up such a table of opposites which he argues Parmenides believed were the divisions of the physical world:[75]

fire	night
bright	dark
sky	earth
hot	cold
dry	moist
rare	dense
light	heavy
right	left
male	female
soft	hard

The members of each column have a connection with one another as well as being paired with the members of the opposite column. The first two words in each column may be combined, since fire is bright and night is dark. Hot and dry naturally go together in opposition to cold and moist, since heat removes moisture. Rare and light (in weight) form a pair in contrast to dense and heavy, since what is dense is heavy in relation to its size. We may also justify the combination of earth and female in contrast to sky and male, because earth ($\gamma\tilde{\eta}$) is a feminine noun in Greek and sky ($o\dot{\upsilon}\rho\alpha\nu\acute{o}\varsigma$) is masculine. Moreover, according to Anaxagoras (A42) earth is of a feminine nature and the sky and sun are fathers and progenitors. Earth brings forth fruit, as women bear children. (Cf. also the myth which Aristophanes relates in Plato *Symposium* 190b, in which he explains that women are the offspring of Earth and men of the Sun). We can now simplify the original list:

fire, bright	night, dark
hot, dry	moist, cold
rare, light	dense, heavy
sky, male	earth, female

75. W. K. C. Guthrie *A History of Greek Philosophy* (Cambridge 1965) vol. 2, p. 77. For Pythagorean opposites, see vol. 1, p. 245: brightness — darkness; right — left; male — female.

We have not yet grouped from the original list soft-hard and right-left. Soft and hard might very well be regarded as functions of rarity and density, since what is dense is harder to the touch than what is rare. Right and left possibly have a connection with east and west. When Polydamas points out an omen to Hector and gives advice based on it, Hector retorts that it is of no concern to him "whether [birds] go to the right towards the dawn and the sun, or whether to the left towards the dark west" (Il. 12.239-240):[76]

εἴτ᾽ ἐπὶ δεξί᾽ ἴωσι πρὸς ἠῶ τ᾽ ἠέλιόν τε
εἴτ᾽ ἐπ᾽ ἀριστερὰ τοί γε ποτὶ ζόφον ἠερόεντα.

This suggests that for purposes of divination, at least, one faced north and had the east on the right and the west on the left. (It is interesting to note that right is associated with brightness and left with darkness in the Pythagorean opposites, too, see n. 75). The members of the left-hand column, hot, dry, rare, light, bright, male, sky, all belong to the upper atmosphere, the aether; whereas the members of the right-hand column, cold, moist, dense, heavy, dark, female, earth, all belong to the earth. There is a description found in Homer and many later poets, expressed in a variety of ways, but generally translatable as "dark earth." Why the Greeks called the earth dark and whether this is relevant to the contrast between the characteristics of earth and those of sky is our next question.

Earth is frequently described as dark in epic and lyric poetry and even occasionally in drama.[77] Many reasons have been advanced to explain the epithet and we shall re-examine some of them now. The most natural interpretation seems to us that dark

---

76. Other references to the "dark west": Il. 15.191, 21.56, 23.51, Od. 11.57, 155, 13.241.

77. Γαῖα μέλαινα: Il. 2.699, 15.715, 17.416, 20.494; Od. 11.365, 587, 19.111; h. Ap. 369; Hes. Theog. 69; Bacch. 13.153; Theogn. 878, 1070b. Μέλαινα γαῖα: Alcman fr. 89.3 PMG, Alcaeus fr. N1. 12-13 PLF. Δῆ μέλαινα: Sappho fr.1. 10, fr. 16.2 (cf. Page Sappho and Alcaeus p. 53); Solon fr. 24.5, fr. 26.4-5. Μέλαινα γῆ Simonides fr. 159.2 D. Χθὼν μέλαινα: Archilochus fr. 58.2, Alcaeus fr. G2.29, B6^A10 PLF, Semonides fr. 1.14 D., Pind. Olymp. 9.50. Πέδον μέλαν (μελάγχιμον): Eur. Bacch. 756, 1065, Rhes. 962. Ἤπειρος μέλαινα: Od. 14.97, 21.109; h. Dem. 130, h. Hom. 7.22. Ploughed land: Il. 18.548; Pind. Nem. 11.39. Other variants: Il. 16.384 κελαινὴ χθών; Od. 24.106, h. Herm. 427 ἐρεμνὴν γαῖαν; Pind. fr. 33b κυανέας χθονός, cf. chapter three.

earth was fertile as opposed to lighter-coloured clay or sand which is relatively infertile.[78] This is the connotation of "black earth" for us. We find support for this explanation in references to food production and the sustinence of man, reading, for example, in *Odyssey* 19.111, "dark earth bears wheat and barley": φέρῃσι δὲ γαῖα μέλαινα / πυροὺς καὶ κριθάς. (Cf. also *Od.* 11.365, Alcman fr. 89.3 *PMG*, Solon fr. 26.4-5D., Pind. *Nem.* 11.39.) In *Iliad* 18.548 the poet describes how, on Achilles' shield, the field grew dark behind (μελαίνετ'), like land which has been ploughed. Water-soaked earth is described as dark (*Od.* 11.587, Pind. *Olymp.* 9.50). In these contexts there is no connection with fertility, but since, in general, well-watered earth is better for agriculture than dry soil, one might argue that earth which was dark was well-watered and therefore fertile.[79]

Kober offers another possible explanation of "dark earth": "land to a sailor looks dark when it is viewed from the sea."[80] She supports this view by referring to the description of the mainland (ἤπειρος) as "dark" in the *Odyssey* (14.97, 21.109) and the *Homeric Hymns* (h. *Dem.* 130, h. *Hom.* 7.22). In this connection we may note that the island of Corcyra is called Melaina in Apollonius Rhodius 4.567-569, and certain islands and headlands are described as "dark-leaved" (μελάμφυλλος). We have, for example, "the dark-leaved heights of Aetna" (Pind. *Pyth.* 1.27), a "dark-leaved peak" (Bacch. 9.33-34), and "dark-leaved mountains" (Aristoph. *Thesm.* 997).[81] Kober accounts for the darkness of the mainland as a contrast to the sea, but it is quite possible, and to the author, more likely, that land is dark against the bright sky. If interpreted this way, the "dark mainland" and "dark-leaved heights" contrasted with the bright sky illustrate the tension we found in the Parmenidean table of opposites.

Wallace argues that "in the *Iliad* (2.699 and 17.416-417) γαῖα μέλαινα is often an equivalent of 'death' and in the expression ῥέε δ' αἵματι γαῖα μέλαινα (*Il.* 15.715, 20.494), the adjective seems

---

78. See Kober p. 32.
79. Cf. μελάγχαιος in Herod. 2.12, 4.198; Theophr. *H.P.* 8.7.2, *C.P.* 2.4.12.
80. See Kober p. 32.
81. Other occurrences of μελάμφυλλος, Anacr. fr. 443 *PMG*; Simon. fr. 519.3 *PMG*; Pind. *Paean* 2.43-44; Soph. *O.C.* 482.

almost to have a predicative force, as blood in these places of slaughter is regularly μέλαν.[82] (Cf. *Il.* 2.699, 17.416-417, and Archil. fr. 58.2). But since a formular expression does not always suit the mood of the passage, it is unsafe to place too much emphasis on this combination, especially since the phrase "dark earth" occurs elsewhere without association with death. That Wallace is mistaken in attributing predicative force to μέλαινα in the expression ῥέε δ' αἵματι γαῖα μέλαινα is perhaps clear from Bacchylides 13.151-154:

> ἐναριζομένων
> δ' ἔρ]ευθε φώτων
> αἵμα]τι γαῖα μέλαινα
> Ἐκτορ]έας ὑπὸ χειρός.

"The dark earth reddened with the blood of men slaughtered by the hand of Hector." If the predicative force had been felt at all in the Homeric line, it would have been impossible for Bacchylides to combine γαῖα μέλαινα and ἔρευθε.[83] One can find other connections between death and dark earth. Theognis says "when I die I shall become dark earth" (878, 1070b): ἐγὼ δὲ θανὼν γαῖα μέλαιν' ἔσομαι. The decomposition of a corpse and its return to earth is a familiar idea to us. Consider Genesis 3.19, "dust thou art, and unto dust shalt thou return."[84] I think that Theognis used γαῖα μέλαινα as a formular expression and that "dark" has no special force in relation to death.

Cole has concluded that dark earth was a cover for the underworld, "that the adjective for earth is really transferred from Hades."[85] He quotes in support Semonides fr. 1.13-14 D., where

---

82. Wallace p. 15. Blood is μέλας: *Il.* 4.149, 7.262, 10.298, 469, 11.813, 13.655, 16.529, 18.583, 20.470, 21.119, 23.806; *Od.* 3.455; *h. Herm.* 122; Hes. *Sc.* 252; Theogn. 349; Aesch. *Ag.* 1020, *Eum.* 980, *Septem* 737; Soph. *Ajax* 919, *O.T.* 1278-1279; Eur. *Elect.* 318-319, *Hec.* 536, *I.A.* 1114. Variations using μέλας in some form: *Il.* 5.354; *Od.* 24.189; Pind. *Isthm.* 8.50; Aesch. *Eum.* 183; Soph. *Ajax* 1412-1413, *Philoct.* 824-825; Eur. *Hec.* 153. Blood is κελαινός or κελαινεφής: *Il.* 1.303, 4.140, 5.798, 7.329, 11.829, 845, 14.437, 16.667, 21.167; *Od.* 11.36, 98, 153, 228, 232, 390, 16.441, 19.457; Hes. *Sc.* 173-174; Aesch. *Prom.* 1025.

83. For ἔρευθε see Jebb *Bacchylides* on 12.151-154: "a solitary but certain instance of the active verb used intransitively."

84. Cf. further Job 34.15, "all flesh perish, men shall turn again to their dust"; Psalms 104.29, "they die and return to their dust."

85. Cole vol. 2. p. 45 and n. 147.

we read that "Hades sends beneath the dark earth those subdued by Ares":

τοὺς δ᾽ Ἄρει δεδμημένους
πέμπει μελαίνης Ἀίδης ὑπὸ χθονός

and Alcaeus (fr. B6A 10 *PLF*) where we find the phrase "son of Cronus, king beneath the dark earth": Κρονίδαις βα [σίλευς κάτω/ μελαίνας χθόνος.

None of these interpretations, however, explains more than a few of the occurrences of "dark earth." The frequency with which this phrase recurs and the variety of ways in which the poets express it (see n. 77) indicate that it is basic to the Greek view of the world and probably very old. Harvey, in a discussion of Homeric epithets in lyric poetry, argues for "some deep religious association behind" γαῖα μέλαινα.[86] He points out that Solon calls the goddess Earth dark (fr. 24.4-5 D.):

μήτηρ μεγίστη δαιμόνων Ὀλυμπίων
ἄριστα, Γῆ μέλαινα, . . .

"Mother of the gods of Olympus, greatest and best, Dark Earth. . . ." If Solon can use dark of Earth, the goddess, as well as of earth, the soil on which we walk, it seems possible that there is a religious association in the epithet. (Recall the sacrifice of a black ewe to Earth in *Il.* 3.103-104). We saw that the goddess Demeter, whose responsibility it was to make crops grow and who was, therefore, closely connected with the earth, was worshipped as Melaina in Arcadia (Paus. 8.42.1, 8.5.8).[87] Dietrich takes Demeter's title of Melaina and Erinys as indications of her aboriginal character as an earth-goddess. It seems likely that in the early stages of Greek religion the Earth Mother was characterized as dark, and if this was so, she would certainly be contrasted with the Sky Father who would be bright.[88] Sky is thought to be the father, because rain and sunshine come from him to make things grow and Earth is the mother, because she bears crops as a woman

---

86. A. E. Harvey in *CQ* N.S. 7 (1957) 216ff.

87. *LSJ* s.v. Δημήτηρ give as one explanation of the name Γημήτηρ "Earth-mother"; cf. *Et. Mag.* 265.54, and also Frisk s.v. Δημήτηρ.

88. The name Zeus, the "father-god," is related etymologically to words for "sky," cf. Sanskrit *dyaús* "sky, day," and to words denoting brightness, cf. Sanskrit *di-de-ti* "shine." See also Frisk, *LSJ* s.v. Ζεύς.

bears children. These two areas of the physical world must have seemed very unlike to the early Greeks; the upper air was clear and bright and pure whereas the earth on which they walked was none of these things.[89] One could not see through it, it did not gleam and it was dirty. It was perhaps this last quality, its dirtiness, that called forth the epithet "dark"; it is common to all types of earth whether fertile or not.[90] (See Appendix III for notes on the etymology of μέλας and its relationship to μολύνω "stain, defile" and the Vedic cognate mála- "filth, dirt").

Let us return briefly to the Parmenidean table of opposites. We have seen that "dark" is a constant epithet of earth in Greek poetry and is very likely opposed to "bright sky" in Greek thought in general as well as in the Parmenidean table. We have seen also that sky is male and earth female, both in their forms as god and goddess and in their functions. We suggested earlier in this section that most of the characteristics in the left-hand column belonged to the upper atmosphere, whereas most of those in the right belonged to the earth. These opposites indicate to the author that the Greeks felt a strong opposition between the upper and lower parts of their world. The formular expression γαῖα μέλαινα and its adaptations are part of this contrast between sky and earth.

VI Other Dark and Light Contrasts

This section comprises three brief studies: (a) dark and white hair, (b) dark and white water, and (c) dark silence and bright fame. Study (a) is interesting in itself but apparently has no broader significance. Study (b) is relevant to our earlier discussion of white in connection with clear weather and the whiteness of calm on the sea. In study (c) we shall find an example of the way the poets compared one state to night and its opposite to day.

---

89. Cf. Bacch. 3.86 where αἰθήρ is ἀμίαντος "undefiled."

90. Certain places are described as "white," probably because of chalk deposits or white sand: *Il.* 2.735, 739; *Od.* 24.11; Anacr. fr. 376 *PMG*; Eur. *Cyc.* 166, *I.T.* 436, *Androm.* 1262; Aristoph. *Thesm.* 856-857 (parody). On "white" used of places, see Kober p. 7.

A. Dark and White Hair

The Greeks described grey or white hair in older people as λευκός or πολιός, sometimes in the same context (Tyrt. fr. 7.23 D. and Anacr. fr. 395.1-2 PMG).[91] What interests us here is the contrast of white hair (λευκός) with dark (μέλας) as a mark of change from youth to age. This focus further reveals the Greek enjoyment of contrast and their tendency to polarity, and probably indicates a predominance of dark hair among the Greeks. (So the popular song, "Darling, I am growing old/ Silver threads among the gold" presents a contrast, but implies that the singer is blond). But the evidence seems to suggest that the poets used the dark/white contrast of hair simply because they liked it.

The poet Anacreon complained frequently in his poetry about his advancing age (cf. fr. 395 and fr. 358. 5-7 PMG). As a younger man, he had looked forward to the day "when white hair will have mingled with dark for me" (fr. 420 PMG): εὖτέ μοι λευκαὶ μελαίνησ᾽ ἀναμεμείξονται τρίχες. Sappho in a poem about Tithonus mentioned a change from dark hair as a characteristic of old age (fr. 58. 13-14 PLF):

πά]ντα χρόα γῆρας ἤδη
ἐγένο]ντο τρίχες ἐκ μελαίναν.

Although the beginnings of the lines have been lost, the general meaning is clear and we may reasonably assume that λεύκαι occurred somewhere in this context.

In the *Antigone* of Sophocles, the chorus of elders tells Creon that they have never known Teiresias the seer to be a false prophet "since my hair turned from black to white" (1092-1093):

91. Hair is neither λευκός nor μέλας in Homer; grey hair is πολιός, dark hair κυάνεος (see chapter three). For πολιός as a synonym for λευκός, see pp. 167-168. There are many instances of πολιός describing grey or white hair. Hair: *h. Aphr.* 228; *Il.* 22.77; Pind. *Olymp.* 4.28; Soph. *Ajax* 634; Aristoph. *Knights* 520, 908; *h. Dem.* 97; Aristoph. *Wasps* 1064-1065; Eur. *Alc.* 470, 908. Beard: *Il.* 22.74, 24.516, Tyrt. fr. 7.23 D.; Anacr. fr. 379(a) *PMG*; Aristoph. fr. 410.2, Eur. *H.F.* 693. Temples and head: *Od.* 24.317, *Il.* 8.518; Anacr. fr. 395.1-2 *PMG*; Bacch. fr. 25.2; Hes. *W.D.* 181; Eur. *Bacch.* 185, *Hec.* 652; fr. 369.3. People directly: *Il.* 13.361; Eur. *Supp.* 166; *Andr.* 613, *Cyc.* 307, *Bacch.* 324; Aristoph. *Acharn.* 600,692. Women: Hes. *Theog.* 271; Soph. *O.T.* 183; Eur. *Helen* 283, *Supp.* 35, *Androm.* 348. Old age (γῆρας πολιόν): *Od.* 24.499; Pind. *Isthm.* 6.15; Bacch. 3.88-89, fr. 25.2-3; Theogn. 174; Eur. *Bacch.* 258, *Ion* 700, *Supp.* 170, fr. 369.2; Aristoph. *Plut.* 1043, *Acharn.* 610, *Thesm.* 190, *Lysistr.* 595, *Wasps* 1192.

ἐξ ὅτου λευκὴν ἐγώ
τήνδ᾽ ἐκ μελαίνης ἀμφιβάλλομαι τρίχα.

In Euripides *Phoenissae*, Iocasta describes her own hair as white in speaking to her son Polyneices (322-323): ἐμάν τε λευκόχροα
. . ./. . . κόμαν. A few lines earlier Polyneices' hair was described as dark (308-309): κυανόχρωτα χαί/τας πλόκαμον. These, then, are examples of contrast between dark and white hair.[92] It is interesting to compare the phrase "white old age" λευκὸν γῆρας (Soph. *Ajax* 625) and πολιὸν γῆρας (n. 91), with a phrase in a fragment of Sophocles (fr. 395 Pearson) which describes the ripening of the mulberry. (The mulberry is like the cow of Minos which changed from white to red to black each day, Aesch. fr. 116 N.). "First you will see the stalk blossoming into whiteness, then the round berry reddening, then Egyptian old age takes it":

πρῶτον μὲν ὄψηι λευκὸν ἀνθοῦντα στάχυν,
ἔπειτα φοινίξαντα γογγύλον μόρον
ἔπειτα γῆρας λαμβάνει σφι Αἰγύπτιον.

Γῆρας Αἰγύπτιον is, as Pearson points out, an oxymoron, since "Egyptian," which we saw had dark associations, is used ἀπροσδοκήτως as a synonym for black, in place of the usual λευκόν or πολιόν.

If the hair of older people is white, then that of youth is dark, particularly in contrast to the whiteness of age. There are two passages in which the first beard of the young man is described as dark. In Pindar (*Olymp.* 1. 67-69), Pelops, son of Tantalus is depicted: "but when about the time of youthful bloom, the down began to mantle his cheeks darkly he turned his thoughts to marriage that was at hand":

πρὸς εὐάνθεμον δ᾽ ὅτε φυὰν
λάχναι νιν μέλαν γένειον ἔρεφον
ἑτοῖμον ἀνεφρόντισεν γάμον.

The fact that μέλαν refers to the first beard suggests that the darkness is comparative; that is the beard showed dark on his cheek but was not necessarily black. There seems to be a reference

---

92. White hair (λευκός) as an indication of age is found in Anacr. fr. 358. 5-7 *PMG*; Eur. *H.F.* 910, *Hec.* 500, *Supp.* 289; Aesch. *Pers.* 1056; Soph. *O.T.* 742, *Ajax* 625.

to the first beard in Alcaeus (fr. F6.9 *PLF*): πρ] ἰν τὸ γένηον μέλαν
ἔμμεναι.[93] In this connection we recall the puzzling passage which
describes Odysseus' beard as dark (*Od.* 16. 176) when he himself is
blond (chapter three, p. 90). It was suggested that Odysseus,
disguised as an old beggar, had a white beard and when he was
rejuvenated even his blond beard appeared to darken in contrast to
the white. The description of the hair and beards of the young as
dark and those of the old as white is given more by way of general
contrast than of literal description.

B. Dark and White Water

It is possible to subdivide the descriptions of water as white into
three groups and of water as dark into two. Water may be white
because of foam, or calm, or purity. The action of oars in churning
up the water is described in *Odyssey* 12.173: ἐξόμενοι λεύκαινον
ὕδωρ ξεστῇς ἐλάτῃσιν "sitting they whitened the water with
their polished blades." A similar picture of oars stirring up foam
(ῥόθιον) is found in Euripides (*I.T.* 1387 and *Cyc.* 16-17; cf.
possibly *I.A.* 283 λευκήρετμος Ἄρης).[94] Euripides mentions
"shores with white breakers" (*Orest.* 992-994): λευκοκύμοσιν . . .
ἠιόσιν. The foam from which Aphrodite sprang is white (Hes.
Theog. 190-191): λευκός ἀφρός. In all these examples a distur-
bance on the surface of the water or along its edge is described,
not the sea itself. But the sea is described as "white" in *Homeric
Hymn* 33. 15, where the Dioscuri "laid to rest the waves on the
plains of the white sea": κύματα δ᾽ ἐστόρεσαν λευκῆς ἁλὸς ἐν
πελάγεσσι. Although λευκῆς is sometimes interpreted as "dis-
turbed, stormy;[95] a different interpretation is arguable. In *Odyssey*
10.94 a calm is described as white: λευκὴ δ᾽ ἦν ἀμφὶ γαλήνη. The
combination is repeated in a lyric fragment (Adesp. fr. 1005.1
PMG λευκᾶς γαλάνας). Our suggestion is that the whiteness of the

---

93. The interpretation of this as a reference to the first beard depends on Page's
suggested reading πρίν.

94. Kober p. 9 remarks: "Λευκήρετμος Ἄρης is used in Eur. *I.A.* 283 of the
Taphian warriors. It is hard to decide whether the colour term applies here to the white
wood of the oars, or to the glistening brightness when they are lifted out of the water, or
to the white foam they raise on the surface of the water. The second of these
possibilities seems the most probable, however."

95. Kober p. 9.

sea in the *Homeric Hymn* is due to the calm brought by the Dioscuri, that is that λευκῆς is proleptic. Recall the frequent epithet of the Dioscuri "white-horsed."

The most common use of white in connection with water is to indicate its purity. Theognis offers to put himself to the test (447-448):

> εἰ μ᾽ ἐθέλεις πλύνειν, κεφαλῆς ἀμίαντον ἀπ᾽ ἄκρης
> αἰεὶ λευκὸν ὕδωρ ῥεύσεται ἡμετέρης.

"If you wish to wash me, white water will always pour down undefiled from the top of my head." Because he is clean, he will not dirty water used to wash him. The point is emphasized by ἀμίαντον. (For other references to washing with or in white water, see *Il.* 23.282, Hes. *W.D.* 739). Springs and streams are also described as white; presumably the epithet indicates fresh, clear running water as distinguished from the sea[96] and from deep "dark-watered" wells (see below). Tucker remarks perceptively that "it also adds an element of cheerfulness."[97] An English-speaking poet might obtain a similar effect with sparkling. In *Odyssey* 5. 70, springs flow with white water: κρῆναι ῥέον ὕδατι λευκῶι (cf. Aesch. *Supp.* 23; Eur. *Helen* 1336, I,A. 1294-1295, *H.F.* 573). With the exception of the last named example, "the white spring of Dirce": Δίρκης νᾶμα λευκόν, the epithet λευκός always describes water (ὕδωρ).

And yet water is also "dark," both because it is disturbed or because it is deep (and perhaps shaded). On four occasions in Homer we read that the "bristling" of the surface of the sea (φρίξ) is itself dark or makes the sea dark (*Il.* 7.61-65, 21.126-127, 23.692-693; *Od.* 4.402). The disturbance of the surface is dark in contrast to the whiteness of calm. Stormy or threatening waves are dark (*Il.* 9.6-7 κελαινός, 21.248-249 ἀκροκελαινιόων). A storm (λαῖλαψ) is also dark: (κελαινός *Il.* 11.747, ἐρεμνός *Il.* 12.375, 20.51). In these three cases, people in a threatening mood are compared to a "dark storm," in a double characterization.

Water is sometimes described as μέλας when it is not stated that it is stormy or disturbed. Iris "leaped into the dark sea" in

---

96. For colour epithets applied to the sea, see n. 28. p. 89.
97. T. G. Tucker *The Supplices of Aeschylus* (London 1889) on line 23.

search of Thetis (*Il.* 24.79 ἔνθορε μείλανι πόντωι). Kober interprets this epithet as indicating the depths of the sea, but the darkness may be caused by Iris' leap which would unavoidably disturb the surface.[98] Compare φρίξ above; the simile (*Il.* 23. 692-693), where a fish leaps out of the sea, falls back again, "and a dark wave covers him"; and the passage (*Od.* 5.353) where Leucothea disappears beneath the sea "and a dark wave covered her" (μέλαν δέ ἑ κῦμα κάλυψεν). These three examples seem to belong to the darkness of disturbed water.

Euripides describes the Euxine as the "black sea" (*I.T.* 107 πόντος μέλας), the name we commonly give to it. Perhaps the Euxine earned this epithet because it was often rough. (Cf. the euphemistic Εὔξεινος "hospitable," sometimes given more accurately as Ἄξεινος).

Besides the description of sea, waves, and storms as "dark," simple water (ὕδωρ) is also dark, although it should be noted that all these occurrences are found in epic or passages modelled on epic. "Dark water" far from being unpleasant or polluted (as "dark" might indicate), was commonly used for drinking (see *Il.* 2.825, *Od.* 4.359, 13.409). The dark association may be due to the depth of water or to its being shaded, since cool water is more refreshing to drink and trees are likely to grow close to a water supply. It is perhaps more likely to be shade than depth in the case of a spring (κρήνη) which is described as "dark-watered" (μελάνυδρος).[99] We find that the water swallowed by Charybdis is dark (*Od.* 12.104), as is water swirling round a corpse (*Il.* 21.202) and water used by Nausicaa and her companions for washing clothes (*Od.* 6.91). It would have nicely complemented our washing references above if Nausicaa had used white water for laundering, but here it is likely the water as drawn from the river, not the water as used for washing which is described as dark.

98. Kober pp. 26-27.

99. References to "dark-watered spring" (κρήνη μελάνυδρος): *Il.* 9.14 cf. 1.15 δνοφερὸν ὕδωρ: *Il.* 16.3; *Il.* 16.160, cf. line 161 μέλαν ὕδωρ: *Il.* 21.257; *Od.* 20.158; *h. Hom.* 19.20; Theogn. 959. It should be noted that the phrase always occupies the final position in the hexameter, although the case varies.

C. Dark Silence and Bright Fame

The "dark silence" of the Greek poets strikes us as a confusion of visual and auditory vocabulary, with silence, which is perceived negatively by hearing, being described by an epithet appropriate to another sense. (For a discussion of synaesthesia, see chapter one and below Appendix I). Silence (σιγή) seems to be a state of not being noticed, of oblivion, and is opposed to fame. Pindar, for example, says that "the man who has nothing hides his head in dark silence" (fr. 94.9-10): ὁδὲ μηδὲν ἔχων ὑπὸ σι/ γᾶι μελαίναι κάρα κέκρυπται. Unlike this man who has nothing, Hiero is characterized as a man who uses wealth well; "he knows not to hide towering wealth in black-robed darkness" (Bacch. 3.13-14):

> οἵδε πυργωθέντα πλοῦτον μὴ μελαμ-
> φαρέι κρύπτειν σκότωι.

The wealthy man is noticed and talked about; the poor man is covered in darkness and has no attention paid him. It is possible to hide wealth in darkness, probably by not using it.

In Sophocles (*Ant.* 700), reference is made to the discussion of Antigone's fate by her fellow-citizens: τοιάδ᾽ ἐρεμνὴ σῖγ᾽ ἐπέρχεται φαμίς, "such a dark rumour goes about in silence." The epithet ἐρεμνή may refer to Antigone's unhappy fate or it may reinforce σῖγ᾽. The rumour may be dark because it is not stated clearly and openly.[100]

In *Nemean* 7.12-13, Pindar tells Sogenes that "mighty deeds of valour dwell in thick darkness if they lack songs":

> ταὶ μεγάλαι γὰρ ἀλκαὶ
> σκότον πολὺν ὕμνων ἔχοντι δεόμεναι.

Here again silence or oblivion is compared to darkness. In this poem there are several other references to darkness or brightness. Pindar mentions "brilliant deeds of valour" (51): φαενναῖς ἀρεταῖς. In praising Neoptolemus he is "holding off dark blame" (61): σκοτεινὸν ἀπέχων ψόγον. He says that among his fellow-citizens "my glance is bright" (66): ὄμματι δέρκομαι

---

100. Cf. also Ap.Rh. 3.750 σιγὴ δὲ μελαινομένην ἔχεν ὄρφνην and Emped. 122.4 μελάγκουρος [v.1. -κάρπος] . . 'Ασάφεια.

λαμπρόν. Blame is dark, probably because it casts a shadow on the hero's fame. Pindar's glance is bright, because it confers brightness on those on whom he gazes (cf. λεύσσω, Appendix III).[101]

Earlier, we pointed out an interesting connection between brightness and fame in Pindar (*Isthm.* 4.18-19, cf. n. 21), where he compares the former lack of accomplishment in Melissus' family to dark winter and his present victory to the blossoming of flowers in spring. When this fame of old is roused from sleep it gleams like the star of morning (23-24). Elsewhere we find "the beam of noble deeds" (42), "kindle the torch of songs" (43), and the strange statement "it is right to do everything to darken one's adversary" (48), into oblivion, presumably. But all these phrases pale before the description of Melissus' coronation (69-70):

> ἔνθα λευκωθεὶς κάρα
> μύρτοις ὅδ᾽ ἀνὴρ διπλόαν
> νίκαν ἀνεφάνατο.

"There this man whitening his head with myrtle showed forth a double victory." Now myrtle is an evergreen with glossy leaves; it bears a white flower and black berries, but at all seasons green is predominant. Our suggestion is that the whiteness is meant to recall the earlier references to the brightness of fame which illuminates Melissus' head as a consequence of his victory.[102]

---

101. Cf. also Soph. *Elect.* 65-66, "as I trust that from this rumour I also shall emerge in radiant life, and shine yet like a star upon my foes": ὡς κἄμ᾽ ἐπαυχῶ τῆσδε τῆς φήμης ἄπο/ δεδορκότ᾽ ἐχθροῖς ἄστρον ὡς λάμψειν ἔτι.

102. φάος may mean "publicity" as in Xenoph. *Ages.* 9.1: τὸ φῶς κόσμον παρέχει "light is a guarantee for order." or Soph. *Philoct.* 1353 εἰς φῶς ἰέναι, 581 εἰς φῶς λέγειν.

Six
General Conclusions

Our study has been an historical one, tracing the gradual development of Greek colour concepts and discussing chromatic theory from ancient and modern points of view. Studies of other words and word groups could be profitably undertaken, for Greek presents us with many more examples of problematic terminology than could be investigated here. In pursuit of the words we chose to clarify, we began with a brief consideration of the Munsell system of colour measurement which makes possible the accurate description of a colour by three points of reference, hue, value, and chroma. In Munsell's reckoning the power of a colour is determined by multiplying its value (whiteness or blackness) by its chroma (intensity), and the greatest potential power is ascribed to the reds and yellows and the least potential to blues and greens. It is instructive to compare this division with Greek colour epithets. In the red-yellow range we find from Homer on: ξανθός, κροκό(πεπλος), ἐρυθρός, φοινικόεις, φοῖνιξ, μιλτο(πάρηιος) and πορφύρεος. In the blue-green range, on the other hand, there is no definitive representative in Homer; κυάνεος, although later "dark blue," is simply "dark" (for the epic poet); γλαυκός, later "light blue," we found to be indefinite in hue, light in value, and probably carrying the association of "gleaming"; χλωρός, later "green," is basically "moist," with reference to the sap in plants. We conclude that the hue of reds and yellows made more impact on the early Greeks than that of blues and greens. In the phenomena which we would be tempted to describe as green or blue, other characteristics were more compelling. Hence the

201

Greeks were slow to describe the sky as blue and grass as green because qualities other than hue were more arresting. Only with the systematizing of colour was the need felt for creating a blue-green vocabulary (see further chapter one p. 29 and n. 46 on that page).

As a corollary to Munsell's equation we propose the hypothesis that for a people whose colour concept is still undeveloped, hue is most evident in colours of high value and chroma. Moreover, it seems true that colours which are low in value (dark) are likely to be described in terms of value rather than hue. Homer, for example, occasionally calls blood and wine dark (μέλας), although elsewhere he describes them as red. Dark (brown) eyes were described in antiquity as "dark" μέλας in prose, κυάνεος in poetry (chapter three). The epithet μελάμφυλλος "dark-leaved" indicates the same preference for value over hue (chapter two, p. 45, chapter five, p. 190). Whatever the particular meaning of οἶνοψ "wine-like," it is clear that in Homer the redness of wine cannot be the descriptive aim of the epithet, for the word is used of the sea and also of oxen. The common quality hinted at must be other than hue, and since it is likely that all three commodities were low in value (dark), perhaps οἶνοψ means "dark and gleaming," or "dark with highlights." Our conclusion then, is that there was a marked tendency among the early Greeks to emphasize value at the expense of hue.

By reference to the Munsell system we can explain the lack of blue and green terms and the preponderance of reds and yellows and we can suggest a reason for the emphasis on value rather than hue. But even so the problem is not completely resolved, for the use the Greeks made of the terms they had is at times still very puzzling. We suggested in the introductory chapter that the Greeks developed a concept of colour only gradually, and that it was not until the time of Aristotle that their ideas were clarified. The early Greeks described things as they saw them, and similar things were described by the same epithet. The most obvious characteristic might not be hue but, for example, sheen. They seem to have been sensitive to surfaces which were "bright and gleaming" as distinct from merely "bright" and those which were "dark with highlights" as distinct from merely "dark." The suffixes of certain epithets suggest a comparison between an object (forming the root of the epithet) and a similar appearance found elsewhere. In οἶνοψ, the suffix -οψ (from ὄψ "face") gives a meaning "wine-like" for the epithet. In ἰοειδής, the suffix -ειδης (from εἶδος "form, shape") indicates that the epithet means "violet-like." In ῥοδόεις and λειριόεις, -όεις suggests a comparison with the flowers "rose" and "lily." For us "wine," "rose," and "violet" are all colour terms and "lily" carries a strong overtone of "white"; but for the Greeks the colour comparison was not predominant. They described the sea as "wine-like" (*Od.* 5.132) and "violet-like" (*Od.* 5.56), oil as "rose-like," probably in the sense of "fragrant" (*Il.* 23.186), and voices as "lily-like" (*Il.* 3.151-152). Oblique as these descriptions seem to us, we must approach their use in Greek with an open mind. From our investigations, particularly of χλωρός and κυάνεος it becomes clear that colour epithets which seem inappropriate and vague at first encounter do have a precise meaning. If they puzzle our literal-minded expectations, they make perfectly good sense when we broaden our vision to focus on qualities other than hue.

Appendices

APPENDIX I
λειριόεις and λείριος

These adjectives are derived from λείριον, a flower which Boisacq[1] and Frisk[2] identify as *Lilium candidum* and *narcissus*. *Lilium candidum*, the Madonna lily, is, as its Latin name implies, pure white; the narcissus can be either white or yellow, the most familiar species being the *Narcissus poeticus* which bears a white flower with a crimson-edged centre. Λείριον is to be identified as the lily in the *Hymn to Demeter* 427-428, the one being gathered by Persephone along with the rose and the narcissus just before Hades carried her off:

καὶ ῥοδέας κάλυκας καὶ λείρια, θαῦμα ἰδέσθαι,
νάρκισσον θ' ὃν ἔφυσ' ὥς περ κρόκον εὐρεῖα χθών.

The evidence of Theophrastus in his inquiry on plants shows that λείριον could be used for either the lily (*H.P.* 3.13.6, 3.18.11, 9.16.6) or the narcissus (1.13.2, 6.8.1, 7.13.4, and specifically identified in 6.6.9). It is, however, the identification of λείριον as the Madonna lily that is undoubtedly responsible for the common translation "white" for λειριόεις and λείριος. But an examination of the occurrences of these words will indicate that they are not limited to colour, since they frequently describe qualities that appeal to a sense other than sight, such as hearing or touch.

In the discussion of Hector's threat to Ajax — "If you venture to await my long spear which will rend your delicate flesh . . ." (Il. 13.829-830):

1. Boisacq s.v. λείριον.
2. Frisk s.v. λείριον.

205

αἴ κε ταλάσσῃς
μεῖναι ἐμὸν δόρυ μακρόν, ὅ τοι χρόα λειριόεντα
δάψει·—

We suggested that λειριόεις, like λευκός, described the vulnerability of the χρώς, the unprotected flesh (see p. 115).[3]
Pindar likens his poetry to a diadem (Nem. 7.77-79):

Μοῖσά τοι
κολλᾶι χρυσὸν ἔν τε λευκὸν ἐλέφανθ᾽ ἀμᾶι
καὶ λείριον ἄνθεμον ποντίας ὑφελοῖσ᾽ ἐέρσας.

"The Muse blends for you gold and white ivory and a lily-like flower, lifting it up from the sea dew." The Scholiast first interprets λείριον ἄνθεμον as coral, explaining that as long as coral is in the sea, it seems to be soft and plant-like,[4] and most commentators agree with this identification.[5] In support one might argue that "flower of the sea" is an apt and attractive description of coral and that, being a durable substance, coral combines well with gold and ivory, certainly better, shall we say, than an actual flower. (Frisk seems to be the only authority who understands Pindar to refer to a flower; he takes λείριον ἄνθεμον as Lilium candidum.) We are faced with two problems at this point: first, is Pindar describing coral here, and secondly, what is the meaning of λείριον, if he is? Logically one would expect to

---

3. It is perhaps from this Homeric passage that Quintus Smyrnaeus (fourth century after Christ) borrows when he describes the Hesperides as "lily-like." Memnon, son of Dawn, taunts Achilles with his superior birth (2. 418):

ἐπεὶ θεόθεν γένος εἰμί
Ἠοῦς ὄβριμος υἱὸς ὃν ἔκποθι λειριοέσσαι
Ἑσπερίδες θρέψαντο παρὰ ῥόον ὠκεανοῖο

Is this perhaps the origin of the title of Elaine "the lily-maid of Astalot" in the Arthurian legend?

4. καὶ λείριον ἄνθεμον· τινές φασιν εἶναι κουράλιον, εἰρῆσθαι δὲ αὐτὸ ποντίαν ἐέρσαν διὰ τὸ δοκεῖν, ἕως μέν ἐστι κατὰ βάθους, ἁπαλὸν εἶναι καὶ φυτῶι ὅμοιον· ὅταν δὲ ἀνασπασθῆι καὶ γένηται ἔξω τοῦ ὕδατος, ἀπολιθοῦσθαι τοῦ ἡλίου καταλάμψαντος αὐτῶι. οἱ δὲ ποντίαν δρόσον τὴν πορφύραν φασὶ διὰ τὴν τοῦ κογχυλίου βαφήν. λείριον δὲ ἄνθος τὸ ἔριον. ὠαφέρει δὲ ταῦτα ἐπὶ τὴν τῶν ὑφαινομένων ποικιλίαν ταύτην, ἐπεὶ τὸ ποίημα ὑφάσματι παρέοικεν ὡς καὶ αὐτὸς ἐν ἄλλοις· ὑφαίνω δ᾽ Ἀμυθαονίδαις ποικίλον ἄνδημα. A. B. Drachmann ed. Scholia Vetera in Pindari Carmina (Leipzig 1927) vol. 3, on Nem. 7.77-79.

5. Norwood Pindar p. 242, n. 28; Jebb Bacchylides on 16. 94-96 (where white coral is specified), and J. B. Bury The Nemean Odes of Pindar (London 1890) on Nem. 7.79.

handle the first problem first, since the second is dependent upon it. As our interest in this study is in the meaning of λείριον, we shall assume, for the moment, that the "sea flower" is coral, and consider the implications of this identification. Norwood[6] argues that the colour scheme of yellow gold and white ivory would be spoiled if λείριον is translated "white" (as it commonly is), since the combination of two white substances would give no contrast. Norwood points out further that the most highly prized and probably the only variety of coral known in Greece in Pindar's day was red. Theophrastus (De Lapid. 38) informs us that "coral . . . is red in colour": τὸ γὰρ κουράλιον . . . τῆι χρόαι μὲν ἐρυθρόν. Neither he nor Caley and Richards in their commentary on this work[7] mention any other colour. Now, if the "lily-like flower of the sea dew" is coral, it must have been red coral, and λείριον cannot mean "white." With no evidence to show that the ancients were familiar with white coral, it is quite unreasonable to insist that "λείριον must convey a sense of "white" whether the idea of delicacy is present or not" and to be equally firm in identifying the "flower" as coral.[8] If the flower is coral, the characteristic of the lily which it possesses is most likely its fine, delicate texture. At this point, we must pause to consider the one stumbling-block in the way of those who interpret the flower as coral — the fact that the Greeks do not seem to have used coral for decorative purposes. Caley and Richards can offer "little evidence that the Greeks used coral to any extent" (see n. 7.) Higgins in a recent book on Greek jewellery cites only one example of coral decoration, on an early Hellenistic fibula.[9] Farnell hopefully refers to LSJ s.v. κοραλιοπλάστης as evidence for the craft of working coral, but the fact that this word occurs once in a Sicilian inscription is not encouraging.[10] We are left to conclude that there is almost no evidence that Pindar would choose coral as a material for his diadem.

The Scholiast offers a second interpretation which is simply

6. Norwood p. 242, n. 28.
7. E. R. Caley and J. F. C. Richards Theophrastus on Stones (Columbus Ohio 1956) pp. 140-141.
8. Cole vol. 3, p. 43.
9. R. A. Higgins Greek and Roman Jewellery (London 1961) p. 176.
10. Farnell vol. 2 on Nem. 7. 77-79.

ignored by commentators, that the "lily-like flower of the sea dew" is wool dyed by sea-purple (see n. 4). On this view Pindar is here comparing his poetry to weaving indirectly as he does elsewhere explicitly (fr. 179): ὑφαίνω δ᾽ Ἀμυθαονίδαις ποικίλον ἄνδημα. The reference to the sea in Nemean 7.79 is clear, the famous and costly purple dye being obtained from a sea-creature, the purple-fish.[11] As far as the composition of diadems is concerned, we have archaeological evidence from the seventh century on for the existence of diadems made of bands of cloth or leather to which were attached rosettes, usually of gold.[12] A band of purple cloth, decorated with gold and ivory, would almost certainly have been familiar to Pindar, an advantage not shared by the diadem of gold, ivory, and coral. Recall Sappho fr. 98(a) PLF, for a purple head-band. The description of purple cloth as the "flower of the sea dew" (ἄνθος meaning "dye") may seem unlikely unless we call to mind the close association of purple with the sea in the Greek view (see n. 11). It is significant that the Scholiast sees no difficulty in the epithet λείριον, although both his interpretations require a meaning "fine, delicate" rather than "white." It is, I think, the use of λείριος to describe a non-white surface that makes commentators dismiss out of court the possibility that the "flower" is purple cloth. But if the Scholiast is right, and he may very well be, Pindar used λείριος for texture rather than colour.[13] (See further below).

Most commonly λειριόεις and λείριος describe the voice. In Iliad 3.151-152, the old men of Troy observing the battle from the walls are compared to crickets. They have ceased from war because of age, but are good orators, "like crickets who sit on a tree in the woods and send forth their lily-like voice:"

τεττίγεσσιν ἐοικότες, οἵ τε καθ᾽ ὕλην
δενδρέωι ἐφεζόμενοι ὄπα λειριόεσσαν ἱεῖσι.

---

11. Variously called πορφύρα, κογχύλιον. For its connection with the sea, see Aesch. Ag. 958-960.

12. Higgins pp. 105-106, 121-122.

13. With Pindar's use of λείριος for a non-white surface, cf. English "clear" which can mean "translucent" whether it describes a colourless or coloured liquid (ONED s.v. clear.)

The Greeks obviously liked the shrill "song" of this insect, just as they liked a clear, high-pitched voice in an orator or a singer.[14] Nestor, who was famed for oratory, was a "clear-toned speaker" (*Il.* 1.248 λιγὺς ἀγορητής); the same adjective describes the "clear-voiced" Muse (Terpander in Plut. *Lyc.* 21.5, 3.2.37, Alcman fr. 14(a)1 *PMG*, Stesichorus fr. 240 *PMG*).[15] The lily-like voice refers not to the thin piping of old men, but is a compliment paid to their oratory. Hesiod depicts the Muses singing on Olympus (*Theog.* 40-42):

> γελᾶι δέ τε δώματα πατρός
> Ζηνὸς ἐριγδούποιο θεᾶν ὀπὶ λειριοέσσηι
> σκιδναμένηι.

"The palace of their father, Zeus the thunderer, gleams as the lily-like voice of the goddesses spreads abroad." Observe in these lines the visual imagery used to describe sound. The palace

14. W. B. Stanford says that the Greek voice was and still is higher pitched than the northern European (*Hermathena* 61 [1943] 16-18). He draws a contrast between λιγύς, λιγυρός, a pitch which pleased the Greek ear, and the noise of a flock of birds which fled "with a woolly cry" (*Il.* 17.756): οὖλον κεκληγότες. (Stanford says this noise is compared to the cry of "barbarians," but here he is mistaken since it is the "sons of the Achaeans" who cry in a woolly manner. His particular point, the difference in pitch between Greek and barbarian voices, is not supported, but the phrase supplies an interesting contrast to ὄπα λειριόεσσαν). Stanford refers to an article of his in *Comparative Literature Studies* (July 1942), in which he explains ὄπα λειριόεσσαν as a synaesthetic metaphor "lily-voiced" (cf. n. 17). Cf. also his *Greek Metaphor* pp. 50, 53-54.

Stanford's most recent comment on lily-like voices may be found in "The Lily Voice of the Cicadas *Iliad* 3.152," *Phoenix* 23 (1969) 3-8. There he discusses the problem on two grounds, semantic and aesthetic. Semantically, he decides that λειριόεσσαν is derived from λείριον "a lily," that the lily in question is the *Lilium Candidum*, and that the τέττιξ is the cicada. Then, at greater length, he considers the point of comparison between the voices of old men and cicadas. He suggests a resemblance between the "song" of the insect and "the pure white colour, the elegantly curving outline, and the soft, smooth texture of the lily's perianth" (p. 4). He than turns to the aesthetic problem: why the Greeks liked the sound of the cicada when many later commentators and even Vergil (*Georg.* 3.328, *Ecl.* 2.12) found it so unpleasant (pp. 5-6). He notes that the Greeks had no reason to object to the "machinelike, mechanical quality and intensity of their [the cicadas'] noise . . ." "since noise-emitting machines hardly existed in their day"; that they "seem to have liked shrillness in tone better than we do"; and that "cicadas were associated with hot sunny weather . . . a symbol of pleasant days" (p. 6).

15. L. Woodbury in *TAPA* 86 (1955) 37 lists references of λιγύς, λιγυρός, to pleasing sounds of words and music: e.g. *Od.* 10.254, 12.44; *h. Hom.* 19.19; Theogn. 939. He also refers to the Peripatetic discussion of voices which are λιγυραί in [Arist.] *De Aud.* 804a21-28.

"gleams" as the Muses sing;[16] their voice "spreads" or "scatters"; and that voice is like a lily. This remarkable passage indicates that λειριόεις is no idle epithet. Synaesthetically, the voice of the goddesses is compared to an all-pervasive light. We can find many examples in Greek poetry of this descriptive crossing from one sense to another,[17] and strangely enough, they probably seem more forceful to us than to the Greeks who first heard them. Stanford has this to say: "Synaesthesia in words is a survival of the physical synaesthesia of primitive man when sense perceptions were far keener and far more efficiently co-ordinated than in more domesticated times." A poet combines a "sound word" like ὄπα with a "sight" or "touch" word like λειριόεσσαν "because he feels the inner concord in a way that the average man cannot."[18] For the Greek poets of our period, then, the divisions between the senses were not barriers, requiring a conscious transfer of particular vocabulary from one to the other; instead there was an overlapping between senses such as sight and touch, so that something seen could be described naturally in terms of touch. The affinity between such sensations as whiteness, smoothness and clarity was obvious to them. They also saw the likeness of auditory sounds to the visual appearance of fire, as these four examples from Homer to Aeschylus show: οἰμωγὴ δὲ δέδηε "there

16. For a discussion of γελάω, see Stanford *Greek Metaphor* p. 116. He argues that the basic meaning is "be bright, shine," and that "laugh" is a secondary meaning.

17. This is sometimes called an "intersensual metaphor," but this term is a mistake, because synaesthesia is not a metaphor but a "way of looking at things." Metaphor implies the conscious use of a figure of speech, see chapter one, pp. 17-22. A Latin term showing a similar breadth of reference is *argutus*. C. J. Fordyce comments on Catullus 68.70-72: (*Catullus* Oxford 1961)

> quo mea se molli candida pede
> intulit et trito fulgentem in limine plantam
> innixa arguta constituit solea. .

"*arguta* is probably best taken of sound, the sudden tap of her shoe, but it might refer to shape 'neat'; 'quick-moving', 'twinkling' is less likely here. *Argutus* and *argutiae* can be applied to anything that makes a sharp impression on one of the senses -- most often of hearing (Verg, *Ecl.* 8.22 *argutum nemus*, *Georg.* 1.143 *arguta serra*, 1.294 *argutum pecten*, Prop. 1.18.30 *argutae aves*) but also of sight (Cic. *Leg.* 1.27 *oculi arguti*, quick eyes, *de Or.* 3.220 *manus arguta* restless hands: Verg *Georg.* 3.80 *argutum caput* with clear-cut lines) and even of smell (Pliny *N.H.* 15.18) and of taste (Palladius 3.25.4 *argutus sapor*): their metaphorical uses correspond -- of quickness of mind, incisiveness of style, expressiveness in art."

18. Stanford pp. 47-62. Cf. also I. Waern in *Eranos* 50 (1952) 19-20 for synaesthesia of sound and light in λειριόεις.

is a blaze of groaning" (*Od.* 20.353); παιδικοὶ θ᾽ ὕμνοι φλέγονται "hymns in honour of boys blaze up" (Bacchyl. fr. 4.80); φίλαν πόλιν ἐπιφλέγων ἀοιδαῖς "setting the dear city on fire with songs" (Pind. *Olymp.* 9.22); σάλπιγξ ἄυτηι πάντ᾽ ἐκεῖν᾽ ἐπέφλεγεν "the trumpet set all those shores ablaze with its sound" (Aesch. *Pers.* 395). These few quotations should serve to show that Greek poets did not distinguish sharply between objects of sight and objects of hearing. When Hesiod described the song of the Muses as if it were visible, he was expressing what he felt about music. We are using imagery, akin to the Greek, when we speak of song "filling the air."[19]

Three late poets describe the voice as "lily-like." Apollonius Rhodius (4.902-903) depicts the Sirens calling to the Argonauts:

ἀπηλεγέως δ᾽ ἄρα καὶ τοῖς
ἵεσαν ἐκ στομάτων ὄπα λείριον.

"Straightforwardly also to them they sent their lily-like voice." The Orphic *Argonautica* (253) employs λείριος of the voice. A verse inscription (*IG* 14.1934.f6) describes the song of the cricket as λειρά (n. pl. of λειρός): τέττιξ γλυκεροῖς χείλεσι λειρὰ χέων. These poets felt a likeness between the white, delicate, fragrant lily and a clear, pleasing song, although our analytical minds distinguish between the flower which can be seen, touched, and smelled and the song which can be heard.

We glean from Aristotle (*Top.* 106a25) the information that the voice is called "light" λευκή and "dark" μέλαινα – the same terms that are used for "white" and "black" in colour. When λευκός is applied to the voice, it means "easily heard" εὐήκοος (*Top.* 107a12-14). We remarked earlier on the Greek enjoyment of clear, high-pitched voices. Nero's voice is said to have been "small and dark" βραχὺ καὶ μέλαν φώνημα (Dio Cassius 61.20). The association of lightness with clarity and darkness with the lack of it is not, then, confined to poetry.[20] We have seen in our

19. For more examples of φλέγω, ἐπιφλέγω, λάμπω describing sound, see H. W. Smyth *GMP* 447-448.

20. On voices and colour, see further W. B. Stanford *The Sound of Greek: Studies in the Greek Theory and Practice of Euphony* (Berkeley and Los Angeles 1967) p. 34 and p. 46, n. 35-42. For colour terms applied to music, see Plato *Laws* 655a, where he objects to εὔχρων "well-coloured," a choirmasters' metaphor applied to tune (μέλος) and form (σχῆμα).

discussion the division the Greeks felt between "dark" and "light," not only in the field of sight, but of sound and touch as well.

Last comes an occurrence in Bacchylides in which the eyes of the Athenian companions of Theseus are described as λείριος. Although an epithet of the eyes might well refer to colour, logic tells us that in this case the eyes are not "white like a lily," but are "lily-like" in some other way. Bacchylides describes the scene on board ship from Athens to Crete, when Theseus leaped from the vessel into the sea in order to prove his paternity to Minos (17.94-96):

ка-
τὰ λειρίων τ' ὀμμάτων δά-
κρυ χέον, βαρεῖαν ἐπιδέγμενοι ἀνάγκαν.

"They shed a tear from their lily-like eyes, awaiting heavy necessity." Jebb takes the epithet λειρίων to indicate "eyes of delicate beauty," "the bright eyes of youth"; he compares Shakespeare's "young-eyed cherubims."²¹ More probably, the delicacy reflects not youth and beauty, but rather a need for protection (recall the sense of "vulnerability" in the combination of χρώς and λειριόεις or λευκός, discussed above in Hector's threat to Ajax). The details of the story bear out the dependence of the young Athenians on Theseus for leadership and protection. When Minos ventured to touch Eriboea's cheek, it was Theseus who came to her aid (17.14-18). It is interesting to contrast the "delicate" eyes of the Athenian youths with the "dark" eye of Theseus as he turned on Minos in anger:

ἴδεν δὲ Θησεύς
μέλαν δ' ὑπ' ὀφρύων
δίνασεν ὄμμα.

In chapter four we interpreted the darkness of his eye as suggesting agitation and emotion — the very opposite of the passivity of his companions. This contrast is surely deliberate and is a further argument in favour of translating λειρίων as "bewildered, helpless." The Suda's gloss tends to confirm this

21. Jebb *Bacchylides* on 16.94-96.

translation: λειρόφθαλμος · ὁ προσηνεῖς ἔχων τοὺς ὀφθαλμούς, "with gentle eyes" conveying a fitting tone of helplessness.[22]

To conclude, λειριόεις and λευκός illustrate for us the unity the Greek poets saw between high, clear sounds, fine, delicate surfaces, and "whiteness" or "lightness."[23]

APPENDIX II
Terms Combining Brightness and Movement

There are several words in Greek which show brightness and movement in their meaning. This has given rise to some difficulty since many commentators are unwilling or unable to approach these words from the viewpoint of the ancient Greek who used them. They tend, therefore, to divide the occurrences of these words into (a) brightness and (b) movement, like so many sheep and goats. This approach gives a false impression; a more fruitful one is to attempt to see how the Greeks thought of the words, as evidenced by their use of them, and to try to understand the unity they saw between brightness and movement. One of the keys to the meaning of these words is the effect of changing light or the play of light on a polished surface. This shimmer, sheen, gloss, or gleam seemed to the Greeks to be like the blurring of animals' feet in swift flight, the flash of lightning, the gnashing tusks of wild animals or the vibrations of an insect's wings. In the first set of examples, the objects could be completely still or moving only enough to reflect the changing light; in the second set, swiftness of

22. It may be relevant here to mention Hesychius' gloss s.v. λειρώς (Bechtel λειρός): ὁ ἰσχνὸς καὶ ὠχρός "one who is weak and pale."

23. For further discussions of λειριόεις, see F. Bechtel *Lexilogus zu Homer* (Halle 1914) p. 213 s.v. λειριόεις; he refers in turn to Fick (*Beitr.* 26.320) as analysing Ποδαλείριος as τὸν πόδα λείριον ἔχων. Podaleirios is one of the two sons of Asclepius, the physician, and is mentioned twice in the *Iliad* (2.732, 11.833). M. Leumann *Homerische Wörter* (Basel 1950) pp. 27-28 takes Ποδαλείριος as opposite to Μελάμπους (Melampus the seer, *Od.* 15.225). He suggests that for flesh and foot the meaning of λειριόεις, λείριος is *zart* ("soft, delicate, fine"). Cf. our discussion of λευκὸς πούς pp. 121-129.

movement seems to suggest the brightness as it does in an English expression like "flashing hoofs," or a "blue streak." (In the case of the tusks of the boar, it may be the gleam of the teeth, but is more likely, I think, to be the movement). We can see why words like αἰόλος and ἀργός came to be translated "swift." Swiftness was an essential part of the application, but we can also see why there is a close association with brightness and whiteness, especially in ἀργός, as white or light colours reflect light well. Below are given some of these epithets with examples of their occurrences in literature.

αἰόλος

In Homer various pieces of armour are described as αἰόλος or are compounded with αἰόλος: a shield (*Il.* 7.222), arms (*Il.* 5.295), the breastplate, αἰολοθώρηξ (*Il.* 4.489), the mitre, αἰολομίτρης (*Il.* 5.707) and the helmet, κορυθαίολος (*Il.* 2.816). Horses are αἰόλοι about their feet (*Il.* 19.404), wasps about their middle (*Il.* 12.167), and worms which devour corpses (*Il.* 22.509). The adjective is converted into a proper name for Aeolus, king of the winds.[1] Page wants to prove that the primary meaning of αἰόλος is "gleaming, shining" and that the idea of movement is a later development;[2] whereas our argument stresses the unity the Greeks saw in swiftness and changing light. Αἰόλος is "gleaming" whether that gleam is caused by a bright surface reflecting light (like armour) or a swiftly moving object. Page offers the fact that in a Linear B tablet, an ox is named Aeolus, and since no man ever named an ox "Speedy," argues for the primacy of the meaning "flashing." One finds a similar problem in the description of a goose (*Od.* 15.161) and cattle (*Il.* 23.30) as ἀργός. Since ἀργός frequently associates brightness or whiteness and swiftness, commentators sometimes behave as if Homer were being completely unreasonable in using the epithet to describe waddling geese and sluggish cows. Undoubtedly Homer would be surprised at their consternation. Just because some Mycenaean Greek called his ox Aeolus, we can hardly conclude that αἰόλος had no connection

---

1. W. B. Stanford *The Odyssey of Homer* (London 1950) in his note on *Od.* 10.2.
2. Page *History and the Homeric Iliad* pp. 204 n. 22 and 288-289 n. 93.

with moving. In our opinion it was more probably the light moving back and forth on the glossy coat of the ox that brought the name Aeolus to mind. It is a matter of interest that the verb αἰόλλω which first occurs in *Odyssey* 20.27 has the definite meaning "move back and forth." This back and forth motion resembles the movement of light on a polished surface. Moreover, a similar motion is seen as one watches the feet of running horses and the vibrating wings of wasps.[3]

A few occurrences from later writers are given here: αἰόλα νύξ "star-spangled night" (Soph. *Trach.* 94), perhaps descriptive of the "twinkling" of stars; αἰόλα σάρξ "discoloured flesh" (Soph. *Philoct.* 1157); αἰόλα κακά "varied ills" (Aesch. *Supp.* 328); αἰόλον ψεῦδος "a shifty lie" (Pind. *Nem.* 8.25); and in prose, αἰόλαι ἡμέραι "changeable days" ([Arist.] *Prob.* 941b24).

ἀργός

The combination of brightness and movement is also found in ἀργός. Dogs are ἀργίποδες (*Il.* 24.211) or πόδας ἀργοί (*Od.* 21.11) as horses are αἰόλοι πόδας. Odysseus' hunting dog is named Ἄργος (Stanford suggests "Flash")[4] and Jason's bright, swift ship is Ἀργώ (*Od.* 12.70).[5] But the brightness in ἀργός is not always caused by swiftness of movement; in some of the occurrences it apparently describes a sheen on the surface. For example, a goose is ἀργός (*Od.* 15.161). Since geese are not famed for speed, the epithet is generally translated "white," but this misses the particular effect of the sheen of white feathers. Cattle are also ἀργός (*Il.* 23.30), because their coat is glossy. A good example of the combination of whiteness and movement is found in the name of the eagle πύγαργος (see pp. 139-144). Anyone who has watched birds knows how distinguishing tail feathers, such as this eagle evidently possessed, are hidden while the bird is at rest, but flash out brightly and suddenly when it rises in flight.

---

3. Some commentators understand the adjective to apply to the "nimble waists" of wasps, but a reference to the swift vibration of their wings seems more likely.

4. Stanford *Odyssey* in a note on 17.292.

5. Cf. Diod. Sic. 4.41.3: τὴν δὲ ναῦν Ἀργὼ προσαγορευθῆναι ... ὡς δ' ἔνιοι λέγουσιν ἀπὸ τῆς περὶ τὸ τάχος ὑπερβολῆς, ὡς ἂν τῶν ἀρχαίων ἀργὸν τὸ ταχὺ προσαγορευόντων.

Ἀργός also describes lightning (*Il.* 8.133, *Od.* 5.128); the teeth of a wild boar (*Il.* 9.539, *Od.* 8.60); and animal fat (*Il.* 11.818, 22.127). In the first two cases, there is a suggestion of speed with brightness, in the third of glistening. It would be possible to go into much greater detail in the occurrences of this epithet, but the brief discussion here will indicate the lines along which further examination might proceed.

ἀμάρυγμα, ἀμαρυγή

These words occur only nine times in classical Greek. Most commonly it is the bright flash from the face, particularly the eye, as in Sappho fr. 16.18 *PLF*: κἀμάρυχμα λάμπρον προσώπω; *h. Herm.* 45: ὅτε διηθῶσιν ἀπ᾽ ὀφθαλμῶν ἀμαρυγαί; Hesiod fr. 43 (a) 4 MW: Χαρίτων ἀμαρ[ύγμ]ατ᾽. Bacchylides uses it for the "flashing movements of the closing wrestling bout" (9.36): τελευταίας ἀμάρυγμα πάλας; Aristophanes for the blurring brightness of horses (*Birds* 925): ἵππων ἀμαρυγά. See also Hesiod fr. 73 MW, Theocritus 23.7, Apollonius Rhodius 3.288,1018. The occurrences of this word are rare and interesting, and the discussions in Gow[6] and Page[7] are full and illuminating.

αἰθύσσω

Stanford has a good discussion of αἰθύσσω and its compounds (κατ-, δι-, παρ-).[8] He discusses with sensitivity several of the occurrences of this word, pointing out the double connection of movement and light, especially in its use by Pindar.[9]

---

6. Gow *Theocritus* on 23.7.
7. Page *Sappho and Alcaeus* p. 54, n. 18.
8. W. B. Stanford *Ambiguity in Greek Literature: Studies in Theory and Practice* (Oxford 1939) pp. 132-133. He refers to discussions by J. W. Donaldson *New Cratylus* (3rd ed. London 1859) and T. L. F. Tafel *Dilucidationum Pindaricarum Volumina duo* (Berlin 1824-27) on Pind. *Olymp.* 7.95.
9. For a discussion of φρίσσω, see Bowra (*Pindar* p. 244), who sees both motion (ruffle) and light (ripple) in Pind. *Pyth.* 4.182-183.

APPENDIX III
Notes on Etymology

In this appendix will be found a discussion of the following terms or groups of terms: (1) ἀργός (2) δνόφος, δνοφερός, κνέφας, κνεφαῖος, (3) ἐρεμνός, ἐρεβεννός, (4) κελαινός, (5) λευκός, (6) μέλας. The etymology of χλωρός is examined in chapter two, of κυάνεος in chapter three, and of λειριόεις and λείριος in Appendix I. Cognates in other Indo-European languages and in Greek are considered to see whether etymology sheds any light on the basic meaning or connotations of these terms.

ἀργός

There are a number of adjectives related to ἀργός: ἀργεστής, epithet of wind, see chapter five; ἀργεννός from *ἀργεσ-νος, epic adjective chiefly used of sheep and clothing; ἀργήεις (and its contracted form ἀργᾶς), Aeschylus in lyric, see chapter four, p. 142 and Pindar; ἀργιόεις v.1. ἀργινόεις in Il. 2.647,656, epithet of places (cf. also νῆσοι Ἀργινοῦσσαι in Xenoph. H.G. 1.6.27). The element ἀργ – appears as a prefix in such epithets as ἀργίπους "white/swift footed," ἀργικέραυνος "with white/swift lightning," and ἀργιόδους "with white/swift teeth."

Other Greek words, mostly late, show this stem: ἀργαίνω "be white," (first in Euripides); ἀργῖτις sc. ἄμπελος "vine with white grapes," ἀργᾶς, ᾶ and ἀργόλας "serpent." Two proper names in the *Odyssey* are also related to this epithet: Argos (Ἄργος) Odysseus' dog, and Argo (Ἀργώ) Jason's ship. (For the significance of these names, cf. Appendix II).

Ἀργός is related to Sanskrit *rjrá-* which has the double meaning "bright" and "swift," the same double meaning which we see in ἀργός (see Appendix II). Ἀργός is formed by dissimilation (the tendency in a language to change or omit a sound because of its proximity to that sound) from *rgró- through *ἀργ-ρός. Frisk debates briefly whether there is a relationship between the meanings "bright" and "swift" and agrees with those who see a connection.[1]

---

1. Frisk s.v. ἀργός.

Other cognates show a connection with brightness or white-ness. Compare ἄργυρος "silver," Sanskrit *árjuna-* "white, light," Tocharian A *ārki* B *ārkwi* "white," Hittite *ḥarkiš* "white, bright," and an Illyrian river named *Argao*.[2]

δνόφος, δνοφερός, κνέφας, κνεφαῖος

The nouns δνόφος and κνέφας "darkness" and their corresponding adjectives δνοφερός and κνεφαῖος "dark" are particularly related to the darkness of night;[3] compare later Greek (prose) γνόφος, and various Indo-European words for "night": Indo-Iranian *ksap-*, Avestan *xšap*, Hittite *išpant*, and Latin *creper, crepusculum*.

Δνόφος is formed from *δνέφος found in the compound ἰοδνεφής (epic adjective). Frisk suggests a connection between these words and ψέφας "gloom, darkness," νέφος "cloud," and ζόφος "darkness," particularly "the dark quarter, i.e. the west."[4] It is not at all surprising to find a connection between the specific darkness of night and adjectives meaning "dark" generally. We saw in chapter five that one of the most arresting experiences of the early Greeks was the daily submersion of the world in the darkness of night.[5]

ἐρεμνός, ἐρεβεννός

Erebos (Ἔρεβος) the darkness of the underworld gives us two adjectives both meaning "dark": ἐρεμνός from *ἐρεβ-νός and ἐρεβεννός from *ἐρεβεσ-νός. Cognates are found in Sanskrit *rájas-*, Armenian *erek* and *erekoy*, Gothic *riqis*, Old Norse *rǫkkr*, Indo-European *régw*, all of which mean darkness. It is interesting that the Greeks narrowed this connection with darkness to the underworld, which as we saw in chapter five, was for them the place of the dead, dark and sunless.[6]

---

2. See also *LSJ* and Boisacq s.v. ἀργός and R. d'Avino "La visione del Colore" *Ricerche Linguistica* 41 (1958) 103-104, and P. Chantraine.
3. Κνεφαῖος can mean "dark" or, more usually, either "at dawn" or "in the evening," *LSJ* s.v. κνέφας.
4. For the west as the "dark quarter," see chapter five, p. 189.
5. Frisk, Boisacq, and *LSJ* s.vv. δνόφος, κνέφας.
6. Frisk, Boisacq, Chantraine, and *LSJ* s.v. ἔρεβος.

κελαινός

Frisk comments that this epithet and its compound κελαινεφής are morphologically isolated and therefore their etymology is hard to determine. He compares Sanskrit *kalanka-* "spot, dirt" and Latin *columba* "dove" (from the colour). Within Greek he sees a possible relationship with κηλίς "stain, spot, defilement," κόλυμβος a water bird and κιλλός "ass-coloured, grey" (from κίλλος "ass"). (For the νος element in κελαινός, cf. ἐρεμνός, περκνός). It seems, then, that κελαινός has a connotation of "spotted, stained" and in this respect it is similar to μέλας (q.v. below).[7]

λευκός

Λευκός is said to be related to three Greek words, two of which are of only passing interest: λύχνος "lamp," λοῦσσον "white heart of the fir tree," and λεύσσω (*λευκιω) "to see." The first two words show a connection with "whiteness" or "brightness," but it is the third, the verb λεύσσω, which is significant in our understanding of the Greek view of the nature of seeing and of brightness. (Cf. further chapter five, section three on seeing and brightness). Frisk notes Indo-European cognates which relate to brightness: Sanskrit *rocá-* "bright" and *rócate* "give light." He also notes Latin *lucus* "wood," strictly "clearing," i.e. the part of the forest where the trees are thinning out and light can reach (but see "lucus a non lucendo"); Lithuanian *laukas* "field"; Old High German *loh* "overgrown clearing"; Sanskrit *loká-* "open space, the world" (not certainly cognate), *locana* "eye." We see here not merely brightness, but clarity and openness, elements of significance in connection with the description of air as λευκός (see chapter five, section two). The atmosphere stretching out overhead is λευκός because it is clear and open; there is nothing to obscure.[8]

μέλας

Μέλας (*μελὰν-s, μέλαινα [⟨αν-ια], μέλαν) is related to a number

---

7. Frisk, Boisacq, Chantraine, and *LSJ* s.v. κελαινός.
8. Frisk, Boisacq and *LSJ* s.v. λευκός.

of Indo-European words which have a connection with dirt: Vedic *mála-* "dirt," Sanskrit *malina-* "dirty," *mála-* "smut," and Lettish *melns* "black" (note, however, that Lithuanian *mélynes* means "blue," not "black" and Russian *malína* does not mean "black-berry" but "raspberry.") It is also connected in Greek with μολύνω "stain, sully, defile, corrupt" as well as μώλωψ "mark of a blow, bruise" and μελίνη "millet" (a grain). The association with "bruise" is suggestive, as a bruise may appear "dirty" against the skin. The connection between darkness and dirt is also found in κελαινός (q.v.).[9]

APPENDIX IV

Supporting Evidence in the Colour Vocabulary
of Some Other Languages

There have been studies of colour terminology among primitive tribes which attempt to find a pattern of development. Many of the earliest commentators on the subject of Greek colour perception referred to other languages which seemed to them to parallel the Greek development of colour terminology (and in the case of some commentators, of the ability to perceive and distinguish colour). One can undoubtedly find instructive parallels, but what one finds is influenced, it seems, by what one hopes to find. The author was able to obtain information about the colour vocabulary of a New Guinea tribe, the Omie, from John Austing, a translator and member of the Summer Institute of Linguistics (Wycliffe Bible Translators), who has been studying the Omie language for the past five years.

The tribe has basically four "colour" terms: *ajive'e* – "bright, white" (related to *ajie* "light" and used for the light of the sun); *hove'e* – "yellow" (used for the light of the moon); *kave'e* – "red" (used for fire-light or artificial light); and *rove'e* – "dark, black, brown, dark green, dark blue." There seems to be a

9. Frisk, Boisacq, and *LSJ* s.v. μέλας.

gradation from the first to the last term in the matter of brightness (aside from hue); e.g. *hove'e* can mean "less bright than *ajive'e* but brighter than *kave'e*." This is a very simplified form of the view we find among the Greeks that colour ranged from "light" to "dark." The Omie distinguish people within their tribe as *hove'e* or *kave'e* ("yellow" or "red") although they describe themselves generally as *rove'e* ("dark") in comparison with the Austings who are *ajive'e* ("light"). Foliage is either *hove'e* "yellow" or *rove'e* "dark." (This is very like the Greek use of χλωρός or μέλας to describe foliage, pp. 44 f.).

The tribe has added to its colour vocabulary a term for "blue" – *niogu'e* from *nioge* "rainbow." That it is a later coinage can be told from its form and from the fact that a neighbouring tribe which speaks a cognate language lacks this term. It is also interesting to note that the word for "colour" is the same as the word for "skin." This reminds us of the etymological relationship between χρῶμα "colour" and χρώς "skin" in Greek.

For a study of colour terms in different language groups, see B. Berlin and P. Kay, *Basic Color Terms, Their Universality and Evolution* (Berkeley and Los Angeles 1969). On the basis of their study they argued that there are eleven fundamental colour categories (white, black, red, green, yellow, blue, brown, purple, pink, orange, and grey) and that from these the eleven or fewer basic colour terms of any given language are drawn. Moreover, they have drawn up limitations on these categories.

1. All languages contain terms for white and black.

2. If a language contains three terms, then it contains a term for red.

3. If a language contains four terms, then it contains a term for either green or yellow (but not both).

4. If a language contains five terms, then it contains terms for both green and yellow.

5. If a language contains six terms, then it contains a term for blue.

6. If a language contains seven terms, then it contains a term for brown.

7. If a language contains eight or more terms, then it contains

a term for purple, pink, orange, grey, or some combination of these.[1]

The confidence one can feel in such findings goes only as far as the areas with which one is familiar, in our case Homeric Greek, which Berlin and Kay analyse as having four basic colour terms: white (λευκόν), black (γλαυκόν), red (ἐρυθρόν) and yellow (χλωρόν).[2]

There are several surprises in this list: the choice of γλαυκόν rather than μέλαν for "black," the assumption that χλωρόν is yellow, and the absence of terms for which a case could be made such as purple and grey. The particular term chosen to represent "black" would certainly be hard to defend, but no one would argue with the authors' conclusion that terms for "black" (or "dark") and "white" (or "bright") were known to the Homeric Greeks. The rest of the list which fits nicely into the authors' scheme ignores the problem in the meaning of χλωρόν which, after all, is infrequent in Homer and hardly deserves to be a "basic" colour term. Purple and grey are, according to the authors' tables, characteristic of only the most advanced levels of colour vocabulary. Ignored are the Homeric occurrences of φοινικόεις, describing a cloak dyed with sea purple at Il. 10.133 (for φοῖνιξ "sea purple," see Il. 4.141-142, the simile of the woman dying ivory with purple), and of πολιός, describing hair grey with age (Il. 22.74).

If Aristotle's list of seven basic colours had been brought to their attention (De Sens. 442a), they would have discovered that he recognized white, black, crimson (φοινικοῦν), green (πράσινον), yellow (ξανθόν), blue (κυανοῦν), and purple (ἀλουργόν). Contrary to Berlin and Kay's point 6, Aristotle's list contains no brown, but it does have a term for purple which belongs at point 7. Other conclusions in Basic Colour Terms must be read in the light of these obvious inaccuracies in Greek terminology.

---

1. Berlin and Kay, pp. 2-3.
2. The source for this information is given as A. Capell, Studies in Socio-Linguistics vol. 46 in Janua Linguarum N. R. (The Hague 1966) pp. 70-71.

APPENDIX V
A Discussion of Pindar fr. 123

χρῆν μὲν κατὰ καιρὸν ἐρώτων δρέπεσθαι, θυμέ, σὺν ἡλικίαι,
τὰς δὲ Θεοξένου ἀκτῖνας πρὸς ὄσσων
μαρμαρυζοίσας δρακείς
ὃς μὴ πόθωι κυμαίνεται, ἐξ ἀδάμαντος
ἢ σιδάρου κεχάλκευται μέλαιναν καρδίαν

ψυχρᾶι φλογί, πρὸς δ' Ἀφροδίτας ἀτιμασθεὶς
    ἑλικογλεφάρου
ἢ περὶ χρήμασι μοχθίζει βιαίως
ἢ γυναικείωι θράσει
ψυχὰν φορεῖται πᾶσαν ὁδὸν θεραπεύων.
ἀλλ' ἐγὼ τᾶς ἔκατι κηρὸς ὡς δαχθεὶς ἕλαι

ἱρᾶν μελισσᾶν τάκομαι, εὖτ' ἂν ἴδω
παίδων νεόγυιον ἐς ἥβαν.

"It is right to pluck the blooms of love in season, in one's youth, my heart. Whoever beholds the dazzling rays from the eyes of Theoxenus and does not swell with passion, has had his dark heart forged from adamant or iron with a cold flame. He is dishonoured by dark-eyed Aphrodite and either is compelled to labour for money or is borne along all the road nurturing his life with womanly courage. But I melt because of her, like the wax of the sacred bees when pricked by heat, whenever I look at young-limbed boys in their prime." The unresponsive man to which Pindar refers in these lines has his "dark heart forged by a cold flame." It was suggested (in chapter four) that the epithet μέλαιναν represents the normal state of the heart and the unnatural reaction is indicated by ψυχρᾶι φλογί. It is interesting to consider Pindar's further characterization of such a man. He is dishonoured by Aphrodite and spends his life in one of two ways.

He may be driven by a desire to make money: περὶ χρήμασι μοχθίζει βιαίως. The Greeks were very much aware of the compulsion felt by a man who was obsessed with gain. We have the example of Simonides (fr. 541. 8-9 *PMG*.):

ἢ γὰρ ἀέκοντά νιν βιᾶται
κέρδος ἀμάχητον . . . ,

"Either irresistible gain forces him against his will . . ."; Bacchylides (fr. 1):

ὡς δ' ἄπαξ εἰπεῖν, φρένα καὶ πυκινάν
κέρδος ἀνθρώπων βιᾶται,

"To speak once and for all, gain overcomes even a wise mind"; and Aristotle (*Eth.* 1.3):

ὁ χρηματιστὴς [βίος] βίαιός τις ἐστιν.

"The money-making life is one of violence." The alternative way of life for one dishonoured by Aphrodite is expressed thus by Pindar:

ἢ γυναικείωι θράσει
ψυχρὰν φορεῖται πᾶσαν ὁδὸν θεραπεύων.

This is, with one exception, the text as reported by the manuscripts of Athenaeus (13.601d) in a discussion of erotic poetry. (The exception is the correction by Musurus from φορεῖτε to φορεῖται, a necessary change to parallel μοχθίζει in the previous clause.) Almost every word in these two lines is debated with regard to meaning and grammatical relationship. Van Groningen has considered the lines exhaustively, reporting the various interpretations that have been made.[1] Three problems face us in these lines. First, the reading ψυχράν is suspected by most editors because it is separated by only three lines from ψυχρᾶι, it is a strange epithet for ὁδόν, and ὁδόν is modified by two adjectives, the other being πᾶσαν, this being a departure from Pindar's usual practice. In answer to these objections we must state that the mere occurrence of the same word within a few lines is not grounds for emendation. The Greeks were not so obsessed as we with variety in vocabulary (see n. 21 to chapter four). Examples of repetition can be found in Pindar's own work: *Pyth.* 1.78,80 κάμον . . . καμόντων, and 9.112,114 κλεινότατον γάμον . . . ὠκύτατον γάμον. It might be objected that these examples are common words, whereas the earlier occurrence of ψυχρᾶι is in a striking oxymoron, which, to our way of thinking, is weakened by the repetition. This, I think, is a reasonable point, although we cannot

1. Van Groningen *Pindare au banquet* (Leiden 1960) pp. 59-67.

be sure that the Greek audience would react in the same way as we. Our suspicions about ψυχράν are undoubtedly strengthened by its strangeness as a description of "road." Van Groningen supposes that an antithesis exists between the "cold path" and lines 10-11 where Pindar compares himself to wax melted by heat when he sees young boys, i.e. between passion as heat and its lack as cold. More specifically, he explains the "cold path" as heterosexual love as opposed to the homosexual love to which Pindar responds. We shall consider later whether van Groningen is justified in seeing two loves in opposition. Van Groningen answers the third objection to the reading ψυχράν, the modification of ὁδόν by two adjectives, by quoting Nemean 6.2, where πᾶσα is one of two epithets modifying a noun: διείργει δὲ πᾶσα κεκριμένα δύναμις. There, he says, πᾶσα determines and reinforces κεκριμένα (which, however, is a participle and retains verbal force).[2] From this parallel he argues that in ψυχράν ... πᾶσαν ὁδὸν, πᾶσαν intensifies ψυχράν "an altogether cold path." The three objections to ψυχράν are weightier together than any one by itself. They cast grave doubt on the correctness of the manuscript reading, and in spite of van Groningen's attempts to justify it, we consider it doubtful.

The second problem which faces us is the matter of grammatical structure. If, with van Groningen, one retains ψυχράν, ὁδόν serves as object of both verb and participle: "he is borne along an altogether cold path, serving it." Most editors however follow Schneider in reading ψυχάν.[3] Some group ψυχάν with φορεῖται "he is borne along in life" and θεραπεύων with ὁδόν "serving (or courting) every path" or "in every way."[4] We have not found parallels for such a construction and use of ψυχάν. It would be possible to take ψυχάν as the object of θεραπεύων "nurturing, caring for, his life," with the implication that he takes good care of himself. This, I think, gives good sense in combination with one interpretation of γυναικείωι θράσει (see below).

2. *Ibid.* p. 64.

3. Other emendations proposed for ψυχράν: βληχράν Schroeder; αἰσχράν Ahrens; σύρδαν Wilamowitz. Schneider's emendation commends itself to most editors, differing as it does by only one letter from the mss. reading.

4. As e.g. L. R. Farnell *The Works of Pindar* (London 1932) vol. 2 p. 442 on fr. 123. 5-7.

The third problem concerns the phrase γυναικείωι θράσει. It has been taken as ironic "with women's courage" i.e. "cowardice" or quite differently "with [or by] the boldness of women" i.e. "bold women." Van Groningen bases upon it his interpretation of the "cold path" as heterosexual love, translating "he is carried by the impudence of women along a path. . . ." Van Groningen has made a commendable attempt to extract sense from the manuscript reading (ψυχράν), although I do not agree with his decision to keep it. He presents two categories of men who do not respond to Theoxenus — those who are involved in money-making and those who are susceptible to women's charms. Could a Greek think that a man was "dishonoured by Aphrodite" if he felt love for women? Van Groningen, in an attempt to reconcile the two states, describes Aphrodite as "déesse de l'amour homosexuel."[5] The title seems to me to be quite unjustified, since Aphrodite herself was involved in heterosexual affairs and, being female, could hardly represent homosexual love to *men*. Moreover van Groningen regards homosexual and heterosexual love as mutually exclusive, but the Greeks apparently did not find it so. From Zeus, who had many affairs with nymphs and mortal women, yet kept his favourite Ganymedes by his side, to Socrates who had a wife and children, yet was known to admire Alcibiades, Greek men seem to have been able to appreciate the attractions of both sexes. It seems highly unlikely that Pindar would have suggested that men did not respond to Theoxenus for this reason. To speak of the "impudence of women" implies that women were aggressive in wooing and this seems quite foreign to what we know of fifth-century Greece.

I suggest that it is better to translate γυναικείωι θράσει ironically "with women's courage." We then translate the lines "he either is driven to work for money or is borne along all the way caring for his life with women's courage." Both types lack the capacity to love: the first is thrust into profiteering, the second is overly careful of himself and cannot act a manly role. *We* say that the first type "loves" money, but the Greeks probably thought he

---

5. Van Groningen p. 59, but cf. p. 58, n. 1, where he recognizes Aphrodite's essential function.

lacked the ability to love, not recognizing what we regard as a redirection of his affections. Clearly this fragment, and in particular these lines, are difficult; it seems, however, that Pindar is describing a man who is passive. unresponsive, and unable to behave like a man.

Bibliography

Grant, Allen *The Colour Sense: its Origin and Development* Boston, 1879

André, J. *Etude sur les termes de couleur dans la langue latine*, Paris, 1949

Beare, J. I. *Greek Theories of Elementary Cognition*, Oxford, 1906

Bowra, C. M. *Greek Lyric Poetry from Alcman to Simonides*, 2nd ed. Oxford, 1961

Capelle, W. "Farbenbezeichnungen bei Theophrast," *RhM* 101, 1958, pp. 1-41

Cole, R. A. *Adjectives of Light and Colour in Greek Lyric Poetry from Alcman to Bacchylides* (unpublished Dublin dissertation 1952)

Dalton, J. "Extraordinary Facts relating to the Vision of Colours with observations," *Memoirs and Proceedings of the Literary and Philosophical Society of Manchester* 5, 1798, pp. 28-45

D'Avino, R. "La visione del colore nella terminologia greca," *Ricerche Linguistica* 4, 1958, pp. 99-134 (Univ. of Rome, Inst. di Glottologia)

Dryoff, A. *Demokritstudien*, Munich, 1899; "Exkurs, Zur Farbenlehre des Demokrit," pp. 176-184

Ellis, Havelock *The Colour-Sense in Literature*, London, 1931, reprinted from the *Contemporary Review*, May, 1896

Fahrenholz, Horst *Farbe, Licht und Dunkelheit im Alteren griechischen Epos*, Hamburg, 1958

Gaiser, K. "Platons Farbenlehre," *Synusia*, Festschr. Schadewaldt, pp. 173-222

Geiger, A. *Zur Entwickelungsgeschichte der Menschheit*, Stuttgart, 1871

Gladstone, W. E. *Studies on Homer and the Homeric Age*, Vol. III, Oxford, 1858

— — "The Colour Sense," *Nineteenth Century* 2, 1877, pp. 366-388

Goethe, J. W. *Zur Farbenlehre*, in *Sämtliche Werke*, Vol. XXII, Munich, 1913

Gottschalk, H. B. "The *De Coloribus* and its author," *Hermes* 92, 1964, pp. 59-85

Gow, A. S. F. *Theocritus, with Introduction, Text, Translation and Commentary*, 2 vols, 2nd ed., Cambridge, 1952

Harvey, A. E. "Homeric Epithets in Greek Lyric Poetry," *CQ* N.S. 7, 1957, pp. 206-223

Hermann, A. s.v. "Farbe" in *Reallexicon fur Antike und Christentum*, 1969, pp. 358-447

Kober, A. E. *The Use of Color Terms in the Greek Poets, including all the poets from Homer to 146 B.C. except the Epigrammatists*, Geneva, N.Y., 1932

— — "Some remarks on color in Greek Poetry," *CW* 27, 1934, pp. 189-191

Kranz, W. "Die ältesten Farbenlehren der Griechen," *Hermes* 47, 1912, pp. 126-140

Lloyd, G. E. R. *Polarity and Analogy*, Cambridge, 1966

Lorimer, H. L. "Gold and Ivory in Greek Mythology," *Greek Poetry and Life*, Oxford, 1936

Magnus, H. *Die geschichtliche Entwickelung des Farbensinnes*, Leipzig, 1871

Marty, F. *Die Frage nach der geschichtlichen Entwickelung des Farbensinnes*, Vienna, 1879

Mensching, G. "Die Lichtssymbolik in der Religionsgeschichte," *Stud. Gen.* 10, 1957, pp. 422-433

Meyer, K. *Die Bedeutung der weissen Farbe im Kultus der Griechen und Römer*, Freiburg, 1927

Meyerson, I. (ed) *Problemes de la couleur*, Exposés et discussions du Colloque du Centre de Recherches de Psychologie comparative tenu à Paris les 18, 19, 20 Mai 1954, Paris, 1957

Morelli, J. *Etude sur les adjectifs de couleur en grec ancien, leur valeur evocatrice, leur emploi metaphorique*, Leige, 1943

Müller-Boré, K. *Stilistische Untersuchungen zum Farbwort und zur Verwendung der Farbe in älteren griechischen Poesie*, Berlin, 1922

Osborne, H. "Colour Concepts of the ancient Greeks," *British Journal of Aesthetics* 8, no. 3, 1968, pp. 269-283.

Onians, R. B. *Origins of European Thought*, about the body, the mind, the soul, the world, time and fate. New interpretations of Greek, Roman, and kindred evidence, also of some basic Jewish and Christian beliefs, 2nd ed., Cambridge, 1954

Platnauer, M. "Greek Colour Perception," *CQ* 15, 1921, pp. 153-162

Prantl, C. *Aristoteles über die Farben*, erläutert durch eine Uebersicht der Farbenlehre der Alten, Munich, 1849

Radke, G. *Die Bedeutung der weissen und der schwarzen Farbe in Kult und Brauch*, Jena, 1936

Reiter, G. *Die Griechischen Bezeichnungen der Farben Weiss, Grau und Braun*, Innsbruck, 1962

Schultz, H. "Das koloristische Empfindung der älteren griechischen Poesie," *NJA* 14, 1911, pp. 11-22

Schultz, W. *Das Farbenempfindungssystem der Hellenen*, Leipzig, 1904

Stanford, W. B. *Greek Metaphor*, Oxford, 1936

— — *Ambiguity in Greek Literature*, Oxford, 1939

— — *Aeschylus in his Style*, Dublin, 1942

— — *The Sound of Greek*, Berkeley and Los Angeles, 1967

— — "Pelias and his Pallid Wits: on ΛΕΥΚΑΙΣ ΦΡΑΣΙΝ in Pindar *Pythians* 4.109," *Studies in Honour of Gilbert Norwood*, Toronto, 1952

— — "The lily voice of the Cicadas (*Iliad* 3.152)," *Phoenix* 23, 1969, pp. 3-8

Tarrant, D. "Greek Metaphors of Light," *CQ* N.S. 10, 1960, pp. 181-187

Wallace, F. E. *Color in Homer and in Ancient Art*, Smith College Classical Studies 9, 1927

Weise, O. "Die Farbenbezeichnungen der Indogermanen," *Bei-*

träge zur Kunde der Indogermanischen Sprachen, ed. A. Bezzenberger, Gottingen, 1878, vol. II pp. 273-290

— — "Die Farbenbezeichnungen bei den Griechen und Römern," *Philol.* 46, 1888, pp. 593-605

Werner, J. "Blauer Himmel bei Homer?," *Forsch. u. Fortschr.* 33, 1959, pp. 311-316

West, M. L. *Hesiod Theogony edited with Prolegomena and Commentary*, Oxford, 1966

Indices

General Index

Index of Greek Words

Index Locorum

This is a select index to passages from the poets quoted and discussed in the text. It does not include indirect references or prose authors.